HUMAN 365

Jade Teta

DEDICATION

Unlike a lot of kids growing up, I did not pretend to be superman or worship a professional athlete. My heroes were my father and mother. They are the most successful people I have ever met. Not in money or career, but in another, more important way. This success came from clarity of their mission, which was to support, teach, love, and coach my siblings and me.

My parents were not college graduates or visionary, business people and I did not grow up wealthy. They made one choice regarding their kids: They decided they would create a different reality and belief system. One that said, "You can do, or be anything, and we are here to help make your dreams a reality." That made them special, but there are many parents who have done the same for their children. What made my parents extraordinary is how they expanded that mission beyond their children. They were this for my cousins, my friends, and complete strangers. To this day people stop by my parent's home to say hello and offer thanks for the generosity and kindness they spread.

It took me some time, but I eventually took this to heart, owned the creation of my life, and sought to give in the way my parents had modeled. Between the two of them, I now recognize that they harnessed six POWERS. I have made it part of my purpose to pass this understanding on to others.

I have used this framework with top-level athletes, high-performance executives, visionaries, and every-day people looking to grow and enhance the world around them.

My mother was a master at Perception, her own kind of Wisdom, Engagement and Sharing of her spirit and soul. My father was her perfect compliment, with his ability in Ownership, his practical Wisdom, Resolve, and Sharing of his stability and comfort, centered around making sure everyone was fed and healthy.

Together, my parents showed me the formula for my own success. I would like to share, and hopefully illustrate, that we all inherently have what it takes to be superheroes. I dedicate this book to my parents and hope to honor them by passing on what they helped me realize, and build.

My parents are Next Level Humans. The six "superpowers" in this book will help grow you to your next, best level as well.

I adore you Mom. I love you Dad. Thank you for not just giving me life, but for showing me how to live it.

INTRODUCTION

As a human you have a job to do. Actually, you have four jobs:

1. To earn a living and manage money (finances).
2. To connect with others and manage people (relationships).
3. To gain and maintain good health (health and fitness).
4. To create meaning in life and make a difference (mind and spirit).

These "jobs" are not taught in school, and becoming good at any one of them can be a lifelong pursuit. Someone who has mastered them all is incredibly rare indeed. Most people struggle in one or more of these areas, and because we all struggle, we often accept mediocrity as a normal part of life. We think, "Those people over there don't have much money either." Or we surmise, "My friends, Bill and Clara, both have the worst relationships, mine are not that bad." And we justify, "Everyone else I know is overweight and feels crappy too. At least I eat halfway decent and exercise some."

I have this theory about, we, humans. We are dreamers. From the time we are little, we have an inkling that we are meant for something great: That we are here to complete a task that we are uniquely suited for; something that makes a difference and contributes in a meaningful way to the world, and our fellow human tribe. And then, somewhere along the way, we get told we are not smart enough or not skilled enough. The tribal directives of prom, marriage, and kids sidetrack us. We succumb to our own natural tendencies toward fear, laziness and delusion. We all fall into things in life we are not fully aware of. We make choices before we understand them. Life happens before we can plan. Plans fall apart in the messy confusion of reality. Our own journey often, and sometimes rightly, becomes diverted for the betterment of another.

But don't be dismayed; we have superpowers that are always there, waiting to help us return to our quest for meaning and creation in our lives. That imperative never seems to disappear. It is always there, in the background, and if you look closely, you will find a small subset of individuals who thrive and have achieved immense success. They have mastered their finances, have taken definitive steps to have real and meaningful relationships, and they are healthy, fit, and can remain so. They have careers they love, lives of their own making, a deep sense of meaning, and feel they matter and are making a difference.

That is what this book strives to do: teach you, support you, and help you become aware of these super POWERS. I was taught by my parents that we all have signature strengths that these POWERS are meant to illuminate; I have seen it play out for others, including myself, and I have spent many years defining, categorizing and frame-working this approach, this lifestyle, for you.

There are six key areas of practice for the Next Level Human. I have given them the acronym: POWERS.

They are:

- Perception
- Ownership
- Wisdom
- Engagement
- Resolve
- Sharing

Each of these areas involves the mastery of certain insights, tools and behaviors. Each is something you can, and will learn, if you focus your attention on it. This book takes you into a world that may make you uncomfortable and challenge the box you currently live in.

It is very much like learning magic; a way of being that creates what you want. I am going to give you a glimpse into this world.

It's not for everybody. In fact, it's not for most. Only a very few ever take this path and even fewer finish. There are settlers, and there are seekers. There are conformists and visionaries. Some people want safety, predictability, and certainty, while others crave to push their limits and pursue extraordinary lives; lives of their own conscious creation, far removed from culture, norms, and societal dictates adopted by the masses.

This book is for those people. The ones that never lost that inborn desire every kid feels when in touch with their higher selves; to be great; to do something of deep meaning that is specifically suited to their unique talents and personal attributes. It's a harder path, and often, a lonelier road to travel, which is why so few take it. Yet, there is nothing more rewarding than becoming a Next Level Human; living and working in full expression of your creative power.

Imagine if you were able to go back to school and be taught about money, relationships, health and meaning. All the things that life is about. Your path would be pretty different, right? This is what this book strives to do: Help you delve into a new education in personal development. Prod you with new ways of thinking and being. Help you recognize, grow, and harness these six POWERS to change your life.

It is my honor to have the chance to present this to you. Thank you for picking up this book and allowing me to Share the POWERS.

HOW TO READ THIS BOOK

There are things that happen to us in life that cause hurt, pain, scars, and more. How we see what happened to us, and handle that pain, is what defines us. Pain can be an incredible teacher. It can also be a powerful dictator. We are the ones who ultimately decide whether our pain will grow us or degrade us. Next Level Humans filter their pain through the six principles in this book. They go by the acronym, POWERS.

Each day has a short meditation or musing to introduce you to one or more of The Six POWERS. The days are labeled by date and the dominant concept or power/s. Read one thought per day. Think on it and try to incorporate it over the following 24 hours.

Some of these writings will inspire you. Others may provide great insight. Motivation and clarity are sure to be found in some. Fair warning, there are passages that may invoke anger, aggravate, or challenge you. That is entirely on purpose. Your emotional responses are a critical element of this journey. Those reactions are your higher-self poking you to pay attention. When that happens, you have just run into core beliefs that, if examined, often become the catalysts that propel your Next Level Self. That is exactly the point.

Throughout the year, you will develop mastery over The Six POWERS and incorporate them into your thoughts and actions. Here are the POWERS:

P= Perception. This is about seeing your pain as a manifestation of the stories you tell yourself. Change your story and your life must necessarily change as well.

O= Ownership. This is about owning your pain and your scars, not as a victim, but in an empowering way. This is about defining your code of honor and the values you will live, fight, bleed, scar, and even die for.

W= Wisdom. This is about learning and growing from your pain and using the experience to gain insight. It is about overcoming bias and being a life long student.

E= Engagement. This is about making choices and taking actions, about exposing yourself purposely to that which is unknown and uncomfortable. It's not, leap and the net will appear; it's, leap and weave the net as you fall.

R= Resolve. This is about getting through the acuteness of pain. It is about overcoming fears and failures. Each time you do it gets easier. It's not, rise to the occasion; it's, create the occasion. Easy is earned.

S= Share. This is about your legacy. Not legacy in the sense of ego, but legacy in what you selflessly leave behind for others. Your creations, words, and deeds create energetic ripples in time that can lift others long after you go.

PERCEPTION

Your whole idea about yourself is borrowed – borrowed from those who have no idea of who they are themselves.

~Osho

I love dreamers, and we all dream, for a while at least. But what makes those who keep dreaming and keep achieving different? I have been consumed by this question since my early twenties. Every time I meet a successful dreamer I ask question, after question. "How did you do it?" "What made the difference?" "What kept you going?" They often answer in a very dismissive way: Saying something like, "You know, I just got lucky. I was in the right place at the right time." Or maybe they will give credit to someone else who gave them their "lucky break."

But when you push a little harder, something else emerges. It starts with this unique quality of knowing their signature strengths, having a hunger to use them for something bigger, and having the ability to assess how good they really are. They have, or develop, the superpower of Perception. This is what gets them started. And then, almost like a road map, they begin to develop the 5 other superpowers along the way.

These elements of success can be learned, practiced, and mastered. Most people fail to manifest because they fail to grasp these concepts. They are either too insecure or too arrogant, and Perception eludes them. They blame and complain, skipping the skill of Ownership. They stop learning and seeking out new experiences; therefore missing Wisdom. They can't make definitive choices and don't take decisive action. As a result, they never learn Engagement in pursuit of their dreams. They are overwhelmed by fear and unable to view failure as a requirement in the learning process. They don't finish what they start, avoiding the power of Resolve. They never teach their process, ignore the less fortunate, and underestimate the power of kindness. They fail to recognize Sharing is their path to meaning.

Success is a teachable process. There is a path to follow and behaviors to model. It all starts with **Perception**: The ability to see the world and your place in it accurately. To see the story you have written, or has been written for you, and write something new.

To rewrite your story you first have to be aware of the stories you are "buying into" or telling yourself. Ironically, we do not always write these stories; instead they are written for us. They are so pervasive and common we don't even think to question them; we just embrace them. One example of these stories is fairytales about "happily ever after." We see and hear these as children, then believe them; whether conscious or not, and we set expectations accordingly. I call it the PMK syndrome: Prom, Marriage, Kids. It is almost as if the path is set for you and you need to "experience" these things as a right of passage to be "happy." Most people don't even give it a second thought.

Changing your perception and rewriting your story as a result is a human superpower far too few possess; yet, it is one that we are all capable of.

OWNERSHIP

Everything can be taken from a man but one thing: the last of the human freedoms—to choose one's attitude in any given set of circumstances, to choose one's own way.

~Viktor Frankl

Let's say you are walking through a narrow mountain trail with sheer rock walls on both sides. A large boulder breaks off the cliffs above and crashes in front of you, blocking your path. Whose fault is that? Only a crazy person would sit on the ground in front of the boulder and yell and scream at it. Only someone completely delusional would look up at the cliffs above and blame them for "dropping a boulder in the path."

Let's say you come home early from work, walk in your bedroom and find your best friend having sex with your husband or wife!!

Here is my challenge: What if you could see finding your best friend and spouse together in bed the same way you saw that boulder in your path? If you could do that with something this difficult, you would be an extraordinary human, a superhero even.

Now to be certain, it is normal to be sad, mad, and torn to pieces by this situation. But what if, after dealing with the fallout you could see this as an opportunity for personal growth as opposed to an opportunity for blame.

Confronted with this scenario of betrayal you have some choices. You could sit in front of the "boulder" and wallow for years about what happened. Many people have done this until all semblance of life and meaning, is sucked out of them. That type of self-perpetuated suffering can ruin any potential for future happiness. But still there are others who figure a way around, through, or over.

This is what those who have mastered the power of Ownership do. Not just with some obstacles, but ALL obstacles they face. No matter what happens they take ownership of the situation. They don't expect any one else to fix it. They fix it themselves. They know if it is something in their sphere of awareness that impacts them, they are responsible for it no matter whom or what may have caused it.

They don't react in the way society dictates; they react according to their own honor code. They understand one of the key tenants of success in life: "I can't always control what happens to me, but I can control how I think, choose, and react to it."

You are nothing without your word. If you don't know what YOU stand for, you have no chance of mastering **Ownership**. Without an honor code, a set of guiding principles for yourself that define how you will behave, your life will be devoid of meaning and your choices will lack follow through.

What do you stand for? Can your friends trust you? Can you trust yourself? Do you know what you want your life to mean? What legacy do you want to leave behind?

WISDOM

The less people know, the more stubbornly they know it.

~ Osho

Information that is learned is knowledge. Many educated individuals put all their faith in knowledge, but knowledge can be one of the major sources of delusion if that knowledge is not applied and tested in the real world.

The first two powers, Perception and Ownership come in to play here. They enhance both the gathering and testing of knowledge. However, they can themselves be blocked by distraction and delusion. Distraction is about outside influences that keep you from your truth. Things like other people's needs, emotions, agendas, and beliefs. Delusion is about your own internal biases. Things like jealousy, judgment, self-righteousness, and arrogance.

It is not what you don't know that is the biggest block to wisdom, but what you are convinced you already know that is the problem. So what is wisdom? Information learned and applied overtime generates Wisdom.

Information + Learning + Experience= Wisdom

Here is a key thing to remember about Wisdom. Opinion is often self-perpetuating, while questioning is self-correcting. This practice is very much in line with what the ancient philosopher, Socrates, taught. The Socratic method is based on questioning the validity of ideas in a logical, rather than emotional way. Here is how this technique works:

1. Create a statement you believe to be true or "common sense."
2. Look closely for examples where this statement is NOT true.
3. If an example is found, reject the statement as false.
4. Rephrase the statement in a more accurate way to account for the exception.
5. Repeat this process again and again until you can no longer find an exception.

A man with Wisdom realizes that he, by his very human nature, is delusional. A wise man knows there is always more to learn and experience. He knows that his truth may not be THE truth. He realizes that by adopting a posture of open-mindedness, he can learn more and gain more knowledge and wisdom in the future.

ENGAGEMENT

The Lion Is Most Handsome When Looking for Food.

~Rumi

The day I learned to swim, I was walking around the edges of the deep-end of the pool dipping my toes in the water and then quickly pulling them out. I would look back at my uncle and he would say, "Just jump in, that's the only way to learn." The next thing I knew he scooped me up and threw me dead center into the pool. Before I could even think about it, I was kicking and screaming and swimming toward the ladder. I got out of the pool and went running, kicking, punching, and crying at my uncle. But in the middle of my tirade he said, "Jade! Jade! Did you see that? You were swimming! You swam in the deep end!!" It stopped me in my tracks. I looked around in astonishment. I did swim! My cry turned into a smile and then into laughter. I often wonder how long it would have taken me to learn to swim had my uncle not done that?

That is the power of Engagement. The idea of acting before knowing; the action mindset; Success and happiness come not from wishing for it, but acting on it. But don't get it twisted. The "success" I am speaking of has little to do with money.

My favorite definition of the verb, engage, is to "involve oneself." Engagement is involving oneself in something. It's a choice to act. Most people go their entire lives making decisions instead of choices. A choice comes out of your own truth and desire in that moment without any consideration for anything or anybody else. Taking other people's opinions, expectations, emotions, wants, or needs into account is a decision; this is why so many people are lost.

To master the Engagement power means you need to start making choices NOT decisions. These choices come from your truth and therefore you MUST know what that truth is. Engagement is about decisively taking action based on your own choices, without any considerations. Engagement is not: Ready, Aim, Fire; Engagement is: Fire, Aim, Aim, Aim, Aim!!!

You have probably heard the saying, "Leap and the net will appear." Engagement takes things one-step further because there is an element of control (Perception) and Ownership in it. Those using the power of Engagement sub-scribe more to the idea of, "Leap and weave the net as you fall."

The interesting thing about Engagement is that it is one of the only approaches to life that simultaneously builds knowledge and experience, which is the very definition of Wisdom. In other words, Wisdom allows us to take better aim and to be more correct in our actions; and taking action also builds more Wisdom. It is a feed forward loop.

Make more choices; Take action; Remember nothing is permanent; Allow no regrets (Regret is nothing but the conscious decision to hold yourself back from further growth).

RESOLVE

What stands in the way becomes the way.

~Marcus Aurelius

Perception, Ownership, and Wisdom all increase the power of our actions. Perception allows us to accurately see the possibilities. Ownership allows us to use our signature strengths, personal declarations, and boundaries to lock-in on what is right for us. Wisdom allows us to focus-in so we are headed in the right direction and have the knowledge and experience to increase our chances of hitting the target. Engagement takes the energy of these other powers and supercharges them through the force of choice. It is like someone pulling back the string on a bow and arrow. The force of the bow is Perception, Ownership, and Wisdom; the arrow is choice. The one thing that can stop Engagement is fear. To deal with fear, you need the fifth power, Resolve.

Resolve is the concept that you can feel fear and move forward anyway; the idea that, you have doubts and act regardless; the premise that, when you're fatigued and worn down, you dig in and complete the task despite it all. Engagement is powerful, but it is unstoppable when it has Resolve behind it. Resolve is about the ability to keep going, to get up after you fall down, to stick it out, to not quit. Resolve is about persistence in the face of failure and fear. Successful people have an uncanny ability to stick to their commitments.

Dedicated commitment to a course of action is Resolve. People who are most successful in life have the capability to make things happen in spite of obstacles like fear, or not yet having the know-how. Success comes from continuing to move forward. Those who achieve success often have the same thing in common: a string of failures. Failures don't hinder success, they expedite it. In other words, failure may be the most important element on the path to success. Obstacles are the stepping-stones to accomplishment. Sometimes failing is the only way to get the lessons needed to achieve what you are after.

Most people believe that we fail and take steps backwards, but it really works the other way. The mindset shift begins by recognizing that failing takes us forward. Failures are directly responsible for successes, and people with Resolve know this. They do not let failure stop them, but in fact use each and every failure as an opportunity to learn.

Resolve is the ability to endure failure and get back on your feet. Resilience is embedded in Resolve, to develop the skill of Resolve we must constantly confront our fears, get knocked down, and get up again and again. Fears have an interesting, energetic magnetism. When we avoid our fears, they tend to seek and find us. When we turn and confront them, those same fears have an interesting way of beginning to dissolve.

The way to confront fear is the same way you confront failures. It's the same way we talk about obstacles. When we say, "the obstacle is the way," we should also hear, "failure and fear are the way." Resolve is about seeking out failures and fears, not avoiding them. It is not "rise to the occasion," it's "create the occasion."

SHARING

We don't accomplish anything in this world alone...and whatever happens is the result of the whole tapestry of one's life and all the weavings of individual threads from one to another that creates something.

~*Sandra Day O'Connor*

O f all the POWERS, there is one that stands out above the rest. This power is the culmination of all the others and a force multiplier for good. That power is Sharing. We have a limited time on this planet. As morbid as it sounds, you and I will be dead very soon, perhaps tomorrow. Many people ask themselves how they will be remembered. I see it differently and want to share this perspective with you.

The chances of you or I being remembered in any significant way, beyond our small circle of friends and family, is silly. Even if we are, we won't be remembered long. We, as individuals, are largely unimportant. We are but a small drop of water in the vast sea of life and time. And yet, we are immensely powerful in the context of collective history. We can exert monumental impact if we choose. When we see accurately (Perception), declare our power (Ownership), master our chosen domain (Wisdom), and choose and act courageously despite our own limitations, fear, and failures (Engagement & Resolve), we are in a position to contribute something unique to the universal collective. By pursuing our highest, best, Next Level Human selves, we also push the human tribe we are a part of further than it could move on its own.

Our vibrations can touch, move and inspire those around us to become their best selves. This forms energetic ripples, which can turn into power-wave forms that positively lift others and forever alter the landscape for everyone who comes after. We have that magic within us and it starts with every single interaction and every singular piece of work we produce. Your kindness, the giving of your time, your laughter, a smile, the sharing of your authentic self, signature strengths given freely, without need for recognition or acknowledgment — those are the things that make all the difference.

Meaning in life is not found or granted. It is not earned and it is not stumbled upon. Meaning is generated automatically when the first 5 powers finally flow into the 6th. In this life there are only three imperatives, to learn, to teach, and to love. None of these things have any meaning without other people. We are social creatures above all else and the way we matter at all comes down to the way we share; the way we love our fellow humans.

PERCEPTION/OWNERSHIP/WISDOM/ ENGAGEMENT/RESOLVE/SHARING

10 Guidelines For Living:

1. Be honest with compassion and qualification, especially when it matters most for your growth or someone else's.
2. Say no to anything that distracts you from loving, telling the truth or following your passion and purpose.
3. Listen first. Assume you are the most ignorant person in the room. Be willing to learn and stay open to everything. Life is more fun that way.
4. Fact check everything, especially your own beliefs, biases and assumptions.
5. Take action. When in doubt or fear, act. Do something right now even if you do not yet know what good it will do.
6. Be generous. Fully give what you can, when you can without holding back. Give without expectation for acknowledgment or reward.
7. Know when to be stingy with your energetic resources. In other words, invest in and share freely until you recognize that person or thing is draining your emotional reserves.
8. Declare your power to yourself. No one is going to do that for you. Remain humble, but never ever stop believing in yourself
9. Never give up. Always get up. Never be afraid to slip up.
10. Whatever you fear, do more of it. Attack your fear. Make your fear your new comfort zone.

OWNERSHIP/ENGAGEMENT/SHARING

In my way of thinking the greatest struggle we face in life is the battle between our base human selves. The part of us that wants to sit on the couch, gossip about others, eat chips and do nothing against the part of us that desires to build a life and a legacy that feeds our souls and makes a difference for others.

I have always viewed those who pursue their dreams and are conscience of creating meaning in life as warriors. If they are successful, we get to see the outward creations of amazing lives. What we don't see is the internal struggle it took to get there.

Warriors dedicate themselves to fighting and devoting their lives to an ideal. The term is usually associated with physical battle, killing and death. For the Next Level Human, it is the relentless pursuit of meaning they fight for. Not only for themselves, but to show others that change is possible. The life you imagined can be reimagined. The life you have created can be recreated.

The death for this type of warrior occurs in the voluntary rejection of our less evolved selves - the dishonesty, delusion, lies, gossip, jealousy, blame, ignorance and other lesser human traits.

The rebirth is in harnessing our creative power to remake ourselves and manifest something greater than what we used to be; and that makes a difference in the world. Creation, communication, generosity, kindness, education, integrity, courage and all other powerful traits every human has within them are the focus.

The full, powerful development of the self for the greater good is the path of the Next Level Human. Their weapons are thought, knowledge, choice and action.

PERCEPTION/OWNERSHIP/RESOLVE/SHARING

I don't know who you are and who you are working to become, but I can tell you I am behind you 100%.

The fact you are on the journey and are working to become something of your own creation is what excites me about you. It's what makes you unique. And I love that you are different than I am. I need that fresh perspective. It is what makes me feel alive and challenges all my preconceived notions about life.

I don't want the same. I don't want comfortable ignorance. I would rather have challenges from life so I am forced to learn and grow. My advice to you is that you seek the same. Embrace the change, cultivate the uncomfortable, and challenge your fears. Love that person who is so distinct from you but who you feel drawn to anyway. Chase that career you want, the one everyone says is "not realistic." Do what matters to you.

In the end you are the one who has to live your life.

I love the path you are on and I will always support you in making your passion a reality. When you dream it helps us all dream. You are not just fantasizing for you, but for all of us.

Fear? Yes please!!! The only thing I truly fear is being more excited by a TV show or a sports team than I am about my own life.

Chase it and let people know you love them. More importantly teach them how to love themselves by loving yourself more than anything else.

Here is to you...the dream chasers. The believers. The magic makers. The lovers. The ones who run toward the scary; and the ones who inspire us all to dream. You have that power. You are much more powerful than you can fathom.

PERCEPTION/OWNERSHIP/WISDOM/ ENGAGEMENT/RESOLVE/SHARING

There are six "superpowers" every human must master to be able to create change and elevate their life. Sadly, these skills are severely lacking in most of us and rarely does a person possess more than a couple of them.

I have this theory about we humans. We are dreamers. From the time we are very young we have an inkling that we are meant for something great- that we are here to complete a task that we are uniquely suited for. Something that makes a difference, that contributes in a meaningful way to the world and our fellow human tribe.

Then somewhere along the way we get told we are not smart enough or not skilled enough. We get sidetracked by the tribal directives of PMK (prom, marriage, kids). We succumb to our own natural tendencies toward fear, laziness and delusion.

Of course this is normal and there is no judgment. We all, including me, fall into things in life we are not fully aware of. We make choices before we understand them. Life happens before we can plan. Our own journey often, and rightly, becomes diverted for the betterment of another.

But the superpowers are always there, waiting for us to return to our quest for meaning and creation in our lives. That imperative never seems to disappear. They are always in the background.

I call them the 6 Powers. They follow the acronym POWERS:

P. Perception - The ability to view the world and your place in it accurately. To see the story you have written, or has been written for you, and write something new.
#

O. Ownership - To declare who you are, what you stand for and what you are willing to bleed and die for.
#

W. Wisdom - The skill to decipher good information from biased, dishonest information, that is the norm today.
#

E. Engagement - The ability to choose and take decisive action.
#

R. Resolve - The ability to act, despite fear; to move forward, despite obstacles; and to get back up after each and every failure.
#

S. Share - To take your pain and turn it into creations that enhance your growth and the lives of others.

See clearly. Own your life. Gather wisdom. Choose and act. The obstacles are the way.

January 5

PERCEPTION

C onfidence is easily misinterpreted as arrogance.
The way people react to confident individuals can cause those confident people to want to play small, so as not to stand out. Just as no human is immune to compliments, they are also always impacted by insults.

The thing to know is that confidence, achievement, and uniqueness are inspiring to secure individuals while simultaneously threatening to insecure people.

This is no small concept. We humans are social creatures at our core and will unconsciously adjust our behavior, and look, to be more "acceptable" to those around us.

Do everything within you to NOT do that. Own your power fully including your look and your way. See it as a vetting process. I no longer take the compliments or the hate personally. To me those things are about them, but I do choose the secure - those who empower me and allow me to empower.

Comments from critics are some of my favorite interactions because they allow me to more fully see and own my power. I also have zero place for them in my world. I hope you realize the same thing. Your dreams are important and believe it or not, "your way" is usually "the way" to get there.

PERCEPTION/OWNERSHIP/WISDOM/ ENGAGEMENT/RESOLVE

I have very few regrets in my life, but the ones I had involved leaving things unsaid or undone. There is maybe an episode or two where I wish I had just kept my mouth shut, but these are exceptions.

I don't really believe in regrets anymore. To me, regret is a choice. It's like saying, "I messed up; I will never be able to get that back and my life is worse as a result."

I don't like that thought process. First, it is depressing and defeatist. Second, it simply is not true. If I change my perception just slightly, I can see that these were learning opportunities. I gained what not to do. I learned how not to be. Perhaps, as a result of these "mistakes" or "failures," I learned something more valuable and experienced something more fulfilling? I am better for it; at least I could be if I allowed it.

Or I can stay stuck, depressed and regretful. But how does that help me? How would that serve you? This is why I decided I will not do regret anymore, period. I love my success. I love my failures. I especially love my cuts, my pain and my scars. Nothing I have experienced in life has shaped me more than my pain. I think pain and suffering are our greatest teachers. Now I embrace and use them.

If you want to try this for yourself, think of it like rinsing off in the shower, except this is an "emotional cleansing." Simply recall those hardships. Let the emotions come back and say, "I forgive you, thank you, I will own this and use it." It's part of your power now; take action with it. Be kinder. Be braver. Be more than you were before.

That's it. You write your narrative. You can either be reduced and defeated by your experience or go Next Level with it. For me, it's an easy choice and the practice is worth it.

January 7

OWNERSHIP/ENGAGEMENT/RESOLVE

P ain in life is inevitable. Life is nothing if not change. The only way to conquer a thing is to confront a thing. If your pain still haunts you, it is likely because you continue to avoid it.

Weight training is a great metaphor. The body gets stronger with incremental increases in stress and strain. In time you learn to love the pain of training. Is life not the same?

See your pain differently, own it fully, learn from it, open yourself up to more of the lessons pain can teach and realize that exposure is the only thing that makes us less fearful. People never became less fearful by avoiding their fears.

PERCEPTION/OWNERSHIP/WISDOM/ ENGAGEMENT/RESOLVE/SHARING

To my mind we are on this planet for three reasons, to learn, to teach and to love.

When you are in tune with this reality, you start to perceive life as something much more than what you can get out of it. It becomes a journey of meaning, gratitude and generosity, rather than the sleepwalking search for pleasure or power.

I call those on this journey "Next Level," because they view this mission more clearly. What is a Next Level Human? Simply a person who looks at life for what it is; an opportunity to learn, teach and love. Their main concern is controlling the distractions of the outside world and guarding against the delusions of their inside worlds so that they reach their next, best level of life.

To do this they train the body to be physically capable and mentally strong. They train the mind to be discerning, logical, sharp and resilient. They then seek out new, challenging experiences that test these two domains in the real world.

They strive for Next Level personal records in Perception, Ownership, Wisdom, Engagement, Resolve and Sharing. They seek to develop these POWERS to their fullest extent in the time they have to play this game of life.

To them, all this is an opportunity for growth. Their motto: always be growing, always be sharing and always be showing your highest self.

Here is to your Next Level.

PERCEPTION/ENGAGEMENT

If you want to change your mind, change your body.
The two go hand in hand and are inseparable. Change one, and you change the other.

ENGAGEMENT/RESOLVE

There are things we have mastered and are easy, and things we have not and are difficult. It's not by accident. Easy is earned and so is difficult. Nothing ever got easier by avoiding it.

It's the SAID principle...Specific Adaptation to Imposed Demand. In other words, you get better at what you repeatedly practice.

If you want to get good at anything, you need to practice practicing.

There is something I have always loved about someone embracing something new. Anyone can be good at what they are good at; few will continue to find and engage in the things at which they are terrible.

Being good is easy; sucking at something is hard. However, think about why easy is easy, and you will often realize it was once hard as well.

One of the most consistent behaviors of successful individuals is their ability to identify what is arduous, and relish in the process of earning their easy.

PERCEPTION

You fall in love with the feelings created by the thoughts you generate about a person. Those thoughts create your Perception, but reality may actually be different.

This person may not actually be the warm caring beautiful human your thoughts have led you to feel they are.

Actions speak louder than your thoughts? Or do they?

OWNERSHIP/WISDOM/ENGAGEMENT/SHARING

The antidote to hurt is not anger or sadness; it's truth.

- Truth of your behavior. I don't know about you, but in response to deep hurt from another I have done things out of character in hopes of regaining control or defending myself. This has included anger, neediness and other dysfunctional and embarrassing actions.

We are always in a battle between our Base Level and Next Level selves. Often the Base Level wins. Being honest about that, versus further lies or more dysfunction, is the mature path to take. It is also the fastest way back to your Next Level self.

- Truth of perspective. Put your pain in context. First off, you are not special. The pain you feel has been felt by millions of humans since the dawn of time.
- Truth of meaning. Life happens. Now happen back to life. No one cares what happened to you, so stop expecting other people to fix it for you.

Imagine cutting your thumb. Then reacting one of 3 ways:

1. Rather than getting a band aid and patching it yourself, you instead angrily shove your thumb in the face of every passerby and scream "Ow...Ow...Ow!!!" OR:
2. You sit sadly staring at your thumb, as it bleeds doing nothing to stop the bleeding.
3. You ignore the entire incident, don't look at your thumb, don't think about it and never mention it again. In fact, you decide to never use that hand again.

Sound ridiculous? That's exactly how most people treat their psychological wounds.

The proper response is obvious. Cover your thumb, tend to it; heal it. As a result, learn to be more skillful and discerning with your knife. Use the wound to grow, learn and get better. For psychological wounds, this means using the hurt to change yourself and the world in more meaningful ways. Allow your pain to become the path to growth.

When I examine my scars, I want to remember the lessons, not the wounds. Your scars are prominent for a reason; they are for you to see, not for you to show. They are there to remind you how to be better, stronger, wiser, kinder, more open, more communicative, more honest, a better friend and more generous than you could ever have been without them.

January 13

PERCEPTION

The natural default of the human brain is that we fail to notice that we don't notice.

This keeps us from understanding, who we are and from creating, who we wish to be.

PERCEPTION

L ive a great story! It's incredibly difficult to do when we are all stuck in the Matrix.

My opinion? There is nothing enlightened, noble, or evolved about sacrificing your own happiness for the considerations of others. In the end, they all suffer, you most of all.

January 15

PERCEPTION/ENGAGEMENT/RESOLVE

They will tell you the relationship you want could never work. The career you desire is too competitive. The goals you have set are too lofty. They tell you to be realistic. This isn't a fairytale - this is real life.

My opinion? They're right, magic does not just happen; it must be created. It involves risk, discomfort, failures, sadness, cuts, bruises, broken hearts and battle wounds, but is a game we play anyway. It's a choice.

They can sit on the sidelines if they want. No judgment; but, let us play.

Don't let them put their fears and limiting doubts off on us. We won't hear them anyway.

PERCEPTION/ENGAGEMENT

Celia, a woman from Finland who I met in Portugal, was traveling the Camino De Santiago. She started in Lisbon, which is more than double the distance that I traveled.

We humans are inherently fearful, lazy and delusional. It is not a judgment and since I am human I fit that description as well. But knowing this is our natural default reminds me how easy it is for all of us to lead extraordinary and meaningful lives. All it takes is action in pursuit of something, anything, larger than us, and that always means overcoming these default states of the human condition.

I am a big, bald muscle-bound guy and I consider myself, strong capable and brave, yet I don't know if I would have the courage to make that trip alone. Celia is older than me, weaker than me and did the trip by herself.

I had an immediate respect and admiration for her. She left an impact on me simply by her action in the world. I was left stronger, more inspired and more conscious due to this brief moment of meeting and seeing her "in action."

If nothing else it reminded me that the most powerful, creative power we have is to act in pursuit of what we decide matters, whatever that may be.

In the health and fitness fields, there is a lot of talk about how toxic stress can be, but "stress" is also one of, if not the most, transformative powers on earth especially when it is chosen with the intent to grow.

You either choose growth, or you choose fear and stagnation.

Here is to getting out of our comfort zones, escaping laziness and conquering fear.

PERCEPTION/ENGAGEMENT

I t is not about rising to the occasion - it is about creating the occasion. It's not "leap and the net will appear" it's "leap and create the net as you fall."

Most people are afraid of the pain, afraid of the hurt and afraid of being afraid. That is not something to dwell on; it's normal human behavior.

Instead of letting your emotions control you, harness their energy and use them to create what you want. One way to think of this is "emotional alchemy."

We are not without choice in the way we feel. The popular notion in the self-development movement is to think yourself through things. This can work, but it is far more powerful in the other direction. Instead of ready, aim, fire... Try fire, aim, ready.

No matter the outcome, you will be empowered, wiser and, if you learn to control your emotions, more resilient. While everyone else is thinking about how to move forward and attack their fears...you are already doing it and growing exponentially as a result.

January 18

OWNERSHIP

D o you have an honor code?
I would not be surprised if you didn't. Most people don't, and if they do it's usually borrowed - Maybe a religious belief or an adoption of your parents' way of thinking?

That is not what I am talking about. Those types of honor codes often mean little because they don't come from the person themselves. That is why they are so often broken.

A true honor code is built based on what you have decided you stand for. Maybe your parents or your religion say one thing, but you feel something else... think about how religion has been used to justify all manner of atrocities from slavery, to genocide, to trying to convince people their sexual orientation has anything to do with their morality.

Why does it matter?

Because you are nothing without your word and if you don't even know what YOU stand for, then you have no chance.

January 19

OWNERSHIP/ENGAGEMENT

In health and fitness you may say you want to lose weight, get healthier, etc., but without your honor code, a set of guiding principles for yourself that define how you will behave, your choices will lack follow-through.

Let me give you an example. If I tell you I am "going on a diet" and you see me crushing a box of donuts, what do you think? No judgment, but I lose all credibility in your mind don't I?

You may not realize this, but your brain is watching your behavior too. If you say you will do something then behave in direct opposition your own brain says, "You're so full-of-it." You feel this lack of integrity to your core and your brain is no longer an ally. It's doesn't believe you.

There is a way to fix this and it transfers to other areas, not just health or fitness. Construct your honor code and start living it.

For instance, mine is generosity, kindness, honesty, fierce loyalty and clear communication. I then do my best (I am not always successful) to live by these principles. I tip generously; hold doors open, smile warmly, and stick by my friends, despite their crazy dysfunctions (if you haven't noticed, we all are screwed up). No one and no thing can make me break my code. So now, if I say I am going to do something, my brain acknowledges, "Yeah you will, and I am going to help. Let's do this!"

PERCEPTION/ENGAGEMENT

In the pursuit of happiness, losses always loom larger than gains. In other words, psychology research tells us that we are experts at seeing what we will lose by taking an action, but completely inept at seeing the happiness that could come from making a jump.

This natural human trait keeps almost all of us from taking actions we feel deep down are required for growth, happiness and love. The fix for this is surprising to many people because it involves a simple understanding about life that many have heard, but few believe.

Have you ever heard the statement "life is not about finding yourself; it is about creating yourself?" Well, it is the same with happiness. If you wrongly think happiness is something you find, then you will cling to whatever degree of happiness you currently own for fear any change may result in you finding less happiness. However, if you realize happiness is something you create; then you realize that it is always there as long as you are willing to paint the picture and act on it.

I am happy and I love my life. That does not mean I don't have a deep desire to create more happiness in my life and the understanding of what it would take. At that point I simply declare what I know will fulfill me on an even deeper level and I seek to create it.

This is never guaranteed, of course, as creations sometimes turn out much different than we at first envision, but that is the magic of the journey. A creation is ever-evolving and maturing; happiness is the same way.

You have to create it from within first; we all know that. What we sometimes miss, due to our own fear, is how deeply happy we can be with someone else who is also willing to create happiness with us.

Happiness is a state of being you create, not something you find, or just have or don't have.

January 21

PERCEPTION/ENGAGEMENT

There is a principle in psychology called the "as if" principle. It has been studied extensively and may be one of the most powerful tools for change.

The simplest example is, if you want to feel happy, you can think positive thoughts or you can force a smile and laugh. Research shows forcing a smile and laughing is a far more reliable and quicker way to induce happiness.

In the same way, dressing like a successful, smart person (i.e., sport coat and glasses) registers to your own brain and the brains of others that you are successful and smart, which then influences yours and their behavior.

Perhaps you will watch CNBC Money instead of the Real Housewives. People around you will speak to you differently and will start to associate you with other successful people they know. They might say, "Hey, I should introduce you to my cousin - he is a high-end business consultant." Most people think achievement follows a DO-HAVE-BE model. If you work hard, the DO, you will earn and then HAVE money. You can then BE the successful person you want to be.

Others look at it through the HAVE-DO-BE lens. If you HAVE money, you will be able to DO all the things you want and BEcome the person you desire.

Talk to most successful people and they will tell you it works in the BE-DO-HAVE manner. You first have to BEcome the person you want. Then you will begin to DO all the things you need to do, to HAVE the life you want.

Think of it like "method acting." Actors get into character by becoming the character, copying everything from their clothing to their inner emotional states. Successful people also adopt this behavior. They BEcome first and behaviors follow.

PERCEPTION

There are two paths in life:

The one that was carved-out for you, from the expectations of your culture and family. This is the path of the tribe.

The second path is created from listening to the drive of the inner, higher self. This path you choose. This is the path to meaning.

Often the second path is so important to the health of your psyche that it will rebel if you don't follow it or choose to ignore it.

Consider being fired, getting divorced, illness, loss, and depression may be the will of the psyche trying to get you back to your own path.

PERCEPTION/ENGAGEMENT

We humans are our own worst enemies when it comes to personal progress, growth and change. We let ourselves be defined by stories told to us by our culture, family, friends, coworkers, peers, etc. They may have different narratives, but always the same outcome, to hold us back.

Stories like, "I am not smart enough." Stories that echo, "Money is scarce." Mindsets like, "I am too old." Beliefs about how it is necessary to sacrifice our own happiness for our kids/friends/spouse.

When these stories are spotted and analyzed, we realize they are rarely written by us. Our culture and family are the original authors and we accepted these stories as our own without being consciously aware we did so.

It is imperative for self-actualization to find these stories everywhere they exist and begin to rewrite them. Rewrite the stories you are telling yourself and your life begins to vibrate and elevate at a different level.

In the beginning, there is nothing more you need to do. Rewrite the stories you are telling yourself. Slowly let the new story take root and you will soon begin taking action, thinking differently, discovering growth and new people in your life that expand you rather than keep you small and stuck.

Want to know how to start? Simply take out a journal, your mobile device or computer. Think about the three major stories you are telling yourself in wealth, health and relationships. Go back to your childhood and see if you can find the earliest memories you have in these realms. There you are likely to find the origin of the story you have accepted. Once you find it, rewrite it.

Couldn't find it? Rewrite it anyway.

January 24

PERCEPTION

The stories you tell are rarely your own and that is often why you feel unsatisfied with the life you are currently living.

To the uninitiated this sounds like nonsensical new age woo or marketing hype. To those who have ever had the experience of consciously manifesting anything in their lives, it feels just the opposite.

The problem with self-development is there is no road map. We never learned the principles of success in school. No one taught us how to excel in health, wealth and relationships.

Almost everything we believe we know in these areas comes from our family patterns that we absorbed either consciously or unconsciously.

PERCEPTION/ENGAGEMENT

We humans operate from groups of stories we have told ourselves over the years. These stories control us in almost every way because they define how we see the world and our place in it. Ironically, very few of these stories were actually authored by us. Instead they were unconsciously adopted from stories we were told by our culture, family, friends, etc.

Some of these stories go like this:

- Money is the root of all evil.
- I must sacrifice my own happiness and meaning for others (kids, family, friends, etc.).
- I need to be realistic.
- It is arrogant to take a compliment and acknowledge how powerful I am.
- 50 is old.

And so on... These stories then rule our lives and define who we are.

The problem is that in a very real sense these stories are like recordings in our brain that get automatically bumped into our mental playlist when we encounter circumstances where the story is relevant.

If your story is that you're fat, you will play that script when the cookies are placed on the table. If your story is money is lacking, you will unconsciously feel it takes an inordinate amount of work to make it. And on it goes.

When it comes to changing areas of your life around health, wealth and relationships, it is these stories you must identify and rewrite. Yet how many people are even aware their brains work like this?

Identify your limiting stories and begin to write alternatives.

Unfortunately, because of the way the brain works you can never fully get rid of these old stories. What you are doing when you write new ones is giving yourself a choice of which story you play. The more you choose the new version, the more the old one gets pushed back into your playlist until one day you will realize you have not played that story for years.

If you try every year to change the same things, feel stuck or never make personal progress, rest assured the culprit is your stories and it's time to rewrite them.

PERCEPTION

W e all write stories. Stories about what happened to us, about how the world works and what we are capable of.

These stories we write are not necessarily true; they are just our perspective. The problem is that they often were not even written by us. More times than not they come from the things we were told by our culture or our family and we accepted and adopted them without much conscious thought.

Other times, as children we have things happen to us and we write stories out of those experiences about trust, safety, love and worthiness. These stories were written in the past and we bring them with us into the present like books we carry in a backpack. When we encounter new relationships and new experiences what do you think we do? We take out our old stories and follow those old scripts.

Have you noticed repeated patterns in your life? -Things that come up again and again? -Relationships that look the same? -Job situations that continually manifest? -The same old money struggles with the same old frustrations?

When we carry our old stories with us what we are doing is living from the past. It's like walking through the world backwards while watching a video on your phone that's on a continuous loop.

When you are coming from this place, there is no way you will be able to make changes for the future. You are chained to your past, and the only way to escape is to become aware of the stories that are limiting and keeping you stuck.

Write new stories. When you do this, you are shutting off the video, turning around and walking into your future with the possibility of creating something brand new.

PERCEPTION/RESOLVE

The biggest obstacle we ever face is our own fear. We settle for all kinds of "lesser-thans."

We don't tell the truth for fear of being rejected if people knew who we really are, so out of fear we lie, eroding relationships and hurting others. And this fear keeps us from developing real, lasting, meaningful relationships.

Due to the fear of rejection or loss, we miss out on amazing love because we are too afraid to put our hearts at risk. As a result, we choose relationships that are more superficial and refuse to explore deeper possibilities. We become superficial ourselves and create a world where our real friends are few, if any.

Due to fears like, not making enough money or not looking good in the eyes of society, we settle for jobs that bring us neither meaning nor fulfillment. We are constantly creating self-imposed obstacles that weigh us down, dramatically limiting our potential. "I'm too old." "I've already tried that." "I can't make money doing that." "I must sacrifice my own happiness for my kids." "What will people think?" "I am too scared I'll get hurt again." "They'll never change."

This inner story we tell is largely unconscious and we don't even notice that we are doing it. At some point you need to choose what you want to create and resolve that you will confront your fears and deal with the failures.

Staying in your safe, little world for fear you will get hurt is insane and cowardice.

ENGAGEMENT/RESOLVE

Life is nothing if not change. It is filled with fears and failures. The longer you see this as something to be avoided, the further you doom your own personal growth.

In every hardship, every failure, and every time you are confronted by your fears there is an opportunity for you to rise up, face them and create a new perspective. I will chase that career; I will open my heart to that person; I will confront my health issues; I will reengage my family wounds and patterns.

I call it the "fear PR." Attack your fears. Each time you do, you strengthen your resolve, elevate your potential, and move toward a life of your own creation. The weight gets shed or becomes lighter and life becomes something you get to own.

You can't change what you are not aware of and when you become aware, you can't help but change.

The bottom line is we are all afraid on some level. You are not alone in that: We all suffer from a fear of the unknown, fear of not being good enough, fear of failure and rejection.

But look at it this way... almost nothing humanity has sought to change has not been eventually molded to its will.

PERCEPTION/OWNERSHIP

People talk of magic, "gods" and this otherworldly place of miracles and myths. It's funny, because when I look around, all the magic and creative power of any god comes directly from us. We needed light so found a way to harness fire. We needed claws and fangs so we built tools and weapons. We wanted to move faster and further so we trained animals and built cars. We wanted to conquer the sky so we eventually built planes. We wanted to travel to space so we did.

There is nothing that seems impossible with the will and imagination to get there.

Consider the fact that if your life feels stuck, it is really your will and imagination that are stuck. The future you imagined can be reimagined, recreated.

January 30

PERCEPTION/SHARING

Your actions have consequences for you, and everyone around you. I have always thought that the way a person treats others during times of stress or discomfort says much more about their true feelings than anything else. This is especially true of how you treat the people you call your friends.

Just remember these three things that also happen to be principles I believe in deeply:

First, it is you who determines the way you are treated by others.

Next, it's the consistent effort you make despite hardship that builds lasting, trusting relationships.

Finally, a true friend will always be ready to forgive, and meet you halfway.

We humans are excellent storytellers. We are so practiced that we get stuck in the way we see others and ourselves. Your ability to see through your phony stories and write new ones is directly correlated to the quality of your relationships.

PERCEPTION/WISDOM

It's not what you don't know, but rather what you are convinced you know for sure that holds you back.

From health to money to career to romance to relationships, it is these repeated patterns of thought, and the stuck beliefs, that keep you from progressing.

Consider what you have not. Read what you would not. Talk to whom you never would. Act differently than you once did. Go where you have been too stubborn to go.

Life is full of magic, and you are the magician.

Open your mind; act in the direction you would not, and the world automatically expands. Remain in the same beliefs, safe actions, common behaviors and familiar people and places, and there is little, if any, chance for growth.

PERCEPTION

When I was eighteen, I went through my first romantic loss. It was confusing, painful, and in an instant, sent a confident, secure, focused teenager into an abyss of self-doubt, unworthiness and questioning. I could not eat. I could not sleep and I was in pain from head to toe, an inescapable, psychic agony.

It took me two years, and during this time I dated no one, did nothing but study, work and read every self-help book I could get my hands on. All I thought I wanted was this person. I thought she was the key to my happiness. But then I realized she was a story, one I wrote probably before I even met her, a story of fairytales and passion and ever after.

And then I hit the, "What the heck was I thinking?" stage. After having a reconnection with my ex a few years later, I could not understand what I saw in her, or in us.

It was the first of many lessons in my ability to rewrite my story. We humans write stories all the time without being fully aware we are doing it, and often without the right perspective or wisdom to write the right story.

ENGAGEMENT/RESOLVE

Here's why hardships are so powerful and necessary: They give us the experiences that force us to reconsider our stories. The stoics call this philosophy, "The Obstacle is The Way." It is in our struggles that our greatest insights, creations and knowledge are formed. It is in our struggles that our deepest love, love of self, is forged.

An easy life provides no anchor. It's flimsy. It gives no depth, no ability to build your resilience and confidence.

What I have learned is that I thrive today because of my hardships, because of my heartbreaks, because of the things that went wrong that I was forced to suffer through. I am so strong precisely because I had to build strength.

Trust me, it still sucks. It is still painful. But I want the full experience. I trust the process. I lay it all out on the line. I don't let insecurity stop me. I say how I feel. I play all out.

I don't want it easy. I know easy is earned and I know I have the fortitude to endure what life throws at me. So bring on the pain...each time I get stronger and better.

Self-development is a prerequisite to a self, developed life. Herd think or your think? Spoon fed beliefs or your beliefs? Purpose driven? Not if you are a sponge for other people's thoughts and beliefs.

The most powerful choice you can make is to question the flimsy, cultural "hand me downs" on which your choices are based.

Those who don't question their beliefs don't question their behaviors.

Those who don't question their behaviors don't question their lives.

Those who don't question their lives know not whose life to live.

PERCEPTION/OWNERSHIP/ENGAGEMENT/RESOLVE

Your ability to define what you want and dismantle the limiting stories you are telling yourself is key to your success.

Successful dreamers don't blame; they don't complain; they are not victims. They own their beliefs; they define their own code of honor; they know life happens, but they also know they happen to life.

Your ability to gather info, turn it into knowledge, and question your bias and beliefs will make all the difference in your success.

Be someone who chooses decisively, has the ability to stay focused, and takes massive action.

Life is nothing if not change. Things happen, losses occur, failures are experienced; fear is ever present.

Your ability to act in the face of fear and failure and to see them as stepping-stones to mastery is critical.

It's not meant to be, it is created to be.

It's not, "fake it until you make it;" it is, "be it until you see it."

Nothing is easy, easy is earned.

The stories we tell determine the lives we live.

February 4

PERCEPTION/ENGAGEMENT

To be different you have to view the world from a new perspective, from a different angle. You have to change your perception of the world and your place in it by dismantling your old stories and telling new ones.

If you have ever heard the statement "thoughts become things," or "change your thoughts, change your life," you have been exposed to the ideas behind this concept. This is only half of the equation. Thinking alone will not do it.

Many of our thoughts are built from automatic habits beyond our consciousness. These patterns are almost impossible to change with thoughts alone. This is why you can think about it, visualize it and chant mantras all you want with little change.

Your brain works a lot like a water wheel. You need the force of the water to move the wheel and once the wheel is moving, it puts added force into the process.

To get the system moving you must see and be different. Act different and your brain is more likely to perceive differently too. Once you see the world from this different place, the proper action is reinforced.

You don't think your way to change. You don't meditate or visualize yourself there. You act, and the thinking and visualization becomes additive. It first facilitates and then solidifies change.

See Different, Act Different. Act Different, See Different.

PERCEPTION/OWNERSHIP

W hat if you had to carry weights around with you all day? Whenever you went somewhere you had to carry them. Whoever you were with, you had to carry them.

Any new person you wanted to get to know, and any place you wanted to visit, you had to carry those weights.

Obviously, this would become extremely limiting. Going out would be too exhausting. Traveling to other states or countries would be out of the question.

You may start to limit your interactions to only other people who are carrying the same type of baggage or maybe they would be the only people you would attract?

You may find this a silly idea, but it is exactly what we do when we choose to hold onto old, psychological baggage. We have an amazing capacity to insist on carrying old stories, old assumptions, old pain, old fears and untruths.

Why do we do this? The human brain values certainty and comfort above all else. For this reason it will often hold ideas, beliefs and patterns of behavior that are not useful, or even detrimental, just to remain in its comfort zone.

PERCEPTION/OWNERSHIP/ENGAGEMENT/SHARING

How do you know if you or someone you know is carrying psychological baggage? Have you ever interacted with someone and thought, "They are always so heavy?" Or "They always seem so light?" It's funny how even our language points out this truth.

Frustration, depression, anxiety and confusion can all signal you have this mental baggage weighing you down. Especially when these emotions are stuck.

No one is going to release that weight for you. The choice is not easy, but there is a way to begin letting it go.

Do anything different right now. It is not thinking that is most powerful, it is doing. Try cranking up some music and dance if you have never done that. Talk to a stranger and tell them something good. Give someone the psychological love you need. Force a laugh and smile until one day it's genuine.

Regret is a choice. Ideas can be changed. Your perspective may be wrong. The life you imagined can be reimagined. The baggage is not necessary; you just think it is.

February 7

PERCEPTION

I f you are looking for the solution to what is eating you up inside, it is within, not out. There is nothing you can do "out there," you must go inward first.

There is a story you are telling yourself; you have just forgotten you are the author and the reader. Because you have forgotten is why you suffer.

If you have ever had a nightmare, realized you were dreaming and woke yourself up, you have an idea of what I am speaking.

This is a skill you can develop, and the reason self-reflection and self-development are so powerful.

Ask yourself, "What story am I telling myself that shades my experience?"

Then ask, "What other story is possible for me to write?"

Just these questions are often all that is necessary to snap out of your self-generated dream.

PERCEPTION/OWNERSHIP

There is one thing you must master before you can realize your power: self-trust. Unfortunately, like all humans you have a natural tendency to lie, falsify, and avoid. As a result you don't trust yourself very much.

This is the real power of a commitment to honesty and communication. Your ability to be honest and clear with yourself, and the people you choose in your life, is critical.

This was once hard for me, but now if you are a friend of mine, you will find I communicate exactly how I feel. In fact, I often over-communicate so there is no ambiguity.

Why don't we just communicate? Are we afraid it makes us vulnerable? Do we believe people are going to use it against us or hold us hostage with what we said? Are we so asleep we don't know how we feel?

My telling you exactly how I feel does not trap me; it frees me. Your reaction tells me exactly who you are. I can discern your level of trust, honesty and communication as well.

Have you ever met someone who you trusted to tell you exactly how they feel about you? They are able to be 100% while having empathy, respect and compassion for you with no expectations?

Remember how comforting it feels to have a friend that has your back in that way?

That is who you must be for yourself first. When you do, the stories you are telling become clearer and life starts getting a whole lot better.

PERCEPTION

The stories we tell ourselves determine everything about the way we see the world. Those stories are ours to write, to change, and to use if we choose.

Before we can do that, we must first understand where these stories that we tell ourselves come from? Did we write them or did we unconsciously absorb the stories of our family, culture, or tribe?

You have the power at any moment to write a different story about what happened or happens to you.

OWNERSHIP

Like a star, our only choice when surrounded by darkness is to become our own source of light.

PERCEPTION/OWNERSHIP

There are many times, as humans, we find ourselves stuck in certain emotional states. Sadness over loss; Anger over betrayal; Regret over mistakes; Anxiety over uncertain circumstances.

Usually these emotional states are fleeting, lasting only a few days or, at the most, weeks. Yet, there are the lingering emotions that continue to permeate our days. What are those things about, and why do we hang on to them?

These emotions are about our inability to rewrite the stories we tell. Stuck emotional states are almost always about the inability or unwillingness to make a choice, or own that choice, once it is made. If you feel loss, that is normal, but if that loss is with you years later it is no longer about what happened, but rather what you are choosing to do about it.

Your ability to understand this and rewrite your script is critical. Let's say you lose a job you loved and years later you still can't resolve the emotional pain. It's not the event anymore, but your lack of willingness to rewrite who you are. You are no longer that job, it is in the past, so you must rewrite your story, taking the eraser to it and inserting a new reality.

Perhaps you identified so strongly with that job that it defined who you saw yourself as? "I am a nurse or banker or project manager and I am good at it." Or maybe, "I built that company; it is part of me."

Well, that is the problem. That script may have fit and made sense previously, but it does not today. What's wrong with rewriting it?

You can author a new story for your life at any moment.

February 12

PERCEPTION/OWNERSHIP

T he biggest obstacle to getting what we want out of life is our refusal to part with our old identities and the stories tied to them.

People say, "I am a jock," and they may think they are not smart. They stay married to the "dumb jock" narrative.

Another says, "I am an artist," and struggles with money because they don't' believe they can also be a good businessperson. They are trapped in the "starving artist" narrative.

If who you are today is who you were five years ago ask yourself why? People are changing all around you all of the time. If you believe people can't change you probably won't change, but that does not stop them.

I am different now. My identity has changed just in the last few years. Sure, much of the old me is integrated, but there is so much new me that friends from just a couple of years ago no longer know me. Even my family scarcely understands the new me, and is often confused by him.

Elevating your life is about refusing to settle for seeing yourself as the old you. It is about remaking your identity into the thing that helps propel you to your Next Level.

PERCEPTION/OWNERSHIP

One of the great comedies and insanities of the human condition is, wanting change while simultaneously doing and being the same thing.

Get your old self out of the way!!

You want something new? Then your old identity has to go.

You want different relationships? It's you that needs to change first.

You want different finances? Then you need to walk a different direction.

I am no longer the football player. He is gone. I consciously remade him. I am no longer the bodybuilder. I have no use for him anymore.

I have kept parts of the scientist, the physician and the comedian. I have added the entrepreneur, the philanthropist and author.

It is not, fake it until you make it. It's, remake it first and then be it...it's, be it until you see it.

And here is one truth that you will never be able to escape: the entire world is change.

Your destiny like everything else in the world is to change. Resist that and you will die on the inside long before your body does.

You are always becoming, unless you aren't.

OWNERSHIP/ENGAGEMENT

Why do you continue to insist that someone else be responsible for your emotional state? If your heart is broken, it is up to you and you alone to fix it.

What we humans often fail to realize is that our suffering is not unique or special. Millions and millions of people have suffered in the same way throughout history. They, all of them, had to learn the same lesson.

They could either die injured with all the heavy baggage of old wounds and petty hurts, or they could own their pain and do something about it.

It's unfortunate, but most of us insist that it is the old lover, difficult family member, or vindictive coworker who must admit they were wrong in order to fix our pain. It's not going to happen, and even if it did you wouldn't feel any relief until you decide you are taking responsibility for it. How many times have you or someone you know apologized, only to find the offended demanding further apologies?

It is like anything else. You don't expect someone else to design your living space, or wash your dishes, or pay your rent. That stuff is your responsibility and so is your emotional pain.

Only children or adolescents stomp their feet, cross their arms in defiance and whine woe-is-me over old hurts. You are an adult not a teen. It's time to develop some emotional maturity.

If you are stuck and hurt it is your responsibility to fix it. No one can heal your broken heart except you.

You can either shut up and work on it or stay entrenched in your butt-hurt, miserable existence.

The choice is yours. It always has been.

OWNERSHIP

I got up early this morning and walked down to the recording studio. If there is one part of the Internet business I despise, it is recording long, video, sales letters. Needless to say I was doing that very human thing and falling into the victim mindset.

You know what I am talking about, right? Those people with constant complaints about how busy, traumatic or imposed upon they are; the type that blame everything and everybody for their own emotional state?

Just think about how unbelievably egotistical and self-centered it is to assign blame to someone else for the state of your emotions. It's almost comical when you think about it, yet that is what we humans do. I call this the VC or Victim Culture. Being human, I am not immune to the VC. But being practiced at recognizing VC behavior in myself, and others, I quickly noticed what I was doing and made the change.

There is an antidote to the VC that works every single time and it works almost immediately. I call it the GC or Gratitude Culture. It's easy to do; just flip it and realize you have control over your internal state.

No one else is responsible for the emotions around your hurt, regret, misfortune or anything else. You alone are responsible for your heartbreak. Of course some people refuse to relinquish the VC because blaming and complaining can feel so good.

Gratitude feels much better though.

So I just remembered that I manifested this. I am in that recording studio because I had a dream to spread my work and my message and doing that means recording video, sales letters. Then I felt incredibly lucky and grateful to be there for hours, reading marketing copy that will convince someone who needs my work to get it and make a positive, lasting change.

I then started to feel beyond grateful for being exactly where I was and doing exactly what I was doing, and I loved every second of it because I chose to. Oh, and I got to beatbox too.

OWNERSHIP/SHARING

You are too busy trying to figure them out. You want them to know, like, see, admire and respect you. How is that even possible when you don't adequately know who you are or what you want yourself?

Even if you do, you are too busy trying to please everyone else and are unable to say what you really feel. This turns you into someone who trusts no one, because you can't even trust yourself.

Stuck emotions come from the inability to tell your story and own your truth. Anxiety, depression, and frustration often have their origins in the inability to make your own choice or own that choice once it is made. The reason? You are not choosing for yourself but rather for the consideration of others.

Compromise in relationships IS a good thing. In fact it is a requirement. But this means sacrifice of the small things, not the big things that make you who you are or that are about the pursuit of your dreams.

If you find yourself struggling in the dark for any length of time, it is because you have turned your back on who you are, what you want and your own dreams. Turn around; it's still there waiting for you.

One final thing - your worry, about being selfish or leaving others behind? Not following your path is more likely hurting them than the reverse. When you pursue your dreams, others are more likely to be inspired to do the same. It seems counterintuitive, but when you get it, they will usually get it too. You are actually helping no one by sacrificing your truths...in fact you are hurting everyone, most of all yourself.

PERCEPTION/SHARING

Believe it or not, one of my favorite artists is my own mother. I am lucky to have several pieces she has created for me in my apartment. My mom sees art in everything and if you go with her anywhere, you will find that she stops and takes pictures of everything, shadows, graffiti, shop signs, etc. When I was a teen I remember telling my mother I was not an artist. She looked at me and said in a matter of fact tone, "We are all artists, Jade."

I did not quite grasp what she meant by this until the last couple of years. As humans we get to write our stories, paint our pictures, snap our photos and sculpt our clay.

Part of the reason we sometimes get stuck is because we become overly attached to the same stories, paintings, photos and sculptures. We stop creating new and stay stuck in old patterns.

Indeed, we are all artists. The stories we tell and the pictures we paint have unlimited potential. The life you imagined can be reimagined.

Your old stories can be replaced by new stories.

You are an artist of life; use your power.

PERCEPTION

Something's power over you is nothing more than the power of the story you have constructed about that thing. The same holds true for a person. Want to change its hold on you? Change your story about it.

Those who master the art of Perception have mastered the art of telling stories that work for them and move them in positive directions. Those who haven't construct stories that keep them stuck.

We must learn to tell accurate stories that also work for us. The stories you spin about yourself, others and the world are everything. Are you even aware of which stories you tell? Are they stories of fear, hurt, scarcity and regret, or stories of possibility, positivity and growth? Are they about how to deal with insults or difficult people? Insults are someone else's story about you, or their story about themselves or the world projected onto you.

Your job is to decipher if their stories contain truth or a lesson, and then decide if you would like to use it in any way.

Developing the superpower of Perception is about realizing that life is about studying yourself through studying others, and changing yourself through changing others.

People are practice and help you practice your purpose. They are there for two reasons: to help illuminate your purpose and to teach you how to get there.

People can be your teachers. Pain can illuminate purpose. The obstacle can become the way, if your story allows for it.

PERCEPTION/OWNERSHIP

The story in your head- you know the one about why it would never work- is wrong.

Even if there is some truth to it, you have the ability to alter that thought process.

Why are you so afraid to let yourself become a new and better you?

ENGAGEMENT/SHARING

Every Next Level of your life requires you grow into someone else. Parts of you will remain the same, but many parts must be altered.

It's important to remember life is nothing if not change. Change happens to you whether you want it or not. You must happen back to life in order to level up rather than level down.

I know you are afraid and uncertain; so am I. Life does that to us on purpose. Fear is fuel; it's fuel for change.

In nature there are three natural reactions to fear: fight, flee or freeze. One of those will surely get you killed; the other two involve movement and have the potential to advance you to the Next Level.

Here is what I want you to understand. You don't know me anymore. I am different than I was just six months ago. A lot has changed. I have leveled up. I did so on purpose. Life asked me to and I obliged.

Here is my plea to you. Let's go to the Next Level. We can do it together. You already are above me in many areas. You can enhance me. I think I can do the same for you. Think about it.

Change or be stuck. That is what we are really up against.

We want happy, but fail to realize it is like a hamster wheel; you need to move to turn it on and keep it on. If you stop moving forward, it stops moving forward.

ENGAGEMENT/RESOLVE

I have heard people call Fear "False Expectations Appearing Real." Well, I have news for you; it's very real. And that's a good thing because we can use it.

A better way to think of Fear is Find, Engage, Attack and Resolve. That's how you level up. You can't have it all, but you can have a lot...if you will follow your heart and chase your fear.

PERCEPTION

I t's the mindset you have when approaching a thing, not the thing itself, that determines its value. I realize this is a hard concept to accept when so much happens beyond our control. This is especially true of the way others see us. It kills us when someone views us in a way we know we aren't.

Let me give an example:

I was in love with a girl. She decided she needed to follow another path. I was hurt, but supportive of her other relationships. I worked hard to stay in her life. I loved her in the ways she allowed and supported her other relationships. I protected her secrets. I adored her. I saw myself as her protector. She, however, saw me differently, more like a stalker. That devastated me, for a time. Years later, it's a great lesson. The episode taught me so much about others and myself.

It was a perception problem, an inaccurate thought getting in the way of a more beneficial reality. If she could see me for who I really was, she would have realized she had someone who, while preferring a different scenario, was in her corner and had her back, a friend for life.

If my own perception was more accurate, I could've recognized how she saw me and supported her in a way she understood.

Why do we make these assumptions? It's usually about familiarity. The "exboyfriend as protector" story isn't a scenario we know or feel comfy with, but the stalker story is.

The way we see a person is how they will appear to us, even when the truth is something entirely different. The same applies to stress, illness, financial concerns, career difficulties, loss and all the rest life throws at us.

Your ability to see obstacles, failures, fears and even people's negative beliefs about you as education and growth potential, is tantamount. Even if the story you're telling is correct, you can still use it for good. Every great movie or love story has an obstacle to overcome. What we never realize is what's in the way may be our own faulty perceptions, stuck emotions, erroneous assumptions and psychological patterns.

OWNERSHIP/ENGAGEMENT

People can only mirror back to us what we, ourselves, already are.
If you keep saying you attract "toxic people," consider you are the toxic one, not them. I know this is a VERY tough realization, but accepting this will change your life.

Do you want change? Act as if you already are what you seek.

PERCEPTION/OWNERSHIP/WISDOM/ ENGAGEMENT/RESOLVE/SHARING

There is a natural tension between who we are and who we should become. This tension is required for mental health and happiness. But without movement to close this gap there is a danger of moving toward depression, anxiety, frustration, and mental and emotional stagnation. Such negative, stagnant emotions are warning signs that we have deviated from the course toward our Next Level selves.

In order to bridge this gap between where we are and what we wish to become, we must understand particular insights and develop certain, mental skills:

- The skill of right Perception. To see the world, and our place in it, accurately so as to overcome distraction and delusion.
- The skill of Ownership over one's life and all that happens in it. Recognition that we alone set our path in motion.
- The acquisition of Wisdom that comes from learning the unique skills and gaining the experience necessary to advance to the Next Level.
- The skill of Engagement where we exercise independent choice and take decisive action.
- The skill of Resolve where fears and failures are not seen as something to avoid, but rather something we must attack head on in pursuit of our Next Level selves.

Distress and boredom continually revisit those without a why. They will remain fixed, moving back and forth between these two states.

As Viktor Frankl said, "A human is not in pursuit of happiness but rather a reason to be happy." What we often fail to realize is that reason does not fall out of the sky on top of us; we get to choose and create it.

ENGAGEMENT/RESOLVE

It's not what you say; it's what you do. It's not where you've gone; it's where you're going. It's not how bad it feels; it's how brave you are.

Stop searching for easy; easy is earned.

Life is not easy. Life is rarely simple. Life is change and challenge.

WISDOM/SHARING

We go through life looking at ourselves through different lenses. In my way of describing it, these points of view have to do with what level of human we are relating to. We have three levels within us:

Base Level= here we view the world, and everyone in it, as out to get us. We feel insecure and scared, and as a result, shut down and isolate ourselves or lash out.

Culture Level= here we are stuck in adolescence and view the world as one big high school. Are we measuring up? Are we in the popular group? Do we have enough money, career accomplishments, adult toys and other status symbols compared to everyone else? Social media plays an interesting role here. Those who love it and those who hate it are often operating from the same Culture Level position. Remember in high school how some, in response to trying to "fit in," rejected the notion altogether? (Or was that just me?)

Next Level= here it is about growth, connecting and sharing. Here we are in tune with our higher power and purpose. We realize that purpose is not more money, more sex, more toys, more success, but rather how we are using our gifts to grow.

What if today, instead of looking for evidence of whether you are winning or losing by checking your bank account, career success, likes, shares, and comments, you simply shared your Next Level self with the people you encounter? What if you could acknowledge before being acknowledged? Forgive before you're forgiven? Give so freely that it inspires others to do the same?

PERCEPTION/ENGAGEMENT

The ability to reimagine and recreate oneself in the face of uncertainty, pain, and loss may be the greatest superpower of human kind.

The future you once imagined can always be reimagined no matter where you currently find yourself. The only thing stopping you from recreating is you.

You alone can remedy this pain or render it unbearable.

OWNERSHIP

D o you know that question people always ask? "If you could go back, what would you do differently?" No matter how bad it ever was, my answer is always the same, "Regret is a choice. Regretting anything in my past is choosing stagnation over growth. I simply don't do regret. Ever. Period.

I would do the same again. I love my life. I own my lessons. I take responsibility for where I have been and where I am going. I am too busy moving forward to waste a single second on regret."

OWNERSHIP

V C.... It's an acronym I use for something I call the "Victim Culture." This is not a judgment or an "I am better than you" thing. It is simply something I have recognized in others, and myself, that I choose to fight against.

It's that natural human tendency to judge, blame, complain, deflect, delude, and exonerate ourselves from stuff we know we had a hand in. We all do it, and when we are in this place we are in the victim culture or VC. And let's be honest, it feels good to shift the blame, point the finger, put up walls, and pretend they were put up by someone else.

The problem is being VC means simultaneously shutting yourself off from all growth and progress. I choose instead to put it all on my shoulders. If it happens in my sphere of awareness and I want it to change, then I own it... Yes, even if I had no hand in creating the mess.

PERCEPTION/OWNERSHIP

There is no blame in change. I refuse to be part of the VC (Victim Culture)... Every celebrated hero who walked this earth did not leave difficulties for someone else. They did not accept it, didn't point the finger or shirk responsibility. They put it on their shoulders and either took care of business or died trying.

I know my inner VC is going to come out because I am human, just like you, but I refuse to feed it or befriend it. Let it show its face...it's just a reminder that I am not on that team.

You want to blame and complain? That's your choice, but I choose the GC (Gratitude Culture) and I will gladly take responsibility because to me, there is nothing worse than whining, complaining, blaming and being in the VC.

OWNERSHIP/SHARING

What do you have? Think about it. You have your stuff...like your car, clothes, and other "things." You have your career. You have your money. You have your relationships. But do you really own these things? Are they really yours? Can they be taken from you? Do you control them?

As I have aged, I have come to see that there is only one thing I truly own, a thing I can invest in and count on. In fact, when I am unsure, scared or lost all I have to do is check in with it. I can silently check in and say, "Should I or should I not be doing this?" That thing is my word - that I own 100%. No one can take it from me but me.

For a long time I had no relationship to my word. Until very recently I would say whatever I thought you wanted to hear. I thought, "No harm no foul." Now I opt to tell you the truth regardless, because not doing so is an insult to myself. My word becomes my legacy and my legacy is the only real thing I own. No one and no thing can take it or give it to me.

If I know I have been 100% in my integrity, even if it is messy, confusing or unclear, then I can at least take solace in the fact that I was being true to me.

Nothing puts the spirit at ease more than being 100% in line with your integrity.

OWNERSHIP/SHARING

We are liars. We all are. This is not meant as a judgment or reprimand, and as humans, not only do we purposely lie and exaggerate, but we also justify our lies and convince ourselves they are true. Our brain renders that we are unaware of our own behavior.

You have no doubt experienced this with friends or family who manufacture a truth you know to be false. This is one of the more curious aspects of human behavior. The question is why do we do it?

Two major reasons:

1. We want to be liked above all else; this drive is built into our survival system. Because of this we can find ourselves exaggerating things, manufacturing interests or telling outright lies about who we are and what we do.
2. We don't know our own truths ourselves. This is so common. Have you ever asked someone why they did something, only to find their frustration or temper rise when they explain, "I don't know?"

Have you ever wanted so badly to know someone's reasons behind their actions, or their internal thoughts, only to discover they don't actually know their own truth and will even make things up? Contradiction like this suggests they have spent little time in self-reflection. Lying is at the root of interpersonal conflict, but is also the cause of so much personal confusion and despair.

What is wrong with telling someone exactly how you feel? Give them all the information (the best you currently know it), and let them make up their own minds what it means about you and them? I have come to see this kind of honesty as the greatest gift you can give a friend.

By not being honest you rob them from really knowing who you are and you rob yourself of the freedom to be understood and loved for who you really are. Honesty is part of my honor code now.

OWNERSHIP/SHARING

When I know the truth, I speak the truth. I refuse to have anyone, in my close circle, who lies to me. When I am told the truth, even when it hurts, I see it as an expression of love.

A lie, including lies of omission, I see as betrayal. You don't help by making things up; you hurt us both.

Observe these two rules:

1. Honesty without compassion is cruelty.
2. Your truth may not be THE truth.

PERCEPTION/OWNERSHIP/SHARING

If someone lies to you, they are a liar. Only liars tell lies.

Here is the thing about liars and lies: They don't really see anything wrong with their omissions or falsehoods. They often think they are doing you a favor because they don't want to hurt your feelings. In some strange way, they think it helps the relationship.

Research shows that those who lie the most frequently have the most distrust of others. In other words, because they are liars they assume others are also. Now, let us not judge. We all lie. It is an inborn human trait. But your capacity to tell the truth is directly proportional to your capacity to give and receive love.

By way of explanation, if you love a liar, don't expect to receive much love back and don't expect them to feel or recognize how much you love them. Lying erodes relationships. It most importantly undermines your relationship with yourself.

Yes, we all lie. My advice though is to find friends who, like you, are willing to commit to the truth. Find that, and you have found a valuable relationship and real love.

Here is one suggestion: The best way to keep a liar lying, whether that liar is you or someone else, is to judge them or yourself. The way to start is to catch the lie and then correct it back to the truth as soon as you notice, but be gentle with yourself. If you want someone to stop lying, then you need to try your best not to take their lies personally.

People lie because they are distrustful that you can handle the emotions. So make sure you are emotionally centered and present for them.

However, big lies and repeated lies are much harder to deal with and another reasonable strategy is to walk away for good without looking back. A strange thing happens when you make a commitment to the truth - a lot of honest people start showing up in your life.

Nothing spurs personal growth and happiness more than true friends who honestly and lovingly point out your dysfunctions.

PERCEPTION/OWNERSHIP/ENGAGEMENT

It's simple, it's not time yet. That thing you want so badly, it's not the right path, or perhaps you are caught in the "looking mindset."

Here is an insight you might be interested in: Stop looking. Start being.

Looking assumes there is something to be found. You don't *find* your great love, perfect career or the meaning you crave…you create it by consciously choosing who you want to be. That has to come first! From that point you, "behave and become."

Behave AS IF you are that thing in the moment, as you slowly become that thing in the future. This is about trusting yourself, and then trusting the process.

Rumi, one of my favorite poets, has a famous quote, "What you are seeking is seeking you." He wrote poems about love and lovers; it is such a nice thought, although I don't see it this way at all. Two people "looking," equals two people lost. And if they don't consciously create themselves first, they will stay lost whether they bump into each other or not.

I would amend his quote to say, "What you believe in, believes in you." Or, "What you choose to become, becomes you."

Stay in action. Pause often for reflection. Trust the process and the right time and path will "become." It has no choice.

It's not "leap and the net will appear"; it's "leap and weave the net as you fall."

PERCEPTION/OWNERSHIP

S uccess in any area of life requires focus, and all too often, we are distracted by the wants, needs, and desires of others; as well as the cultural norms, expectations and practices of our society.

Distraction is an external obstacle to focus, but delusion also comes from our internal biases, judgments, and wrong beliefs.

Delusion and distraction are the worst enemies of focus.

Clarity, honesty, and alignment are the antidotes to distraction and delusion. Together, these factors become a lighthouse to remind you where you are headed when life gets tough.

Whether you are struggling with health, happiness, mindset, or money, these principles are the first ones you need to attend to.

OWNERSHIP/ENGAGEMENT/SHARING

Have you ever actually written down what you are trying to create in detail? The qualities of the man or woman you seek in a relationship? The specific career achievement you are after? The monetary situation you are hoping to achieve? What happiness might look and feel like?

The most important area in which to develop clarity is your "big why." Viktor Frankl called this the "will to meaning." It is the internal drive all humans have toward leaving a legacy, or purpose in their lives.

Meaning is not something you find, it is something you create.

Meaning varies from person to person; it's a matching of your unique attributes and skillsets with the legacy you want to manifest for yourself or others.

OWNERSHIP/ENGAGEMENT/SHARING

The act of creation is one of the most powerful forces on the planet. As humans, we have what psychologists call, a "drive toward meaning." In other words, we have a psychological imperative to produce meaning in our lives. The primary way we do this is through creation.

Creation is really about putting our signature strengths to use in a way that produces a unique outcome of our making.

One of the simplest, but most powerful acts of creation, is having children. For most people this is where they spend the bulk of their creative energies. They "create" a family.

For others, meaning is generated through intangible creations like their businesses, careers, work, or tangible creations like books and art.

The point to understand is that a meaningful life is directly correlated to the quality of your engagement in creative pursuits.

What are you creating that fills your "will to meaning?"

If you are one of the many people who feel disconnected, disengaged and uninvolved in life, it is likely because you have lost touch with the expression of your creative force.

It's easy to get this back though. The interesting thing about living a meaningful life is we get to choose where and how we will create meaning in our lives.

Will we create it in our children? Will we create it in volunteering? Will we produce art? Will we choose to engage in random acts of kindness? Will we bring laughter and joy to our interactions with people? Will we create a safe place for those who require it? What will we make our charge in life?

Meaning won't fall on you and it is not something you suddenly discover. It is a conscious creation of your own choosing.

OWNERSHIP

The people we choose in our lives are often a direct reflection of our perceived value and worth to ourselves.

The need to be liked and accepted is universal and something we unconsciously seek. This is why we will appease, care for, go out of our way for, and hold on to people who treat us with less respect and consideration than we might normally demand.

The way we get treated is the way we allow ourselves to be treated.

Look in the mirror of your relationships...are you being enlarged or reduced? You alone are responsible for that.

If you see the same patterns popping up over and over again in your life that is a hint for you.

Personal struggles are not "out there"; they are being generated from within.

PERCEPTION/OWNERSHIP/ENGAGEMENT/RESOLVE

Life happens to us all, but some choose to blame and complain (the VC or Victim Culture) and others choose ownership over all that occurs, whether they caused it or not (the GC or Growth Culture).

This growth mindset may be the number one determining factor for success and happiness.

Failure and fear are an inescapable reality of being human, and some believe they should be avoided at all cost. Others see them as learning opportunities... stepping-stones to success.

Life is uncertain and there are consequences on every corner. When confronted with these consequences, we either don't act, act out of fear, or double down on old thinking patterns that don't serve us and keep us stuck.

We don't realize it is within our ability to see and create new possibilities; this is our greatest power.

PERCEPTION/OWNERSHIP/ENGAGEMENT/RESOLVE

A person takes an action that has potential consequences. Their worst fears are then realized and they suffer. These types of life events are some of the worst we encounter...jail, accidents, divorce, job loss, bankruptcy, etc. - Life happens and our choices have consequences, but many people add insult to injury by reverting into old mindsets and thinking patterns that were behind the consequences in the first place.

This is why we see those repeated patterns in our lives. Job lost again, crappy relationship again, unhappiness again, infidelity again, poor health again, etc. - We don't get to change and elevate our lives by climbing back into a shell of regret. We don't get change by doubling down on the same patterns and beliefs we had before.

In every tragedy, event, or wound, lies an opportunity for growth, change, and transcendence to a deeper self-understanding.

Our ability to turn hardship into learning and growth is what will determine our success and happiness. And that is directly connected to learning to think, see, and behave differently than we have been.

We are rejected and we learn to develop worthiness from within, we are abandoned and learn to be self sufficient, we are divorced and turn it to our advantage by seeing it as an opportunity for growth for our children rather than something that will hurt them. We lose that job and turn it into finding or creating something we are really passionate about.

Everything that happens has a hidden choice behind it...do we bet on the old thoughts and behaviors that got us there in the first place?

Or do we create the new? -New people, new thinking and new possibilities?

PERCEPTION/OWNERSHIP/WISDOM

What is your superpower and what is your kryptonite?

We all have several signature strengths that when applied, amplify our chances of success. Some of mine have been clarity of purpose, resolve/resilience, being decisive and having the ability to explain complex ideas in simple terms. These "superpowers" have served me greatly.

But I also have my kryptonite. - Mainly getting into negative and self-defeating thought patterns and behaviors. One is making assumptions. Another is getting caught in my bias and most importantly, putting too much energy and consideration into people who are not interested in the same kind of friendship.

Have you ever had that experience where you are overly concerned about what certain people in your life do say or think about you? As a result you end up feeling drained of your emotional resources, unworthy or "less than?" Of course this is normal human behavior, but it also has the potential to rob you of valuable time and energy. We don't often think of people or places as holding us back. And the truth is it is not really the people who are doing it, but ourselves.

We are our own worst enemies. We may think the problem lies with others, but it actually lies with us. The solution comes from identifying this self-sabotaging, thought process and dismantling it over time.

Here is one technique used in coaching:

- Step 1 is to catch the feeling in the moment and name it. "I am experiencing hurt/sadness."
- Step 2 is to allow yourself to turn inward and feel the feelings fully. Stay with it until the feeling begins to dissolve or reduce. One little known principle about emotions is they are less likely to persist in the light of recognition.
- Finally, replace the feeling with a new thought and feeling. "I am worthy." Do your best to feel this sensation.

At first it may just feel like words in your head, but this technique begins the reprogramming process of removing the kryptonite.

PERCEPTION/OWNERSHIP

I have heard people say, "Life is not about finding yourself, it is about creating yourself."

I have always loved that quote, but at the same time it has always rung a little false for me. Can you really create yourself without knowing who you currently are, and would you be able to recognize your creation without the ability to see yourself accurately?

For me, the journey is about both finding AND remaking yourself. The finding is about avoiding delusion and being able to view the world and your place in it accurately. Once you are able to do this, you can identify the missing puzzle pieces that may be blocking your ability to remake yourself.

In this regard, relationships with others are imperative. Most people see self-development as an individual pursuit, but without others we quickly find ourselves in circular, delusional thinking. Relationships help us discover our blind spots and patterns of dysfunction. Other humans are a mirror to our own internal psyche... the emotions, the assumptions, the fears, and the challenges others bring are nothing more than our own internal, psychological filters being activated. If we see ourselves as unworthy, our filters will easily generate the perspective that others feel the same way about us, whether they do or not.

Have you ever made an assumption about what a person meant only to discover they meant the exact opposite? That was your internal filter altering reality to reflect your intrinsic beliefs regarding self.

Of course this is not always the case. Sometimes people mean exactly what you think they do, but that too is a hint into our internal state.

We often find ourselves in repeated patterns with similar relationships, a self-fulfilling prophecy of sorts. Using these social relationships as a way to self-reflect is one of the most powerful methods for creative human growth. Sadly, many people don't take ownership of their relationship circumstances, but rather blame the outcomes on the other person. Doing that removes your ability to find your dysfunctions and know yourself better.

Know thyself to create thyself.

PERCEPTION/OWNERSHIP/ENGAGEMENT

L ife is a creative choice in every second.
You choose your Perception.

You choose your voice.

You choose the attitude you wake up with and the gratitude you go to sleep with.

You choose... new possibilities are yours if you choose to see them.

The life you imagined can be reimagined...the life you created can be recreated.

OWNERSHIP/SHARING

To feel empty inside is to be human. Loneliness is part of the human condition. It is there on purpose. It should not be avoided; it should be embraced. I have worked with enough people to know this is universal.

No one escapes it.

Victor Frankl spoke about this in the most elegant way. We each have three wills we can pursue: The will to power, the will to pleasure and the will to meaning. There is nothing wrong with indulging all of these wills as they all serve a purpose and can act as fertilizer for self-growth and discovery.

But it is the will to meaning that has the most potential to free us from that emptiness. Setting our minds to transforming ourselves into individuals who contribute to the greater good is the only way I believe the soul is ever truly fed.

You won't ever fully escape that feeling of loneliness because it is part of the human software program...and you wouldn't want to, because it is what drives you to meaning...to do, and inspire beyond yourself.

March 17

OWNERSHIP/ENGAGEMENT

We are in complete control over our thoughts, but have little to no control over external events.

This is simultaneously infuriating and freeing. Infuriating, because our natural human tendencies make us not want to do the work involved in honing and controlling our thoughts. Freeing, because the potential is there for us to take back control at any moment.

We may not recognize it as such, but when we blame, complain, lament, regret, whine, and wallow in self-pity...we are making a choice. Whether it is conscious or unconscious, we are making a choice to see our circumstances a particular way. Yet, we could see them as completely different if we chose. We could envision opportunity and possibility in any setback. We can choose lessons and growth or we can opt for blaming, complaining, and defeat.

This is why I love weight training. When I miss a lift I don't blame the weights, get angry with them, take it personally, or make excuses. I just take a step back, collect myself, and then engage again. Some days I win and some days I am beaten. It does not keep me from coming back though. I would not have it any other way.

Imagine if we approached all of life this way? This is my practice. Why do we expect easy and avoid hard?

Nothing is easy! Easy is earned.

"You have control over your thoughts not outside events. Realize this and you will find strength" --- Marcus Aurelius

PERCEPTION/OWNERSHIP/ENGAGEMENT/SHARING

How do you find passion and purpose? You don't; you chase passions and choose purpose.

We often get confused because we don't realize the thing we love is often just the tool of our purpose, not purpose itself. Let me explain...let's say you are a personal trainer. That may be the tool you use, but what you really are is a teacher or motivator. Or maybe you are a chef. But that is just your tool. Maybe what you really are is a nourisher and caretaker? Perhaps you are an entrepreneur? But your purpose is as a creator.

It's not what you do that is your purpose, but **why** you do it. And that "why," is an evolving, flexible pursuit. You get to choose your "why" to some degree.

The path to purpose is often through passion, but the two are very different. Passion can often become about nothing but pleasure and lead nowhere. But focused passion almost always leads to purpose.

Chase your passions, but not all of them. Undirected passion is not what we are looking for, focused passions are. Through pursuing passion several possibilities for purpose emerge. Then you get to choose, and watch it evolve.

If you have trouble with this concept, look for the thread that weaves through all you do. I am or have been an athlete, personal trainer, bartender, clinician, author, and entrepreneur. None of these were or are my purpose...but if I observed myself in all of these things, the thread is, I was/am a transformer, teacher, inspirer. My personal gift was to touch, move, and inspire people. This purpose I bring with me everywhere I go from my job, to my hobbies, to my individual interactions with people. It is my why and my chosen life's work.

Do you know yours?

OWNERSHIP/SHARING

As humans we all make mistakes. We fall short sometimes in spectacularly embarrassing and destructive fashion. Few who have really lived life escape from this.

Sadly, the real injury is often self-imposed and done after the fact. We hold to our shortcomings, blame, hide, point the finger, avoid, deflect, and build a towering pile of our own nonsense, avoidance and lies.

It's as if we say, "I messed up so I might as well give up."

And that is exactly the point. We can't live our truth without facing our lies. We don't understand day without the concept of night; and we can't truly own our own light without exposure to our darkness.

There is no more inspiring story on the planet than the redemption story. You have lived and learned. Now live again and bring forth your light. We need you. The world needs you. You need you. I need you.

You have the ability to inspire. If you are not here to make a difference, than what are you here for?

PERCEPTION/OWNERSHIP

It's often difficult for us to see our own dysfunctions and blind spots. Being human comes with a certain degree of delusion. One way to illuminate where your dysfunctions lie is in repeated patterns.

Do you continue to have difficulty with coworkers at every new job? It's not them it's you. Does every new relationship eventually suffer from the same type of arguments? It's not them - it's you. Do you get consistent feedback you are selfish or cold or rude? Do you have a history of not being able to communicate well? It's you!

It's funny isn't it? We can spot and judge other people's dysfunctions from a mile away. We are excellent at it...yet, we are horrible at seeing our own.

Life and people can act as mirrors for us. Often the concept we become the most self-righteous about in others is the very trait we can recognize in ourselves and don't like.

The patterns in our lives that repeat over and over are almost always about us. If you want to grow and elevate your relationships, you must be able to spot and correct your own dysfunctions. They are not always apparent until you know where to look.

Our relationship patterns with others are one of the best mirrors for our own dysfunctions.

March 21

OWNERSHIP

N egative emotions cannot exist simultaneously with the feeling of gratitude. A daily gratitude practice has been studied in the field of happiness psychology and is a consistent and reliable behavior that correlates with overall happiness and life satisfaction.

In the studies, participants use a gratitude journal and write three things they are grateful for that day. These should be different each day. This practice shakes the brain out of its default state of judging and negativity. It's a skill you can learn.

Blaming, complaining, and wallowing in past or current hurts or mistakes has the opposite impact, degrading mood, leading to feelings of unworthiness and reducing life satisfaction.

There are few life changes that are easier to institute than this gratitude practice and the results are felt immediately; they grow and magnify as the practice continues.

What are you grateful for?

Write three things down each day. Do it especially when you feel stuck in the negative emotions of fear, hurt, and anger.

OWNERSHIP/WISDOM/ENGAGEMENT/RESOLVE

Freely admitting your dysfunctions while owning your superpowers is critical. It's a skill that drives success and is a predictable trait of high performers. It makes sense; you can't improve if you are not willing to look at your stuff. Having people in your life that can give honest feedback and sincere coaching is paramount.

Creating a new life is exactly like creating a new body. You need to be different than you have ever been before. It's a simple concept, but almost no one seems to be able to do it.

Realize if you are trying to change...whether it is a more fulfilling career, more financial security/freedom, a more loving, stable relationship, or healing from sickness... What you are signing up for is everything different.

It is the height of stupidity to think you can keep thinking, doing, and being the same person in the same ways as before.

Once you understand this, you begin to realize that not only do you need a new mindset, but you also need new skills and knowledge. Whether these skills be understanding investing, better communication, being more empathetic, or another field of study. You must learn and master the new, and that is uncomfortable.

As humans we crave certainty. We don't like being taken out of our comfort zones. We don't want to give up the familiar. We default toward laziness and away from action. We want easy, we are afraid of failure and fear the unknown.

The major insight about life is that **easy is earned**.

OWNERSHIP/ENGAGEMENT

Being stuck in a state of frustration, sadness or anxiety is almost always a result of either one of two things...the inability to make a choice OR the inability to own that choice once it's made.

This is one of the hardest things we can do especially when other people influence so much of who we are and what we feel.

We often torture ourselves by thinking, waiting, and stressing about what another person did, said, or wants. We want them to "just be honest" or "make up their mind" or "behave differently." The truth is, humans lie. We do it for many reasons. We do it to have our cake and eat it too...we do it because we think we are protecting another's feelings...we mostly do it because we are so out of touch and unhappy with ourselves, a lie is better than facing our own two-faced, dysfunctional selves.

If you want to know how deep the lying goes for a person, just look at the level of trust they have for others. Those who live lies think everyone else lies too and therefore, they trust no one.

So what should we do when we are in these places with another human? We take a long, hard look in the mirror and realize waiting for them to spontaneously make the choice we prefer is futile. Instead, we should draw firm boundaries in the sand...choose for ourselves (as hard as that can be)...and stand by that choice despite our doubts, loneliness or uncertainty.

When we do this, it is not only a form of vetting our current relationship, but more importantly declaring to our inner psychology what we deserve and the new type of person we want as a friend in our lives. Not a liar, not a cheat, not a phony, but rather an emotionally evolved person capable of truth and honesty.

Stop waiting for them. They are not going to miraculously come around until we declare through conviction and action what we will tolerate and what we will not. Then, if they want to be with us, they are forced to change.

Sometimes making a choice for ourselves and/or owning a choice we have made is the hardest thing we do in life. But if we want something different than we currently have, we must find the strength to choose for ourselves.

PERCEPTION/OWNERSHIP/ENGAGEMENT

I don't believe in faith or "the universe" or "everything happens for a reason." I believe in the human ability to choose and create. It is our superpower and all we need to make life happen.

It is not, jump and the net will appear; it is jump and weave the net as you fall. The ability to rewrite our stories, to reimagine our lives and to alter our reality through actions is all we really require in life.

The life you imagined can be reimagined.

Your view of the world can be changed. What has happened to you can be the baggage that weighs you down or the lessons that allow you to soar. The choice is always yours.

OWNERSHIP/ENGAGEMENT

Life is suffering. As the Buddhists believe, life is Dukkha, which translates as "pain" or "unsatisfactory." They maintain that it is the acceptance of this truth that leads to understanding and enlightenment.

If you are single, you suffer because of the lack of deep personal connection only romantic relationships can provide. If you are married with kids, you suffer because you lack complete freedom. If you have a job, you suffer because you must work. If you don't have a job, you suffer economic uncertainty. If you are thin and healthy, you suffer because of the lifestyle sacrifices you make to be that way. If you are overweight, you suffer the discomfort and health challenges.

Choice, by its very definition, means you must forego something else in the process of choosing what you desire. The secret to life is in understanding that you get to choose your suffering, but suffer you must. It is part of the human condition.

Life requires that you carry a load. You will never be without discontent and discomfort. In reality, life depends on this suffering. Each choice requires a sacrifice. The trick is to choose what you fight, bleed, and suffer for.

OWNERSHIP/ENGAGEMENT/SHARING

I have this belief that there is a life we ought to be living.
It is something we all feel at a very young age, an understanding that we are meant for something great, something uniquely suited to our signature strengths.

When we are young we know this intuitively, but we don't have the life experience and consciousness to understand it fully. As a result, we dream of being amazing. We dream about being a superhero, a savior of the world, a great healer, or a powerful magician. We dream these things because the outside world provides only fanciful versions of greatness.

Unfortunately, they are all fictional. As a result, as we grow older we may start to see our inner drive to be great as fictional as well, especially when we hear the constant cultural refrain of "be realistic."

However, these dreams matter.

There is a life you ought to be living. It has been called many things, but destiny is probably the most familiar. However, we think about destiny all wrong. We think of it as preordained or planned out in advance. In reality, your destiny is your choice. You have gifts that you are born with and others that you have learned. You have experiences and hardships that inform you further and refine your niche or specialty. From there, you get to choose where you will bring this unique mix of insight, personality, tools, and experiences to life.

Maybe you are a teacher and through your unique set of skills, experiences, charisma, and signature strengths you find a unique area, way, or place in which to teach? It does not need to be your career. It could be your hobby. Your interactions; your volunteer work; your committed engagement in any place in the world.

The important thing is to realize all the pain, work, failures, confusion, mistakes...all of it...is a canvas in which you can paint your destiny to live the life you know you ought to live.

PERCEPTION/OWNERSHIP/SHARING

If I were to tell you that all the hardships, hurts, and heaviness you have endured are the catalyst for a great and meaningful life, what would you say?

I know it's hard to grasp, but it is really about how you see your pain. I have a scar on my right hand from a bar fight back in my days as a bouncer. I have some pretty nasty arthritis in that hand as well. But you know what? I love that scar and the pain. It is one of my favorite things about my physical body. Because as challenging as that event was, delaying my graduation from college, it gave me the time to contemplate my ways, and slowed me down. All of that made me grow. It acted as a psychological ripple through my life that made me kinder, more caring, and more in tune than I would have been otherwise.

I have psychological wounds too. I have been rejected and betrayed by those I saw as some of my best friends. Have you ever had someone whom you love utterly and completely reject you? Have you ever had a family member you trusted come back with a "you owe me?" Have you ever lost someone? Have you ever thought you were loved only to find out you weren't?

We humans desperately cling to this stuff. We hold on to it like a trophy. We point it out and bring it up, whine about it and examine it constantly as if to say, "I was hurt. I am wounded. You should bow at the alter of my pain."

This is what you must see. Wallowing in your pain is not inspiring nor empowering, and it does nothing for the world or you.

I am the happiest I have ever been in my life. It's a result of my pain. I still carry it, but I don't wallow in it; I relish it. It focuses me on my purpose and its ripple effect has made me better. I don't do "you owe me's," because my pain taught me. I don't do indifference, phoniness, and lies because my pain reminds me. I don't dismiss people and I always communicate, because my pain instructs me. I am who I am because of my pain and I love who I am.

Yes, my pain fractured and scarred me. It's still there too. I don't mind looking at it because it makes me better. I have zero need to present my pain like a tattoo for all to see. You will see my pain in my generosity and kindness. I transformed it the same way it transformed me.

WISDOM

I t is not what we don't know that is the issue, but what we are convinced we do know that is keeping us stuck.

Hence the idea that Wisdom is a far greater superpower than knowledge, and the key to Wisdom is cultivating open-minded experiences.

PERCEPTION/WISDOM

S elf-reflection is the beginning of the process of understanding.
We humans have an uncanny ability to assign our own faults to others, to judge others for the same behaviors we lean toward, and to assume we are right and others are wrong. We are so delusional that research shows we actually think we know other people better than they know themselves.

The natural default of the human brain is to judge, make assumptions, and to ascribe the best attributes to ourselves while pinning the worst traits onto others. We are also lazy. There is nothing we love more than letting ourselves be pulled away from reality by fantasy of TV, news, social media, games, food or any other way to hide. This is not a judgment; all humans default to this state, including myself. These are natural traits of being human, but they can be overcome; self-reflection is where to start.

There is no better way to shine a light on your own dysfunctions than to sit quietly with yourself or observe your behavior with others. However, we would rather watch TV, or scroll through Facebook, anything to distract ourselves from ourselves.

When was the last time you sat still to watch yourself and the world pass by? This state is far more useful to self-discovery than the constant to-do-list and social scramble.

Rest, recovery and reflection charge the psychic battery, allow for self-discovery, and have the impact of exponentially raising work capacity and focus.

Rest and reflection is synergistic with work and focus. Distraction, judgment, assumption, business, and TV fantasyland are not.

"To know oneself is to study oneself…" --Bruce Lee

PERCEPTION/WISDOM/SHARING

How do people develop a following and command interest both offline and online?

There is a formula for this: P+P+W (Presence plus Power plus Warmth).

Research has shown (yes, studies show charisma is a learned skill rather than an inborn trait) that magnetic people don't make you feel like they are the smartest in the room...instead they make you feel like **you** are the smartest in the room.

OWNERSHIP/WISDOM

S ocrates. At a time when the Greek way was to conduct everything by commit-
tee and consensus of the popular vote, he was the first to question the logic.
He recognized that "group think" was a danger to the truth. He believed that
humans, by their very nature, were lazy thinkers and could easily be co-opted to
another person's belief through numerous means. He believed that questions were
the answer to finding truth and right action.

The Socratic method is simply a series of questions to test your, or anyone
else's, beliefs.

First you make a statement you believe to be true or common sense. You then
search for examples or exceptions to your statement. When you find them, and
you almost always will, you amend your statement to account for those exceptions. You continue in this way until you arrive at a statement that is most true.

Many people who understand science will recognize the Socratic method as
the precursor to the scientific method. What distinguishes science from opinion is
not that it is necessarily truer at the start, but that overtime, it is self-correcting.
Ultimately, science, when done right, corrects its self and moves closer to the truth.

This is the exact opposite of opinion, which is self-perpetuating. Human nature leans toward confirmation bias, which means we will naturally and automatically seek out information that agrees with us and selectively ignore that which
does not.

Socrates' contribution to self-development is one that warns against the destructive power of bias. He recognized it as one of the primary factors that choke
self-growth and wisdom.

Of course, like most powerful ideas, this scared the establishment in the society he lived, and he was eventually put on trial for his teachings, found guilty,
and killed.

PERCEPTION

The natural default of the human brain is that we fail to notice that we don't notice.

This keeps us from understanding who we are, and creating who we wish to be.

OWNERSHIP/WISDOM/ENGAGEMENT

There is what you know, you know. For example maybe you know that you know how to read.

There is what you know, you don't know. Maybe you know that you don't know how to fly.

But the biggest category of all is what you don't know, you don't know.

In other words, everything you did not even realize existed. It just was not on your radar. Insights that could change your life and open up your world. This is the area that provides the most opportunity for growth.

In this regard there are seekers and settlers. Settlers prefer comfort and certainty. They want the status quo. They gravitate towards conservatism.

Seekers head more towards autonomy and discovery. They purposely push the boundaries of their comfort zones. Their Next Level selves are always inquiring, "What else is there for me to know?"

The most successful are almost always seekers. It is almost impossible to move from where you are to where you want to go otherwise.

PERCEPTION/WISDOM

The two major forces that keep us from ourselves are distraction and delusion, distraction from the world around us, delusion from the world inside us.

I find it useful to remove myself from both as often as I can and as much as is possible.

Distraction is all around and ever present. There is nothing wrong with escapism on occasion, but what happens when the creations of the culture become a greater focus than the creations you manifest in your own life?

PERCEPTION/ENGAGEMENT/RESOLVE

We all are human and therefore suffer with certain psychological tendencies and needs: the need for status; the need for certainty; the need for related-ness; the need for autonomy; and the need for fairness, but our chief need and drive is the need for meaning.

The greater the degree of distraction, the less chance you have to create meaning in your life.

Thoughts of fear and failure may be paralyzing, but when your number one fear is being a coward or not trying, you automatically begin to engage in real life, not the "make believe" distractions of culture.

PERCEPTION/OWNERSHIP/SHARING

If you want quality relationships, you need to be willing to spend time understanding yourself first.

Self-reflection, self-development and self-actualization are not selfish pursuits; they are the psychological equivalent of the airplane oxygen mask: You must put yours on first before helping others.

Neglecting your personal development will degrade your relationships in the same way neglecting diet and exercise can destroy your health.

PERCEPTION/OWNERSHIP

The stories we tell ourselves can lift us up or weigh us down.

Baggage is an unconscious belief system we adopt based on past events that hurt us in some way. We then use that baggage to justify our beliefs about the world and why we can't trust. There is a reason we say, "They have too much baggage."

Responding in the present based on our past pain is very much a victim mentality, and severely limiting. We wrongly assume this baggage is helpful, but these stories severely limit our potential for growth, especially in our career, finances, and personal relationships.

Strong boundaries have the opposite effect.

It's boundaries we need, not baggage. Boundaries provide protection, but rather than weigh us down with bitterness, resentment, regret, fear, and remorse; boundaries allow us to trust, take risks, and interact with others from a place of possibility.

Boundaries equal taking responsibility. We open ourselves up and come from a place of possibility, and only when our boundaries are crossed do we act and adjust our position.

The idea is to have powerful and defined boundaries and ditch the baggage. One serves us; the other holds us back.

PERCEPTION/WISDOM

I ronically, the major obstacle to growth is not what you don't know, but rather what you are convinced you already know for sure.

Being closed off to new information, avoidant of novel experiences or ignoring a different perspective is a choice to stunt your own growth. It shrinks rather than enlarges.

OWNERSHIP/WISDOM/ENGAGEMENT/RESOLVE

We, humans, will often sacrifice our own personal growth simply to be right or prove someone else wrong.

There are several ways to avoid this state of stunted growth. They are:

- Question your own beliefs.
- Be open to the beliefs of others.
- Seek knowledge from different sources.
- Force yourself to have new and sometimes uncomfortable experiences.
- Say yes to that which you have always said no.
- Be willing to give up your need to be right.

PERCEPTION/ENGAGEMENT

Your life is unlikely to expand in any meaningful way without your involvement. We live in a world of unprecedented opportunities for growth, yet we have brains that naturally resist that growth by instead seeking safety, comfort, looking good, or being right.

How do we rewrite this negative programming?

Simply notice!

Then act differently. Whenever you are acting in limiting ways, stop yourself and make a choice to be different than what you have always been. Do this and your life has no choice but to change.

WISDOM

The accumulation of information is an interesting process. We read a book, journal, or article and it becomes our bible, until we read the next source and then that becomes our bible.

This is level 1.0 learning. We don't yet know very much so we have this false security around the "truth" of information. We think, "Well, it was published so it must be the truth." At this stage we are most susceptible to confirmation bias. We read an article, believe it, and then start to naturally gravitate toward only information that supports and bolsters that viewpoint. We also avoid any information that contradicts what we think we know, limiting our ability to learn new things.

In level 2.0 we gain a little more exposure and real world experience. Let's assume we believe in a vegetarian or primal (meat-based) diet. The first time we see someone who is sick as a result of following an all vegetarian or all primal diet, it makes us begin to question things. Of course many, if not most, people choose to ignore these outliers, preferring to keep their blinders on. Often they are too heavily invested in their knowledge base.

Finally there is level 3.0 learning, where we begin to realize that the more we learn, the less we actually know. We start to look at information differently at this point. The black and white dichotomies we created in level 1.0 and 2.0 begin to fall away and are replaced by gray. We no longer make grandiose definitive statements, but start using words like "may" and "it depends" and "that's one point of view." At this point, we reach a degree of wisdom about the information we consume.

We can determine which level we operate from by our degree of certainty and need to defend what we think we know. At level 1.0 we are convinced of our way, level 2.0 we start seeing contradictions, and at level 3.0 we embrace the fact that we don't know much at all.

The point? Books, blogs, documentaries, Ted Talks, articles, etc.; all that information is only as good as our ability to see it in context of the bigger picture.

Don't educate yourself into a box.

PERCEPTION/OWNERSHIP/RESOLVE

R esearch shows that there are three things that determine success more than any other factor.

Can you guess what they are?

IQ maybe? Nope, intelligence is not it.

EQ (Emotional Intelligence) perhaps? Not that either.

Work ethic? That's important, but not it.

The three factors are:

1. Your belief in your own abilities.
2. The belief in you by those around you (family, friends, peers, and coworkers).
3. Your ability to see failures and setbacks as learning and growth opportunities.

PERCEPTION/WISDOM

Sometimes I wake up early just because I can't wait to have coffee.
How can something so bitter, that I literally made a disgusted face over on my first taste, turn into one of the most enjoyable of life's rituals?

In the same way, some of life's greatest hardships can turn into some of our most rewarding lessons that make us who we are.

So...as in coffee, as in life.

PERCEPTION/WISDOM

People always say you need to "think outside the box." And most people view this, out-of-the-box thinking, as a desirable and respectable trait. I agree 100% that we should "think outside the box." All our greatest thinkers and most celebrated luminaries were out-of-the-box thinkers, seeing things others could not.

There is just one tiny issue...do you even know what your box is? If you don't, then how can you know you are thinking beyond it?

Your box comes from the people you grew up with, the shows you watch, the people you work with, the people in your town/state, the stories you have heard, the media you choose, the travel you have done and the books you have read.

There is a funny little psychological glitch called the Dunning-Kruger effect (I call it the dunce effect for short), which says those with the least knowledge about a subject are also the ones convinced they know the most. It is one of the most silly, and yet true, psychological glitches of being human.

Here is how it works: in order for you to know if you are adept at a subject, it requires you to study it and develop a large degree of expertise. This accumulated knowledge is the essential component to decipher whether you actually know what you are talking about. But in a strange twist the more people learn and expand their box, the more they become aware of all the stuff they don't actually know. As result, they underestimate what they know.

So people with the smallest boxes think they have the biggest boxes and those with the biggest boxes think their box is much smaller than it is. And guess which group is more likely to notice information outside their box? Yep, those with the least bias and most experience.

How do you tell the dunces from the rest? Those with the loudest most extreme views are almost always the dunces. Those logical few in the middle are too busy looking to expand their box versus yelling and screaming about what they think they know.

Politics, religion, and now, nutrition; these topics are magnets for the dunces.

Osho sums this up so eloquently, "The less people know, the more stubbornly they know it."

PERCEPTION/OWNERSHIP/ENGAGEMENT

Like all humans, my natural, default state of delusion and distraction is always tugging at me. Before my study of psychology and the natural tendencies of the human brain, I would get incredibly frustrated at my inability to stay focused, my propensity to get emotionally hijacked, or my persistent need for outside affirmation.

I did not realize these things were normal aspects of being human, a natural consequence of not training my brain to see, act, and behave differently.

So, I slowly started monitoring my inner thoughts and creating reminders for myself meant to "snap myself out of it." This started out as single words, my two favorites are IGNITE & ELEVATE. These words represent what I want to be "when I grow up." - Someone who inspires and elevates others and myself. They are psychic reminders of who I am to be.

I use imagery too. When afraid, I call up a vision of a warrior; especially the American GI charging the beaches of Normandy facing his greatest fear for a meaning much larger than himself.

I use technology, like a reminder that shows up on my phone four times daily, buzzing me into an awakening of who I am to be.

When it comes to change, it is not, "fake it until you make it," it is, "be it until you see it." That means making sure your mental maps are primed constantly to oppose the natural default state of human fear, ignorance, and laziness.

ENGAGEMENT

In life you often get what you believe you deserve; and the thing you are told you cannot do is usually the action you must take.

Do your job, learn, get better, and care deeply, but realize personal growth is not a goal of most. If you are not progressing, you are either staying in the same patterns, or regressing.

April 16

PERCEPTION/OWNERSHIP/ENGAGEMENT

Emotions are instructive and directive. They are meant to be felt, not stifled. They are the way your Next Level self snaps you to attention and says, "Hey, look over here. This is where your life needs work."

Some insights can only be gained by feeling. I don't stuff it. I talk about it. I feel it. I go with it. It serves me and moves me.

A stuck emotion is a symptom of a stuck life. An emotion ignored and stuffed away becomes a life of stagnation and bitterness.

Here is to all the feelings in life, and the ability to feel and move, NOT stuff and stay.

PERCEPTION/OWNERSHIP/ENGAGEMENT/SHARING

You can't change anyone, and nobody owes you a thing.

The idea of trying to change a person is not only impossible, but it is emotionally exhausting. It is also a symptom of the worst combination of human traits, ignorance and arrogance. It's normal of course. We all fall prey to the, "I am better than you" trap at times. Of course that does not make it excusable.

Change can't be forced. It can, however, be inspired. That has only ever been done by authentic, aligned actions. In other words, being exactly, and generously, who you are.

People see right through phony behaviors and false stories. We humans have an uncanny ability to sniff out hypocrisy and dishonesty in everyone but ourselves.

We also know real when we see it. Its rarity is precisely why it so often inspires. Take authenticity in action and combine that with true generosity of spirit and you have one of the most powerful catalysts for inspiring change.

But remember, one of the most selfish things you can do is give with expectation. No one owes you anything. Expectation is the antithesis of generosity, and it inspires no one. In fact, it's a repulsive force that achieves the opposite of change.

You want someone to change? Change yourself.

Be fully, unapologetically and honestly yourself. Share that freely without expectation and you will often inspire change without even trying.

PERCEPTION/OWNERSHIP/SHARING

I have been asked why people need self-development. It's my opinion, but I believe the single greatest gift you can give the world is your best self. Being your Next Level self literally changes other people for the better and that makes the world immensely more enriching for us all.

I bet you have a friend that generates that feeling for the people they meet. Let's say you meet someone new: you have a lot in common, a similar thirst for learning and positive vibes. What do you do? You usually say, "Oh wow, so-and-so. You will love them!"

I bet you also know the slight anxiety you feel when a new peer meets a friend or family member who is not warm, friendly or socially adept.

My mother is the person I always want everyone to meet. My mother has a way of genuinely seeing the beauty in people. Her responses to people are so authentic and warm that they can't help but feel that they are amazing and important. She interacts with people with large egos and just lets them have it. She sees people annoyed and overcomes it with positive vibes. She senses those who are doubtful, sad, or wounded and loves them in a way that inspires them to heal.

People can never keep their emotional barriers up when my mother touches them with her unique brand of love for her fellow human. Once, one of my girlfriends admitted she was afraid to meet my mother. I smiled and said, "She is going to adore you. You will feel like you are best friends within five minutes. Don't worry." That's exactly what happened.

My mother went through hell as a kid. She endured a lot of wounds and has many emotional scars. She and I know everything about each other so I know her wounds well. The amazing thing is how she has transformed that pain into magic for others. She uses each of her scars to touch others in that same area of their souls. Not only does she fill their gaps in that brief interaction, but she also imparts something that allows them to begin to fill it themselves.

This superpower came out of her own self-development. Why would you want a perfect physical body but a bitter, empty soul inside? That is why self-development matters.

April 19

PERCEPTION/OWNERSHIP/ENGAGEMENT

What I love about life is how it is always teaching if we allow it. The problem is, lessons are rarely painless and no one voluntarily puts their hand on a hot stove.

Strength comes from speaking and acting your truth, but it also comes from accepting when the truth of life is in direct opposition.

Life is an interesting place where we simultaneously travel alone while traveling together. I believe this is the most important element of learning and change.

Change requires learning to see different, think different, and be different. Input from others helps us see our blind spots, and prevents us from repeating patterns and being stuck in life.

OWNERSHIP/ENGAGEMENT/SHARING

In relationships with others we are able to gain valuable feedback about the world, our place in it and our ability to effect change. Relationships are the way we learn and grow.

If we cheat, lie, and avoid we are voluntarily stunting our own growth while not letting those we say we care about know us at all. Yes, relationships might change as a result and some will even end, but living a life of deception is no life at all.

If you are my friend...if I say I love you, then I will tell you the truth as difficult as it might be. I have learned the hard way this is the only way to truly connect, the only way to truly grow.

To live my truth alongside you with honesty and integrity, that is what I commit to, as your friend, your lover, your family member, as your fellow human.

April 21

PERCEPTION/OWNERSHIP

Y ou are dysfunctional, scared, lazy, and ignorant. I know you are because I am too. It is part of the human condition.

The mistake we make is thinking we are special in some way; that our suffering is unique. It's not. Millions upon millions of humans have gone through the same confusion, doubt, loss, pain, illness and heartbreak since the beginning.

That we are somehow better than or worse than the next person is simply our need to try to make ourselves special. We humans want nothing more than to be seen, understood and loved. It's our prime directive.

So we spend all our time posturing, promoting, and pimping ourselves in an effort to be seen. We look to see who spots us, and as a result, we miss seeing ourselves.

It is the cruelest of all tricks, and it is our own mind that keeps us stuck in it. We are looking at them to see if they are looking back. They are, but the reason has nothing to do with the car you drive, how sexy you are, your money, your status or anything else you peacock with.

They look for the same reason you look: only to see if you are looking.

All the while, you miss the person who needs you the most: you.

Do you know who you are, what you stand for, and what you choose to bleed, suffer and die for? Have you spent any time with you? Or are you content to live a life defined and confined by others?

PERCEPTION/OWNERSHIP/ENGAGEMENT

Purpose before power. Meaning before money. Easy is earned. This is a Perception problem most people have. They think it works the other way around.

This isn't enough of course, but it is the fire that drives the engine to discover how to get there. The other powers must be developed too.

Three critical questions of self-actualization:

- Who are you?
- Who do you want to become?
- How will it drive meaning in your life?

You can't understand how to behave differently if you don't understand how you are currently acting in the world. For example, when I decided I wanted to be a writer I had to be honest about the fact that I did not write. I read a lot, but writers write. So I started writing every day. This was before the days of blogs and most of my writings took place in a notebook. It did not matter to me what I wrote, I just knew writers write and I was not.

This applies to personal traits as well. If you want to be honest you have to be honest about your lies first. If you want to be trusted, you must trust. If you want to be respected and understood, you must first acknowledge where you are not these things and be it yourself before you see it in others.

I remember looking in the mirror one day and saying "You are a liar, a gossiper and a phony. Fine. But not anymore."

Of course for anything to really change, it has to really matter. How does being a writer, radically honest, and always upfront with my friends serve my deepest purpose and meaning?

I am a student and a teacher (a teacher is always both). That is where I derive my meaning and purpose. That is what sustains me and inks my legacy. I am not perfect and I am always becoming, but who I have been, and who I seek to become, is always informing who I must be now.

April 23

PERCEPTION/OWNERSHIP/ENGAGEMENT/RESOLVE

We humans crave certainty above all else and we are often horrible at making the leap to the Next Level because we don't want to leave our comfort zone.

How can we avoid this trap and act much sooner?

Look out for the repeating patterns. Look out for stuck emotions.

Recurring anxiety? Depression?

This is your higher-self giving you clues that it is time to level up, and telling you it's time to expose yourself to the next, great story.

PERCEPTION/OWNERSHIP/ENGAGEMENT/RESOLVE

We are all inherently fearful, lazy and delusional. We can either wallow in this knowledge and deny it, or understand that we have just been given the secret to success.

In any endeavor, be a little less fearful, a little less lazy, and continue to seek the truth without bias or dogma.

PERCEPTION/OWNERSHIP/WISDOM/
ENGAGEMENT/RESOLVE

To fight fear you must confront your fears. No one ever became less fearful by avoiding their fears. Think of FEAR as Find, Engage And Resolve.

To conquer lazy takes unlocking passion and choosing your purpose. If achievement were a car, passion would be the engine, and purpose the navigation. Passion drives you and purpose guides you. Beware of the misdirection caused by chasing passion without a strong purpose.

Overcoming ignorance and delusion is perhaps harder than anything else. Once we make an error, we will justify our behavior and cling to that choice to save face in our own mind. Instead question your motives, dismantle your bias, and always seek to prove your own beliefs and assumptions wrong. Always be learning but not from places that just reinforce what you think you already know.

Here is to attacking our fears, living with purposeful passion and questioning everything, especially our own assumptions and biases.

The ability to see failure, mistakes, loss, heartache, and obstacles as opportunities for growth is what sets the successful apart from the rest.

RESOLVE

The idea that a life focused on health and fitness is supposed to be easy, or anything worthwhile will be, is a mistake.

Easy is earned in the trenches of failure and in the power of Resolve.

Failure is a requirement. The faster and more frequently you fail, the more opportunity you have for learning and growth. Failure is a stepping-stone, rather than an obstacle, to success.

I envision fitness endeavors as the perfect metaphor for life in general. Being frightened of failure is the same as being afraid to succeed, because without failure true success in fitness and life becomes impossible.

The process of chasing a PR (Personal Record) in the gym mirrors the process in life. You must show up again and again and over and over.

When you fail, which you will many times, you must get back up and start over. It's this process you must fall in love with, not the outcome.

If you are not ready to fail, then you're not ready to succeed. You know you have arrived when arrival is no longer the goal.

OWNERSHIP/ENGAGEMENT/RESOLVE

There is what happens in life and there is how we happen back.

Make no mistake; you will suffer. But that suffering can be used to create something beautiful.

Life, by its very definition is movement and change. Suffering most often results from resisting this movement and change. We get stuck because we get too attached to the story of what we had instead of the story of what we can create.

Change is usually forced on us. We are averse to change and prefer comfort and certainty. We think we can avoid suffering this way. Yet, at the same time, we crave autonomy and feel compelled to grow. We have these dual desires, because we want change but want things to remain the same. Yes, it's silly, but also very human.

The first step is acknowledging that we will suffer regardless. Any choice you make means you are foregoing another choice. Choose certainty and comfort and you suffer due to lack of growth. Choose growth and change and you suffer from lack of stability and comfort.

Life is change. Stability and comfort are myths anyway.

The trick is choosing for you, not based on culture, family, friends or expectations. When you do, remember it's not "Fake it until you make it." This implies doing without believing or feeling. Change must happen on the inside as well as on the outside. It's "Be it until you see it." This is the mental state where action and feeling are in alignment, if only for a second. With practice it's the way you slowly become.

The secret to comfort is making the process of change your new comfort zone. Attack life, otherwise you risk being attacked by it.

OWNERSHIP/ENGAGEMENT

W ithout meaning we have no anchor, no lighthouse, no direction. Without meaning we will naturally begin to seek pleasure and/or power instead. These things can't fulfill us and may destroy us.

It is my contention that the single, most important thing we can do as individuals is to create our meaning. I use the word, create, on purpose because meaning is not something that falls out of the sky and knocks you on the head.

When I asked my father why he came to all our games, was always home for dinner, and never sought to chase career concerns, he said, "I chose early on to be the best father, and that meant my job was just a means to support that goal." Wow, the perfect lesson in meaning.

Meaning is a creative choice. To define your meaning you must be an artist of life.

Choose what you will paint and then...paint it.

OWNERSHIP/ENGAGEMENT/SHARING

Without meaning or purpose we will chase pleasure in sex, food, material items, and more. None of these can provide what we are really thirsty for. We all know those who chased pleasure and were broken by it.

Without creating meaning we will chase power in status, money, and knowledge. We all know the miserable, self-righteous know-it-all, whose sole life gambit is to prove they are winning.

Meaning is not fleeting or destructive. It feeds you from the inside out. When all is wrong on the outside, all remains certain on the inside because we know why we are here and what we must do.

Meaning is a choice and a creative pursuit that involves how you will enrich yourself by enriching the world. It is never self-centered and it is always far reaching.

Meaning is what you seek and what you must create.

OWNERSHIP/WISDOM

There is a sweet spot between arrogance and insecurity where you have the audacity to believe in yourself, but the humility to know you don't know much at all.

May 1

PERCEPTION/WISDOM

Many of our beliefs are beyond our consciousness. We don't have a clue what they are, where they came from, or how they are powerfully influencing us in every interaction of our lives.

It takes a rare fish to be aware they are swimming in something called water, and what a powerful, little fishy that is.

I want to know what I am swimming in.

OWNERSHIP/ENGAGEMENT/WISDOM

Those who talk shit are almost never doing shit.

You have a lot you want to do. Do you really have time to waste on what someone else thinks or says?

Learn from others. Consider the feedback. But never let their insecurity become your own.

OWNERSHIP/ENGAGEMENT

M indset is what drives everything.
Victim Culture (VC) vs Growth/Gratitude culture (GC)

The VC wallows in their pain, blaming, complaining, judging and pointing fingers. They are the critics, the jealous types, the self-righteous, gossipers and deceivers.

The GC do their jobs, are grateful for the opportunities they have and turn their pain into powerful catalysts for personal growth. They are all about growing, learning, supporting, creating and taking action.

It's not true 100% of the time, but what I have seen over the years is that those who make effective change eventually make the switch from VC to GC.

The Growth/Gratitude Culture has the potential to move you. It is the best mindset for change.

May 4

OWNERSHIP

We are told, "Find your purpose and work/love/health/fitness will be so much easier." The problem is purpose is not found and it's not static. Purpose is created and it evolves.

You get to choose the purpose you want to create and once you do, it becomes a magical process.

PERCEPTION/WISDOM

Wisdom is knowledge plus experience. But what is it that drives us to accumulate that knowledge and have those experiences? To learn, to teach, to love in the future, is it not?

We humans have an interesting way of hearing a concept and then repeating it without thinking it through. One idea that is repeated a lot in the world of self-development is that we should practice staying in the present moment. We hear that living in the past is not helpful and the future not known.

The thought goes like this: the past is gone so dwelling on it will cause nothing but anxiety; the future is uncertain and therefore thinking about it causes anxiety as well.

I realize this seems to make sense, but I have never found it useful. Sure, remain in the present if you want to stay comfortable. Stay in the present if you want to avoid learning. Stay in the present if you don't want to experience being human.

I recently read a paper by Martin Seligman, the founder of happiness psychology. He dismantled this idea. We are called "homo sapiens," which translates to "wise man." A better name, Seligman points out, is "homo prospectus," because everything about our psychology is driven by considering our future prospects.

It is this singular attribute of considering the future that drives us to create, to seek love, to learn, to teach, and to change ourselves, and the world. As a result of that future prospecting, we often feel fear, anxiety, and depression. That's the point and how we know we're alive. We feel these things, so we seek to change these things.

At our core, we are emotional alchemists. We look back at our pain. We then look forward with our uncertainty, fear, but also hope. We use those positive and negative emotions to fuel the fire of change.

Science now tells us this is who we are. It also tells us that technically, we can't live in the present moment even if we tried. The brain is not actually processing the moment at that moment. In this way, we only really perceive the world in the past anyway. Apparently our happiness depends on it.

PERCEPTION/WISDOM

When you perceive the world; where is that happening? If I tell you to point to where you see the tree, you will surely point away from yourself to somewhere in front of you? But that's not where you see the tree at all.

You are seeing the tree inside yourself. You perceive it as "out there," but in order to see it you had to bring it in through your eyes and process it in your brain. The image sits inside you, not outside you.

During the process of internalization you changed the tree into something that is more than a tree. Perhaps you fell out of a tree and broke your arm as a child. As a result the tree comes along with some fear and caution. It's seen as dangerous or unstable. Perhaps you hike and spending time in the woods is comforting and relaxing. When you take the tree in, you may feel peaceful and calm as a result.

The truth is, it is just a tree, nothing else. You shade this truth by adding things to its story. You do this so quickly and beyond your conscious awareness that you can get the truth completely wrong. Seeing the truth is a critical skill, but it's not easy. Truth is sometimes subjective. Your filter sometimes blurs the truth. My filter does the same.

Many things obscure the truth. Distraction (people, events, places, upbringing, cultural norms etc.) from the world around us can hide the truth. Delusion (dogma, bias, emotion, etc.) from the beliefs inside us can hide the truth.

To find the truth, we have to learn to think clearly, away from the herd and the noise. To see the truth we have to question our stories. Two of the most prevalent stories humans tell are insecurity and arrogance.

To see the truth of a thing we often question the thing. Or we question people about the thing. Questioning is a great start, and the most critical skill. But the most important thing to question is ourselves, and how we see the thing.

"People are not disturbed by things, but by the views they take of them."
- Epictetus

ENGAGEMENT

I asked my mother as we drove across country, "Mom, what do you think you would tell a person about happiness and life, something they could anchor to during the tough times?"

She said, "I don't know, I think you just have to take a lot of long walks and do your job."

I love that. This has certainly been true for me. I love my life and while I have pain, doubt, and insecurities, like everyone else...movement clears my head and Engagement in my work and passion always anchors me back to my source, power and purpose.

WISDOM

always learn most when I assume I am the most ignorant person in the room. This is my practice, not my mastery.

PERCEPTION/OWNERSHIP/RESOLVE

That moment of stress, pain, anguish, and confusion…that is when you meet your true character, and theirs.

Pay close attention. Actions never lie.

You can't love enough for the both of you. They either meet you halfway or you walk away. That is the only way it works. It is the only way it has ever worked. And don't take it personally.

We are all human and some simply don't have the strength, courage, or imagination to create what you know is possible. It's best to find someone who's "all in" with you.

The best person for that job is you.

PERCEPTION/OWNERSHIP/WISDOM/SHARING

Y ou know those people who are always negative, complaining and registering their distaste with something? How about those who only ever have nice things to say? Every person they mention is the best, most awesome, genius person they know?

These people bother you because you know life is not like that. Sure, we like when people say nice things, but we value congruency more. We want to see people describe things as we feel they are. That builds trust. If they tell us something we have experienced differently, we become skeptical and lose trust.

This "all bad" or "all good," behavior is their own way to manage fear and dislike of uncertainty. It's as if they think, "If I am always nice and positive about everything and everyone, I will not have conflict." Or "If I always see the bad, I will be prepared for any negative contingency."

One of the worst things you can be pegged as is dishonest, or not genuine. Being "all good," or "all bad" assures you will be seen as inauthentic or untrustworthy because everyone knows life is not that way.

It helps to know the difference between brutal honesty and compassionate honesty. Brutal honesty means I say whatever I feel without considerations of your feelings. Compassionate honesty means I consider your feelings and qualify my statements.

1. Ask Permission. I say, "Look I have something to say. Are you sure you want to hear?" This gives choice and warning and lets them know you respect them.

2. Qualify. Most truth is subjective so say, "This is my opinion," or "I see it this way. How do you see it?"

3. Decline. Your opinion is not always necessary or appropriate. If so, just say, "I don't have enough information to have an opinion. Or "I would rather not say as I have history with that person that makes me less objective." Or "This is none of my business.

4. Intended kindness. Whether or not the other person is hurt or not, is less a concern. Truth often hurts in the short term, but heals in the long run. Say, "I know this may not be what you want to hear, but I would rather risk hurting you now than lying and ruining your trust."

OWNERSHIP/ENGAGEMENT/RESOLVE

What if I told you the next five years would be the hardest of your life; filled with loss, heartache, confusion, hurt, setbacks and frustrations you can't even imagine?

If I could magically provide the opportunity to avoid these struggles, would you take it?

What if I told you that as a result of all you had been through you would be wiser, kinder, more open, more resilient, better equipped to give and receive love, and have a deeper appreciation for what is most important in life?

Would you want to avoid the pain and hardship then?

This scenario is obviously hypothetical, but what IS true is that we all have the ability to turn hardship into growth. It's not about luck or happenstance; it is about you choosing to turn the pain into fuel for growth.

Too many decide the weight is too heavy and they can't bear it. This is nonsense; you can deal with anything you choose to handle. You have the power to turn any obstacle into a path toward success or turn any pain into fuel for growth. The only thing stopping you is you.

There is no blame or complain in change.

Either you are wallowing in it or doing the work to grow from it.

SHARING

My mother, and all mothers, to me are the quintessence of selflessness and generosity.

If you have ever met my mother you would be struck by the way she makes everyone feel important, noticed, beautiful, and smart. She is the person who will be immediately interested by a person in line next to her and tell them they are so beautiful and give them a hug...they may look at her like she is crazy, but the effect is that everyone who witnesses this, especially the recipient, becomes infused with positive energy, smiles and lightness.

Since I was a boy, I always saw this as magic. I would watch as my mother would "cast a spell" on people and immediately uplift and inspire with just a single sincere act of kindness or word of recognition.

She is an incredible artist and creates art, but I have always seen her greatest creative power in the way she manifests positivity out of thin air for those around her who need it.

The artist and emotional alchemist: that's my mom.

As Bobby Boucher in, *The Waterboy,* says, "I love my momma very much... now you know dat!"

OWNERSHIP/ENGAGEMENT

How do we implement a plan for change? What is the formula we must follow? It's not about goals...it is about a mindset shift that can only be brought to fruition through action.

So you're stuck? One of the most important and powerful lessons I have learned about mental "stuckness" is that physical movement is one of the best cures.

It could be as simple as getting to the gym or as complicated as packing up your stuff and heading across the country.

Many in the self-help and self-development worlds focus on thinking first. They say, "Think positive thoughts" or "Think like a winner and you'll be a winner." This approach can definitely work, but action influences thinking faster than thinking influences action.

Our brains are constantly making meaning, assigning value, and rationalizing our behaviors. If we are sad but force a smile and a laugh, the brain says "Hmmm I am smiling. I must be happy." It then creates the feelings of happiness. This is much faster, and more predictable, than "thinking happy thoughts."

You have to first **be** the thing in your actions before it shows up in your reality. *Be it until you see it*!

OWNERSHIP/ENGAGEMENT

A ctions are spiritual declaratives. They demonstrate everything you need to know about yourself or others.

If you are ever confused about yourself or another, the clarity is in the consistent actions. Actions are a far more honest assessment of who they, and you, are.

You want change? Two things:

1. Act as if you are that thing right now this moment.
2. Surround yourself with only those whose actions consistently say they support, believe, respect, and love you!

ENGAGEMENT/RESOLVE

In weight lifting, as in life, it is a game of challenge and growth. We purposely expose ourselves to greater and greater demands in the weight room, competing with ourselves to better ourselves. We seek Personal Records (PRs) as a way to measure our progress and test our resolve.

Attempting a PR is uncomfortable. You're apprehensive because you have never lifted this weight before and you know it is a little risky. You think, "What if it's too heavy?" Or, "What if I can't control the weight?" Or, "What if I get hurt?" And you let the fear and the doubt wash over you as you silently take in a deep breath, feeling your heart beat through your chest. And there is this little voice in your head...your inner warrior...that says, "F that, I got this. No way I am NOT going to destroy this weight."

Whether you successfully lift the weight or not, the brain has already received the message. You engage. You take action. You're a warrior. You follow through and equally accept success or failure because you know both are required.

There can be no success without failure to learn from.

I have what I call "fear PRs," things I am afraid of, apprehensive about, and feel uncomfortable doing. I know I can only achieve and learn if I attack my personal fear PRs.

One of my fears is flying. For a long time, I simply did not fly. Then I realized I was more afraid of being a coward than I was of a plane. I started chipping away at this fear. I took short flights at first, then longer flights, racking up my PRs. I flew over the ocean, a huge fear and a new PR. I have now done it again and again. I took my longest flight to date, about 11 hours, non-stop from LA to Paris. This was a new fear PR; an opportunity that reinforced my growth mindset and philosophy of attacking life.

PERCEPTION/ENGAGEMENT/RESOLVE

We all have fears, big, small, silly and common, but what few of us do is systematically chase those fears down and conquer them bit-by-bit.

Remember your brain is always watching. What are you teaching it to think about you? How you attempt one action in life is how you do everything.

We humans each have our own internal struggles, feelings of inadequacy, unworthiness, guilt, not belonging, disconnectedness, or loneliness. These are all aspects of the human condition, part of being alive.

The natural tendency is to avoid such feelings. It is understandable to take this approach when confronted with these thoughts and feelings. But if you look a little deeper, you will find that those thoughts are actually pointing you toward the way. If you examine them closely enough, from the perspective of how they might serve you, you can't help but notice the potential for those feelings to illuminate that, which creates the opposite.

In other words, allowing yourself to deeply explore your sense of unworthiness also brings the potential to acknowledge your specialness - the thing that you bring to the world that no one else can bring. Only you.

If you buy into the fact that often the world is a reflection of your thoughts, then you can see those feelings as an embodiment of what you bring to the world. When was the last time you told someone how special they are? Acknowledged their power and beauty and worthiness? If it has been awhile, then there is a hint as to why you feel less of that sense yourself.

Have you ever done a tough workout or a kind deed and felt more resilient and meaningful as a result? Stop waiting for action to be taken by others on your behalf...instead take action for others on your behalf...watch how you change along with them. It's your power that you need most, not others'.

Where the body goes the brain follows. Every physical action has a mental reaction. It's called the "as-if principle." Face your fear by taking one small step toward that fear; your brain watches you and says, "I am an action taker. I face my fears. That is who I am."

It is a strange idea, but you are watching your own actions all of the time in the same way you are watching other people's actions. You know the saying, "actions speak louder than words?" That applies to how you measure yourself as well. Sure, it also works the other way. Thoughts can become actions, but not as readily as actions become thoughts.

PERCEPTION/WISDOM

The vast realm of possibility resides in what you don't know you don't know. In other words, almost all the insights, experiences, to dos, knowledge, tools, techniques, etc., are things you are completely unaware even exist. This is what the wisdom of mentors, coaches and teachers opens up for you. They can point out your blind spots, allowing you a clearer path to your potential.

In one year, I hired three different coaches: one for relationships, one for business, and one that covers success mindset around personal growth.

The insights and movement I gained were monumental. How can you put a price on being shown a possibility that you never comprehended as possible for you? It's huge.

ENGAGEMENT/RESOLVE

"PR" stands for Personal Record. The Fear PR is how you continually take small, directed actions toward your fears.

If you're afraid of being alone, your first Fear PR might be going to a movie solo. The next might be dining alone, the third, dinner without your phone. Soon, you'll reach the ultimate Fear PR of visiting a foreign country where you don't speak the language, alone!! Imagine what that level of Engagement could do for your life?

In fitness we seek Personal Records (PRs) in lifts. In self-development we seek PRs in life. Each time we are rewarded with elevated learning and mental reinforcement that we are courageous, capable, and resilient.

Just as in the gym, we will sometimes miss our PRs and must work to achieve them...it is the same with Fear PRs in life. Those PRs that are the most difficult to achieve are almost always the most valuable.

ENGAGEMENT

I am not a fan of traveling for the most part.

It's a comfort zone thing. I like my routine, my workouts, and familiar surroundings.

But my comfort zone is incapable of teaching me much, creating many memories or producing growth. This is why I have been forcing myself to travel. It's uncomfortable, but my experience tells me that is exactly the reason it expands me so much.

Choosing to live in our comfort zones is choosing to stunt our own personal growth.

ENGAGEMENT

My philosophy of success in any endeavor has always been to focus on my strengths again and again. Then select one weakness at a time and transform it to a strength, or at least move it out of the weakness category.

Most people avoid what they suck at or are afraid of. That is my natural tendency too, but what I have found is that attacking my fears and doing what others won't is the difference between success and mediocrity.

How we do one thing in life is how we do everything.

Our brains are watching and making assumptions about us based on our actions. This is exactly how our brains evaluate others as well.

I don't want my brain to see me as an avoider, lazy, or a coward. I know the watcher is always watching. What I want it to see is a man who is willing to step into discomfort, fear, and pain in order to grow.

By following this process, discomfort zones become comfort zones.

PERCEPTION/ENGAGEMENT/RESOLVE

I am a huge proponent of visualization as a tool for preparing the brain for what I hope to manifest. Weightlifting has always been the perfect practice ground for me. When I was younger and approaching a heavy weight during a workout, I would shut my eyes and see myself successfully lift the weight. I would let my mind "feel" how light it felt before I physically attempted to moved it.

Thinking is powerful. Action is powerful. The two combined is all the proof your brain needs to be convinced you can do, be and have the things you are working and striving for.

Using visualization for other issues works the same way. Imagine yourself sitting in a movie theater watching a movie that features you as the main character. You are watching yourself achieve the thing you want, while at the same time feeling exactly what it feels like. With your brain primed in this way, it says "Oh yeah, I can do this. I already know exactly what it feels like."

It's not the universe conspiring in your favor as many people say...it is more like you are the universe and the scriptwriter. It takes practice, but it is a powerful procedure and one validated by research.

I have experienced firsthand how visualization plus action can move mountains, but the critical piece many miss is that you have to let it show up the way it does. A good movie never unfolds quite the way you expect; it usually turns out better.

Certainty and comfort; they are key needs and fall back positions for the brain. We want predictability, and smooth sailing. We want easy. Life is not that way. The only thing certain about life is uncertainty.

Life has this strange way of jerking you up by the shirt collar just when you thought you had it all figured out. Like that good movie, it keeps you on your toes, and often you don't completely understand until the end. That's when you gain perspective.

If life does this naturally, why are we so intent on resisting it? Why are we afraid of this natural consequence of living?

If we are to learn, grow, and love, we must be willing to confront this uncertainty. We need to develop some degree of resilience and resolve to continue, even when we fail, are in pain, or afraid.

Our brains are always watching us to determine what type of person we are. Our brains look at our actions, not our words.

ENGAGEMENT/RESOLVE

The Fear PR: it's a purposeful exposure to something you fear or is uncomfort-able for you to build up mental resilience and psychological resolve.

Ironically, the gym provides a perfect micro example of this Fear PR lifestyle. Attacking a PR in the weight room often comes along with apprehension and a little fear. It's the attempt, whether successful or not, that convinces the brain you are strong, fearless, and resilient.

Treat life this way. Travel, learn, expose, and jump. It's not, leap and the net will appear; it's leap, and weave the net as you fall.

Nothing is easy. Easy is earned.

PERCEPTION/OWNERSHIP/ENGAGEMENT/RESOLVE

You're watching you. The same way you evaluate the intentions, trustworthiness and capabilities of someone else; your brain makes those same determinations about you. It's not listening to your mental chatter, it's focusing on your actions. It thinks to itself, "Who am I? Do I mean what I say? What do I stand for?" And then it answers those questions by observing and judging its own actions.

Let me explain how this works. When I decided I wanted to be a doctor, I was in my senior year at high school. When I mentioned this new intention to be a doctor, most people could barely contain their laughter. I was a "jock," not a smart kid. I spent all my time reading about and watching sports.

I did not know where to begin, so I started acting "smart" and doing things I thought doctors might. I got fake glasses, started dressing more professionally, and began reading books on anatomy, nutrition, and health.

I was not just thinking about it- I was being it. This caused me to look at myself differently. Overnight I changed the way I saw myself. I used this same method to become an author. I was not a good writer, but I just did what writers do; I wrote every day. This book you are reading right now, some of these thoughts are that daily writing.

I followed these actions with business and money too. I did not know the first thing about running a business; I just started running one. I wasn't "faking it," I was "being it" and this consistent action convinced my brain it was true. Then something strange happened; other people started to see me that way too.

It is not about a bunch of woo like, "think abundantly." It is a lot easier than that...just do your job. Do the things and take the actions. As a result, your thoughts automatically change.

Bonus: your brain won't see you as a phony who talks a good game but gets nothing done; it will see you as someone who conquers mental barriers through action.

Weights do not move by thought; you must walk up to them and physically lift them.

ENGAGEMENT/RESOLVE

The gym is the perfect metaphor for life:

- The weight does not budge without focused action.
- To progress, you must challenge yourself with ever increasing demands.
- You must always balance work with rest and recovery.
- One workout, one week, one month is not enough; consistency is the only thing that gets results.

PERCEPTION/OWNERSHIP/ENGAGEMENT/RESOLVE

You cannot have a thing if you don't declare that thing. In other words, to get what you want, you must be willing to take intentional action in pursuit of the goal. Of course, that does not automatically mean you will be able to achieve what you desire.

Too many people get this all wrong, and their language is a dead giveaway. They have the "if it's meant to be" attitude. Unfortunately, that is not the way the world works. There is no "meant to be." You don't sit around waiting for the stars to align. There is only your committed action in the direction of what you want.

It's not "meant to be"...it's "created to be."

"Meant to be" is a cop-out. It's a way of giving yourself some psychological leeway. It's an excuse to quit. If you are using that phrase frequently, it tells you something about your fears, level of commitment, and ability to manifest concepts in your life.

Big change requires big declarations and even bigger action. You must declare what you want with such conviction that there is no doubt about what you intend to create.

Life has a way of calling your bluff. It will say, "You want that? It's going to cost more money than you can afford." Or, "You want it, it's going to mean your comfort zone is stripped away." Or, "You can try, but it's going to take you swallowing your pride, losing your friends and being more vulnerable than you have ever been."

When you embark on a dream, nothing about that journey is going to be easy. Dreams mean something because they come at a cost. Storms in your life are brewing no matter what; you can turn into them intentionally and direct your life, or you can "meant to be" it, and end up right back where you are, or worse.

Your life follows your committed action...choose and act.

ENGAGEMENT/RESOLVE

One of our core human needs is status. We desire to be viewed by others as competent, confident, and capable. We also want to be respected, admired, and listened to. Psychology research shows we seek status from others in all kinds of ways. Some of those behaviors are successful and some aren't.

One key difference is between talkers and doers. The talkers talk. They talk about what they did in the past. They mostly talk about what they're going to do in the future. They LOVE to talk about others.

Then there are doers. They take action. They move in the direction of what they want. They even move when they are not 100% sure of where they are heading. They let actions guide them. They figure if they just move, they will either succeed, or their failures and stumbles will allow them to self-correct and start heading in the right direction.

What's interesting about these two types is that talkers rarely find the status they seek, while doers almost always do. What is even more fascinating is that talkers seem to obsess more about status while doers intently focus on acting, despite what others think.

In no place is this more apparent than the difference between critics and creators. Creators create and critics talk about what creators create. Creators are almost never critics. They're too busy creating. Critics are almost never creators; talkers practice talking and because of that are poor at doing much else.

Creators dream and create, and critics talk and talk. Creators care more about respecting themselves than seeking outside approval.

In life, achieving, gaining, or arriving all require action. You can simply act, or you can think and talk. You can be a critic or be a creator. One will move you forward, and the other will allow you to talk about what someone else is doing.

I know which option I choose. How about you?

OWNERSHIP

Our greatest power lies, not in who we are, but rather, in who we can become.

ENGAGEMENT

S trength of body or strength of mind? -Action or thought? Which is more important?

Your brain is watching and judging. The person it watches most and judges the harshest is you.

To the brain, actions are less ambiguous and far less open to interpretation. When we speak of others we say, "Actions speak louder than words." It is the same with ourselves.

We can say we want to change. We can talk about change. We can meditate, "Om," and "woosah" all we want. We can say affirmations again and again, but nothing will change until we act.

People say "thoughts become things" and "actions speak louder than words;" I say actions are words in motion.

May 29

ENGAGEMENT

Physical pursuits are only about vanity to the uninitiated. For those that live the lifestyle, physical challenges ARE mental challenges. Physical endurance IS mental endurance. Physical power reflects alignment and personal power.

Those who abide by a fit lifestyle don't push themselves to look good. They push themselves because they have figured out a secret; action here, translates to words, thoughts, and actions over there.

Understand this, and looking good ceases to be a concern and often comes about naturally.

"Security does not exist in nature, nor do the children of men as a whole experience it... Avoiding danger is no safer in the long run than outright exposure... Life is either a daring adventure or nothing" -- Helen Keller

ENGAGEMENT

F ailure is feedback.

Talk is cheap; action is rich. You are defined by what you do, not by what you say.

Ironically, if all you do is talk and never act, you will be defined the opposite way in which you speak.

Action defines who you are; talk degrades it.

The answer rarely comes from dwelling on it. The answer comes by living with it, and working through it. Don't try to think your way out of it; live your way through it.

Live your way into the answer.

May 31

OWNERSHIP/ENGAGEMENT

V ivere est militare (to live is to fight). I have this phrase tattooed down the right side of my torso. I think it is one of the more true statements I have ever read.

Some may interpret it as the physical struggle for survival. Through most of human history, there were predators, including other humans; we needed to fight in order to survive. We also needed to battle an environment that could end our lives at anytime. Then there is the "fight" against age, illness and the rest. I am not referring to those fights.

Being alive in the modern day is not just about having a heartbeat and taking breaths. The people I encounter daily have varying degrees of life in them. Some meet you with smiles and pleasant words. Some make brief eye contact and say little. Some are oblivious and don't see you at all. There are those you sense are barely living, and those who have a purpose of being that is palpable in their energy.

Paying attention to people in this way is extremely instructive.

It's the people who light you up without saying a word that I think this statement applies to. Why do they have this effect on you and others? I think it is because they have learned to create meaning wherever they go.

Some are mothers and fathers who devote their lives to their children; that is their fight and meaning. For some, it's their creations - the books they write, the hair they cut, the canvas they paint, or photo they capture. For others, it's being there for individuals where and when they can. For some, it's experiences and learning they chase. Or it could simply be bringing kindness to all the people they meet. The point is we can sense when someone is just going through the motions of life versus living the fight.

No matter what it is, they know what they stand for, who they are, and what they are willing to fight, bleed, scar, and die for. It's what they have chosen to make their life mean beyond themselves that really feeds them.

The fight is realizing you don't stumble onto meaning. Meaning is chosen in each moment, and true meaning is mostly about a larger purpose, those things outside of ourselves.

To live is to fight for meaning.

ENGAGEMENT

A ction is the antidote, both for your own confusion and when you are confused about someone else. It's actions, not words that have the power to reboot your story if you're stuck, as well as accurately tell the story about another.

We express this understanding in many ways, but my favorite version is "actions speak louder than words." Stuck on a question? Don't think on it, just make a move and the right direction quickly becomes apparent. Want to know if they are a true friend or if they really love you? Simply watch their actions and you will quickly know.

We humans often don't want to believe this universal truth. We would rather talk ourselves into something else; convince ourselves why we don't act. But that is almost always our fear talking. Unlike talk, taking action gets things moving in real time, clarifying for us as we go, allowing us to adjust on the fly.

When it comes to others, we want them to explain their feelings to us when their actions say all we really need to know.

Now don't get me wrong, explanations, thinking, and talking-it-out are hugely important, but when things grind to a halt, confusion sets in and you are stuck in limbo; no amount of talking, thinking, or considering is going to help.

Action is the only thing that will get you moving or clarify your situation.

ENGAGEMENT

One thing that keeps us fixed in our fear is the adage, "leap and the net will appear."

It's not true and we inherently know it's not, but it makes us apprehensive because we know we can fall flat on our faces.

The more accurate way to think of it is, "leap and create the net as you fall."

This version tells you the truth of the situation. That no matter what outcome an action creates, there are always other actions you can take to correct course. However, you can't see them until you make the first move. Your actions, and theirs, tell you everything and guide you everywhere.

PERCEPTION/RESOLVE

No one likes pain.
Did you ever consider that pain is instructive? It has a message for you. Sometimes when I am hurt I think about that.

Sometimes pain is progress.

Sometimes pain is the path.

RESOLVE

The key truth about change resides at the start. It's the only thing you have control of right now. Lasting change requires starting again, over and over, until it no longer feels like starting.

Stop looking for easy. Easy is earned.

OWNERSHIP/WISDOM/ENGAGEMENT/RESOLVE

You don't climb a mountain and then jump off. You climb a mountain so you can climb back down with a new perspective. Sometimes you climb just for the experience. If you want to be a mountain climber you climb for the sake of climbing.

ENGAGEMENT

I sleep with my bedroom door open in the winter and it gets into the 50s. In the summer I cool the room to 65 (the lowest the setting goes). I also finish my morning showers with at least a thirty-second blast of "as cold as the water goes."

I train with weights until my body is burning and my chest is heaving for breath. Sometimes I roll around on the ground after one of these workouts trying to find a position, any position that will take the hunger for air away.

I have a sauna and I will force myself to stay in it until my heart is pounding out of my chest and it feels like the sun itself is in the room; then I will blast myself with cold water. It's a shock to the system that makes me unable to stay still. I stay in that cold until my body becomes used to it and sometimes long enough to turn on the shivering response.

Perhaps strangest of all I purposely recall old, emotional wounds. I bring them to mind with vivid imagery, visualizing them in full detail. I even imagine being on a plane or train or in a large crowd when tragedy strikes. I try to feel the fear and then see myself rushing forward to help, to fight, or to do whatever is required for good.

I am not kidding; I really do this. -But why? In the Stoic philosophy there is something called, negative visualization. This is where you imagine losing a thing so you can appreciate life more and be prepared to act with a plan. My practice is adapted from that, but it goes deeper.

Throughout human existence we have been confronted with uncomfortable situations. Thermal challenges, food challenges (finding it and avoiding being it), and physical challenges. These obstacles kept us mentally sharp, primed our metabolism and helped us grow and adapt. They kept us alive and made us feel alive.

Today we live in perpetual comfort. Threats are small and rare. Yet it seems we are more afraid, more close-minded, and more insecure than ever. These practices guard against that; they help me grow, keep me engaged, and make me feel alive.

We humans do not thrive from perpetual ease. Discomfort forces us to grow. Suffering is the proving ground for meaning.

Don't just rise to the occasion; create it.

OWNERSHIP

Y ou should always refuse to engage with anyone who insists on seeing you in a negative way; one in which you are not, or no longer wish to be.

OWNERSHIP/ENGAGEMENT/SHARING

Part of our human struggle comes from our lack of certainty about who we are and what we want. You don't feel solid and sure if you are just "winging it." Waiting for the right time or situation, more often than not leads to waiting forever.

Life requires real choices and real sacrifice. If you want an amazing career, you need to plan to leave your current one. If you want real love, you need to be vulnerable, get over your fears and hurts, and decide what and whom you want.

With all things in life you need to decide and act. No one is going to figure that out for you, and no amount of time is going to fix an uncertain, confused, or scared mind.

Action is the only antidote. One thing that helps is an honor code - writing down who you are and what you stand for. It is one of the most powerful things you can do.

Want an example? Here is my code I wrote several years ago during some rough times. It has been my mantra ever since:

"I am a warrior. I hold it down for my friends, keep my word to myself, and carry any pain without blame, complaint, or self-pity. I know I can generate happiness for myself in an instant through a warm gesture, a generous act, or a forced, but real, laugh or smile. I am honest, but never cruel. You can trust what I say. I will communicate clearly exactly how I feel. You'll never have to guess. Kindness is my religion, honesty my practice, and generosity my action. But I am a warrior; I do have limits and strong boundaries. I do not associate with rude, mean, greedy, or selfish people. I loathe bias, self-righteousness, gossip, extremism, and dogma; despite, as a human, I know I struggle with them too. The desire for fame is a sickness I have little tolerance for. True beauty does not require attention. I avoid the emotionally selfish. I give freely and never keep score. I will call out racism if I see it. I do not tolerate lies, by omission or otherwise, and will walk away and never look back if a friend insists on lying to me. I am grateful for my struggles, hopeful about the future, and willing to sacrifice everything for those I love and the things I stand for. You owe me nothing. True love does not ask for reciprocation."

OWNERSHIP

Honesty and transparency are good.... the other stuff is too much work!

OWNERSHIP/WISDOM

One of my favorite quotes by Bruce Lee is, "To know thyself is to study thyself in action with another person." As I have studied psychology, as well as studying others and myself, I have noticed three general categories in which people fall: Base Level, Culture Level, and Next Level.

Here is a scenario to illustrate. A troll comments on our post, insulting and calling us out. For most of us, this will ignite a battle between our 3 selves. Base level will want to fight (insult back) or flight (immediately delete the comment). Culture level will look at it through the lens of what's right or appropriate. How will other people watching interpret it? Next Level will see the comment as more about the other person. They will either engage in order to learn more, or delete if it crosses their boundaries. At the Base Level we are triggered. It's emotional, and we feel attacked. At the Cultural Level it's about considerations. How does it make me look? At Next Level it's what can I learn? We are capable of all three responses, but which one gets the most practice? Which do we cultivate? Whichever one that is, becomes the dominant level. Here are some of the attributes from different psychological labels I have assigned each level:

Psychological Attributes	Base Level Human	Culture Level Human	Next Level Human
Major concern:	Safety	Acceptance	Purpose
Emotional driver:	Fear	Rejection	Contentment
Personality style:	Pessimist	Envious	Optimist & Trusting
Reciprocity style:	Taker	Matcher	Giver (With Boundaries)
Relationship style:	Avoidant	Anxious	Secure
Motto:	Me Against The World	Us Against Them	We Are All One
Philosophy:	Eye For An Eye (Treat Others The Way They Treat You)	The Golden Rule (Treat Others How You Want To Be Treated)	The Platinum Rule (Treat Others How They Wish To Be Treated)

ENGAGEMENT/RESOLVE

You will be dead soon.
Focus on the things you want and only what you control. Then be fearless in your pursuit.

June 12

OWNERSHIP/ENGAGEMENT/RESOLVE

S trength is expressed in both muscle and mindset. Each feeds the other. You transform the body by creating obstacles for your muscle.

You transform your mindset by creating obstacles for your mind.

Like the Stoics believed:

"Turn fear into prudence, pain into transformation, mistakes into initiation, and desire into undertaking."

— Taleb Nassim Nicholas

PERCEPTION/ ENGAGEMENT

There is less difference than you might think between overcoming obstacles in the gym and overcoming obstacles in your life... in terms of the mindset. For life change, some will tell you all you need to do is "think positive" or "stay in the now" or some other vague, new age cliché that actually explains little or nothing.

I am not saying these ideas have no merit, but most people have little idea what that actually means. Physical pursuits, on the other hand, are a direct conduit into the emotions. They are like emotional alchemy. Feel stuck? Go for a walk. Feel insecure and weak minded? Go lift something heavy. Feel sad? Don't "be in the now" or try to "think positive;" simply move the muscles of your mouth into a smile.

Research into this "action to emotion to thought" concept is called the "as if" principle. When it comes to moving, enduring, and overcoming obstacles in your life, the easiest step is to move something physically to get unstuck. It is a physical, mental, and emotional trial run towards resilience.

You miss a lift in the gym; you don't cry about it, hold on to it for years, and carry the baggage. You simply lift it again until you get it. And yes, while you're doing it, you can "Om," or "be in the now," or "think happy thoughts" if you want.

PERCEPTION/OWNERSHIP/ENGAGEMENT

If you really want to attain a goal, you must be brave enough to believe, courageous enough to act, and have a focused patience that will carry you through.

The vast majority of people will convince themselves it's not possible, not worth it, or too costly. The human brain resists change. It's a normal part of being human. You are so caught up in all the reasons it could never work that you have forgotten the amazing magic that awaits you if you just make it happen.

Striving for the same type of career, relationship, job, friendship, etc., might feel comfortable to you, but it will never fulfill you the way you really desire. You can go for the ordinary and stay in your comfort zone or get what you really want...the choice is yours.

People will question your motives, doubt your sincerity, and challenge your resolve. It's not personal, it is simply their own internal process of making sense of your actions as it relates to them, and that is the difficulty. We are not immune to the emotions, opinions, and judgments of others. We would not be human if we were.

However, if we are ever to succeed in our goals, we need to stay focused on what we require and guard against the distractions of others. That requires the ability to distinguish our own needs and wants from those of other individuals. In the end, if you are true to yourself, others will quickly follow your lead.

It's conviction and confidence that leads the way and teaches others how to treat us. Waiting for someone else to catch up is wasted time. Love them, coach them, and meet them halfway if you must, but never pretend to be anything except exactly what you are.

If you don't stay true to you, not only will others not respect you, but most importantly, you will never be able to accept yourself.

OWNERSHIP/ENGAGEMENT

How do you know you are following your passion/purpose...If you were the last person on earth, would you still do it?

If I were the only person left on the planet I would still show up to workout, week in and week out. It's in me - I have no choice.

Would you?

OWNERSHIP/SHARING

I am not a father, not in the traditional sense anyway. I have never had any desire to have children and doubt I ever will. Yet I have a good sense of what that kind of commitment takes.

I have been lucky to have a very strong, masculine presence in my life from day one. By "strong, masculine presence," I mean a man who derives his power through action. He is not a talker. He has no need to tell you what he has accomplished. He is not a fighter. He has no need to show you his guns or biceps. He is not a status seeker. He could care less what car he drives, what clothes he wears, or how much is in his bank account.

And he is not an avoider. He has no fear of expressing his emotions, setting firm boundaries, or letting people be exactly who they are. He is also not trying to return to some imaginary time when life was supposedly better. He could care less if you are gay or straight or black or white. He judges you on how you act in the world the same way he judges himself.

Also, he adores women; he loves their power and he is in awe of their beauty. He has no problem supporting them or being supported by them.

To me Father's Day is synonymous with Man Day. To be a good man is to know what you stand for and to stand for something more important than you or your small circle of family or friends. To be a man is to realize you are human first and you have a role to play and a job to do. That job is to take your signature strengths and use them in a way that enhances the entire human tribe.

A weak man tries to hold others back, beat others down, suppress individuality, tolerate intolerance, and pretends he is better than anyone else. A strong man knows what he stands for, what he will fight for, bleed for, scar and die for. He is aware that thing must be something more than just his own offspring or creations.

To my pops, thank you for showing me what a man is. To all the male fathers and creators, who have taken on the job of furthering the growth of the human tribe - Thank you.

June 17

OWNERSHIP/ENGAGEMENT

To those who live the fitness lifestyle, it is more like a creative pursuit; the same way a movie enthusiast will describe the latest film they watched as the best ever. The same way painters might take a video of themselves painting, to display their creative process. The same way a foodie might post a picture of an incredible meal.

When the pursuit of health and fitness becomes a lifestyle, the last thing that person is thinking is how much weight they need to lose or whether or not you think they have a nice body. What they are pursuing is a unique, creative process that feeds their sense of meaning at a very, deep level.

This is why they crave that workout at 5am or will spend their Saturday evening on the beach working out. Fitness is very much a metaphor for life. You grind, you pursue, you fail, you prevail and as a result of that Engagement you feel alive.

People often ask, "How do you make health and fitness a lifestyle?" The answer is, find a way to tie the pursuit of movement and healthy eating to your life's meaning and legacy.

For me, I want to teach, move, and inspire people to see their power and know that change can be theirs if they desire. I see the pursuit of health and fitness in complete alignment with that message. Because I have attached my deepest purpose to that pursuit, it makes it effortless to live in this way. I have no choice.

This reminds me of Nietzsche's words, "A man with a why to live, can bear with any how." In this case I would amend the quote to say "A person with a strong why to live will naturally pursue any how they feel serves that why." Not only that, but...fitness just feels good.

ENGAGEMENT/RESOLVE

If you want change in life you must be a warrior for it.

I know the term "warrior" is confusing for some because it conjures images of battle and violence. The definition of warrior is, "one who is engaged aggressively in an activity, cause, or conflict." The two most important words in the definition are "engaged" and "aggressively."

Most people play at change. They dabble around the edges, only dipping their toes in to test the waters. Then they wonder why they make no progress.

This is not how you make things happen. That is the Ready-Aim-Fire approach. When using this approach, most people never even pull the trigger.

Being aggressively engaged means pulling the trigger first and figuring out the rest later. It's the Ready-Fire-Aim-Aim-Aim approach. That's the most difficult part, because making big moves comes with big risks; it's natural to feel apprehension or even fear in that regard.

There are two quotes I have been drawn to whenever my inner warrior starts to waiver, one by Seneca and the other from Frank Herbert, who wrote the novel, <u>Dune</u>:

"No man is more unhappy than he who never faces adversity. For he is not permitted to prove himself" --Seneca

"I must not fear. Fear is the mind-killer. Fear is the "little death" that brings total obliteration. I will face my fear. I will permit it to pass over me and through me. And when it has gone past I will turn the inner eye to see its path. Where the fear has gone there will be nothing. Only I will remain."-- Litany Against Fear: <u>Dune</u>

June 19

PERCEPTION/OWNERSHIP/WISDOM/
ENGAGEMENT/RESOLVE/SHARING

The success mindset is something that can be taught, learned and mastered. It's not something you are born into and it's not some type of inherited talent. It is not easy. In fact, it is probably one of the hardest things a human can do. That's because it requires a mindset and focus that is likely very different from that of your family, friends, peers, and coworkers.

We are social creatures above all else. Humans were not designed for isolation and we will unconsciously resist anything that isolates us from our support group. Due to this connection, those of us who are trying to elevate our lives will often make one of two critical mistakes:

1. We will try to take people with us to the Next Level.
2. We will limit our growth so we can attempt to have the best of both worlds.

Both of these approaches hold us back. Those who truly love and support you will always be there. They will see your success and growth as a source of pride.

Trying to inspire those around you, spur them to change or elevate their life before you, yourself, have made it is like shooting yourself in the foot. You have to get there first before you can help someone else do it too.

The next issue is our own fear and the desire to stay in our old world. But old and new can't exist at the same time. You can't play at change. You have to jump in. This may require being alone for a while.

Here are two ways to circumvent these issues:

1. Consciously recruit a new support system, one that is already where you want to be. This is where paid mentorships and coaching are critical. The knowledge and insight gained help you leapfrog into the next world more quickly.
2. Practice being alone. Many people spend zero time alone, yet this is a critical skill if you ever want to elevate. Plan hikes, workouts, dinners out, movies and vacations on your own.

This practice cultivates self-trust and self-awareness; it gets you acclimated to the discomfort of what can be a lonely transition from one income bracket, career, relationship, lifestyle, etc., to the next.

Create a life of which you can be proud; one for which you can be grateful, one of your own making. Start now.

ENGAGEMENT/RESOLVE

Life is analogous to fitness and sport. You train, you prepare, you get right in the head. You are consistent and you give it 110%. And after all that effort, you can still get beaten down and lose; it is disturbing.

There is a secret the successful have. It's not so much a secret as it is a learned skill or mental trait...this disturbing reality about life does not disturb them.

Sure, it's as painful for them as the next person, but every time they encounter this nasty fact, they get back up and charge into the storm again. Why? Because suffering enlarges, if you let it. They see it as a teacher and a way to grow. Comfort, certainty, and letting the fear keep them from taking risks is more painful to them in the long run.

There is a will that burns inside all humans; it's been there since we were children. It's the desire to create something meaningful using our own signature strengths, something that expands beyond our self. Suffering is a requirement to growth and therefore becomes a source of that meaning.

In fitness, in body change, and in life shortcuts don't exist. You want a shortcut? Here it is...shut up and do your job!

PERCEPTION/OWNERSHIP/ENGAGEMENT/RESOLVE

The ability to see failure, mistakes, loss, heartache, and obstacles as opportunities for growth is what sets the most successful apart from the rest.

The belief or idea that anything worthwhile will be easy is a mistake. Easy is earned in the trenches of failure and in the power of Resolve.

If you are not ready to fail, then you're not ready to succeed.

Limits are almost always self-imposed. We humans construct a psychological box of beliefs and behaviors. This box represents the way we perceive the world.

Is the world safe or not? Are women or men to be trusted? Does money represent possibility or evil? Do we constantly think we are the smartest person in the room or are we open to learning from others?

Sometimes our boxes serve us, help us learn, grow, and see possibilities. Other times our boxes keep us stubbornly fixed in the same life patterns again and again.

Life will provide enough obstacles; why would we want to create so many self-imposed limits by choosing to stay in our own idle mindset?

The only way to grow and break through these self-imposed confines is learn to think and act differently. When life happens, more often than not, we retreat back to the comfort of our box. We act and think the same as we always have and end up getting the same as we have always gotten.

Breaking through our self-made obstructions and elevating to a Next Level in health, wealth, and relationships means confronting life without our old box of behaviors and beliefs.

Once you can accomplish this, the limits you have placed on yourself begin to fall away.

ENGAGEMENT/RESOLVE

Fitness is a metaphor for life:

- Knowing how to build muscle is not the same as building muscle. In other words, talk is cheap and action pays.
- Lift the same heavy weight over and over and day after day and it magically gets lighter. In other words, easy is earned.
- Progress does not mysteriously occur. You must always seek to beat your own personal record (PR). In life there are PRs in fear. Attack your fear PRs.
- Results and change come from getting out of your comfort zone and pushing your limits
- A universal truth to stay safe and keep the results coming in fitness and life: "push until you can't, rest until you can."
- Movement is life.

PERCEPTION/OWNERSHIP/WISDOM/ ENGAGEMENT/RESOLVE

What you don't know about yourself can and does hurt you. The only thing certain about life is uncertainty. It's not if you will deal with pain and loss, but when and how often.

Your fears will either find you or keep you from finding yourself.

The typical approach is to suck it up, work harder and stuff the pain away. But these are examples of refusing to look inward to determine who you are and who you wish to become.

From examining the stories of those who have turned pain and loss into growth, several behaviors are recognized and arise more than any other:

- *Visualization*: a practice of deep mental focus on imagining what they want and who they will become. This involves almost a meditative focus on the feelings of the eventual desired outcome.
- *Gratitude*: a practice of owning and being grateful for all the things that have happened, even the worst of them. This practice is how we turn dark stories to stories of redemption. Own and be grateful for the dark, because it can be a path to the light.
- *Reading*: those who read non-fiction are better critical thinkers and problem solvers. Those who read fiction are more empathetic. Reading is also a shortcut to accumulating the knowledge and experience to get you where you wish to go.
- *Committed action*: to choose with intention, to move in any direction despite the fear, uncertainty, or lack of a plan. Staying still and behaving the same way you always have is a self-constructed, mental prison.
- *Meditation*: the conscious choice to be alone in your body without the distraction of people, technology, or anything else. This practice is the single greatest way to focus on you, and what keeps you stuck. It is also the single greatest tool in balancing and calming the seas of your mind.
- *Physical challenge*: the purposeful exposure to that which challenges the physical. The psychological principle of "as if" says, as the body goes, so does the mind. Of course this works in reverse too, but action has been shown to be a greater mental mover than the reverse. A physical PR in the gym often translates into more mental PRs in life.

PERCEPTION/OWNERSHIP/ENGAGEMENT/RESOLVE

D eclare what you want, and be brave enough to take the actions needed to get there; the world will have little choice but to bend to your demands.

"Impossible is just a big word thrown around by small men who find it easier to live in the world they've been given than to explore the power they have to change it. Impossible is not a fact. It's an opinion. Impossible is not a declaration. It's a dare. Impossible is potential. Impossible is temporary. Impossible is nothing."

— <u>Muhammad Ali</u>

PERCEPTION/OWNERSHIP/WISDOM/
ENGAGEMENT/RESOLVE/SHARING

Everything you need to know about the principles of success, in any endeavor, is what is called the SAID principle: Specific Adaptation to Imposed Demand.

It's the reason you might be the fittest, strongest powerlifter or bodybuilder, yet perform like a 2-year old in a Crossfit workout. If you ever want to be humbled in fitness, just go work out with someone who trains differently than you.

Take that same principle and realize if you want to have a thing, you need to learn how to be that thing. Someone who wants to be an author needs to be reading and writing all the time. That's what authors do. They don't sit around saying I am going to write a book; they are writing it everyday in some form or another. The same goes for wealth, relationships, and personal growth.

Do the thing that needs to get done to have the result. This is the hardest thing we do in life, and there are no shortcuts. But, there is a process. Just like in fitness you plan, you periodize (building in work and rest) and you systematically and incrementally chip away at your personal records (PR).

The same is true in all other endeavors. If you want a great relationship, then you need to be the person you are hoping to meet. You don't get to be a liar, con artist, and avoider...then expect an honest, authentic, expert communicator to show up in your life.

You don't get to make money off of your mental resources, and work when you want, without first building your work and education PRs in the areas that can deliver this reality.

You don't get to be seen as kind, warm, generous, and caring until you build up your PRs in these categories as well. How about a new generosity PR with a $100 tip; or a new kindness PR with 10 heartfelt compliments to strangers?

How you show up in one area of life is often how you will show up in others. If you want to make a difference for you and others, you have to be that difference first. Attack life like this and you will keep reaching new happiness and success PRs again and again.

June 26

RESOLVE

People never become less fearful by avoiding their fears. The more we let one fear hold us back, the more that fear amplifies and the more additional fears we will be faced with.

I have a theory about fears. You can't run from them. They have a strange way of always chasing you down.

When I was a kid, I had a recurring nightmare about a man breaking into my room and kidnapping me. The dream always had him at my door, trying to get in and I would be so scared I would wake myself up. Someone gave me the idea that if I was aware I was dreaming, instead of waking myself up I should confront the man.

So that night before I went to bed I put a butter knife near my pillow. When the dream came, and the man was at my door, I looked down and that butter knife was now a huge machete. I was still scared but I took the knife, slowly walked to the door, and quickly opened it. The man had no face but he looked at me and I showed him my knife. He then vanished and I woke up. I never had that dream again.

This experience is one of the most memorable and vivid of my childhood. It has become a symbol for me to confront the things I am most afraid of. Like you, I am afraid of a lot of things. Will I lose someone I love? Will the money run out? Will I get sick? Am I worthy? Will I end up alone? The first rule of courage is identifying your fears and then confronting them.

These conscious forays into attacking my fears are "fear PRs." A PR in the field of fitness is an acronym for a "Personal Record" on a lift. A fear PR is the conscious confrontation of a fear. I have been attacking my fear of flying. So I have been flying more, not less, and taking longer flights. As a result, I fear flying much less. In fact, I think the fear is gone and now there is simply the discomfort of travel.

My next fear PR may be to conquer my fear of sharks and learn to surf. The point is, as I get older, my fears are becoming less intense and I have fewer of them. That is almost always the opposite for people as they age.

ENGAGEMENT/RESOLVE

If you were to tell me something was impossible, I might believe you. But I would ignore you just the same.

Impossible has nothing to do with my intention. If I believe in my chosen pursuit with the full magnitude of my spirit, then I chase that dream whether to failure or success.

June 28

OWNERSHIP/ENGAGEMENT/RESOLVE

When people say it's impossible, impractical, unrealistic, or can't be done, I know what they really mean. It's impossible, impractical, unrealistic, and can't be done for them.

The impossible never became possible through inaction. Magic happens when you declare who you are, what you want, and where you are willing to go to get it.

Talk to most successful people and they will reminisce about how improbable it was for them to succeed. Pry a little more and you will find they were compelled to act through a sort of clarity of focus that was so strong they could not ignore it. They will tell you it was the pursuit of their dream or nothing. The possible was discovered in the journey.

So when people tell you it won't work or you can't do it, just look at them and say, "I know." Then go do it anyway.

Dream chasing makes no sense to someone without a dream.

ENGAGEMENT

A nd as my mother so wisely tells me... "Jade, when life gets hard all you need to do is take long walks and do your job."

PERCEPTION/OWNERSHIP/ENGAGEMENT/RESOLVE

When you are in pain, it is useful to keep in mind that your destiny requires change...it is NOT to remain the same. And change is uncomfortable.

We humans can be a little dense at times. We want so badly to have something different, yet we simultaneously desire to remain comfortably in the context of what we know.

News flash, those two things cannot exist together. Either you choose comfort or you choose change. You can't have both.

If you find yourself in an unfamiliar place struggling for something you believe in, do not let your fear shake your Resolve. Fight on...you are in the process of change and the champion of your own legacy.

If you have regret, lied, cheated, sold out, embarrassed yourself, failed, gave into fear, and made mistakes...you are in good company. No human has ever escaped these conditions. You suffer precisely because that is what is required to find your truth. There is nothing more inspiring than the redemption story. It is always available to you.

All you need is to redefine who you are, and what you choose to bleed for. Then pick up your weapons and charge into battle.

OWNERSHIP/WISDOM/ENGAGEMENT/RESOLVE

If there is one thing I have learned about life, it is that the only thing I have ever been able to control is my own, internal state of being.

Life happens. I am no longer too surprised when things don't go as planned. I lose little sleep when things go against me. I don't get too excited when things are heading my way either.

I have grown to see times of uncertainty as the perfect opportunity to further define and practice my beliefs. I am not going to pretend these times are pleasant, but I have learned through experience that discomfort is what births growth and change.

The world happening around me does not threaten or scare me. I don't believe in conspiracy theories and doomsday scenarios. I believe in one thing, and one thing only: my ability to choose my own state of mind at any time.

Allowing an outside event beyond my control to impact my mood and affect my Resolve is a symptom of a lack of clarity, focus, and purpose.

If I wake tomorrow and find I must fight for what I stand for, I will be the first into battle and the last one out.

Until then, I do my work. I love. I practice kindness. I give in big, unexpected ways. I tell the truth. I work to become my highest self. I believe the greatest thing I can do for the world is to be the best version of myself as possible.

So if you are scared, uncertain, disappointed, or frustrated, the solution is to go to work on yourself. Change always meets resistance from fear, but you are always in control if you choose.

WISDOM/ENGAGEMENT/RESOLVE

"Please Do Not Feed the Fears"
I love this idea, but I think the meaning is backwards. Starve your fear and it will starve you. Turn into your fear, understand it, engage with it, and yes, even feed it; and it will more likely transform from fear to friend.

PERCEPTION/ENGAGEMENT/RESOLVE

Fear has been called many things. It has been made into an acronym: False Expectations Appearing Real. It has been called "the mind killer." It is this state of being we are told to avoid or try to explain away.

I hate to say it, but fear is real. It is also only a mind killer if you allow it to be. In my mind, it's the misunderstanding and avoidance of fear that perpetuates it.

Fear has a strange way of following you around. No one ever became less fearful by avoiding their fears or trying to pretend they are self-generated delusions we can dismiss.

Fears will find you if you don't find them first. In my opinion, the correct acronym for fear is: Find Engage And Resolve.

Being without fear is impossible, you're human. Realize fears are there for a reason and can be used to your benefit.

To do this, start small. I use a concept called the fear PR (Personal Record). Slowly and incrementally find and engage your fears. Start with the small ones and build to the large ones. There is no more powerful way to build wisdom, courage, and perspective.

Turn fear to your advantage by appreciating why it is there in the first place.

PERCEPTION/OWNERSHIP

As humans we seek control and stability. We desire above all else comfort and certainty. This is completely normal. We all do it. At the same time it can be one of the biggest obstacles to growth and change.

You can't make moves by not making moves.

The internal state of frustration is brought on by a desire to grow but held static due to our need for stability. That's something every human knows. And yet, there is a very easy way to circumvent this issue. It is simply a matter of knowing when to take control. The key mistake is focusing on controlling the world around us when the only world we can control is the one within us.

Your need to change your surroundings; Your desire to change someone's mind; The upset you feel if someone else does not like or trust you; Your constant worry about who is doing what, why they are doing it, and how you can get them to do it differently - That game is one you can never win and should not be playing in the first place.

Your inner world is where you hold sway. How you react. How you choose to feel. The ability to choose to see the world from a different angle; your honor code and code of conduct, whether you choose to carry baggage or instead set up clear boundaries; All of this you CAN learn to control.

The control of your inner world is the base of a psychological pyramid that remains strong through the storms of life. It's the stability you seek, and it provides the support to anchor you through the most difficult of life's changes.

Life happens and there is not a damn thing you can do about it. But you happen to life as well.

Building your internal strength is like building a strong fit body. It requires thought, questioning, and practice. It's not easy, but it is the only way to control anything, because it is the only thing you can control.

OWNERSHIP/WISDOM/ENGAGEMENT/RESOLVE

Life happens and it is that happening that informs us... why would we want to stick our face in the sand or run from it?

Find your fears or they will find you. Confront your demons or they will consume you. Speak your truth or lose it. Celebrate your failures, knowing only they can lead to future success.

Stop being afraid of what stands in your way because those things show you the way.

OWNERSHIP/ENGAGEMENT/RESOLVE

I have a concept that I like to relate to the idea of "warrior": the journey to self-actualization, the process of pursuing our greatest potential or "higher selves," and fighting against our Base Level selves.

My use of the word "warrior" in my work with those I coach can at first be confusing due to the connotations of war, death, and destruction. The warriors I am speaking of fight battles as well, but the battles they wage are against themselves. They rally against their fears, limiting stories, and entrenched biases that keep them forever stuck. The fight is mostly within.

It is also not just a domain of the male. This fight is one employed by men and women alike. In fact, judging by those who read and pursue self-development, "warriors" are more likely to be women.

In the warrior spirit there is the idea of "dying a good death." This happens when you confront your enemy and fight to the finish, despite your fear. It happens when you stick to your mission and are clear-headed and solid in why you fight in the first place.

There is one thing that has the power to sustain you in the battle of life. It's not the love of others, it's not the control over others, and it's not money, or any worldly pursuit. It's what you choose to make your life mean. What you choose to leave as your legacy.

When you choose your own meaning, the fight, the blood, the sweat, the scars, and the pain will not only be worth it, but ironically, will go down in your history as the most enjoyable and memorable parts of your life.

All there is to dying a good death is living an excellent life of your choosing.

OWNERSHIP/ENGAGEMENT/WISDOM/SHARING

A happy person is not someone who is without pain or hurt. They just know how to integrate that pain and hurt into their deepest meaning and purpose. They use it as fuel to make positive magic happen in their lives and the lives of others.

It's not *if* you will suffer, but rather what you choose to suffer for. What will you choose to make that pain mean? What will you learn from it? What will you teach from it? How will it enhance the way you love?

Your suffering is not unique or special, but you can make it so through what you bring forth from it.

PERCEPTION/WISDOM

We may think we are free from the tribe, but our biases are incredibly difficult to see.

It is not ignorance that keeps us stuck; it is our inability to consider any point of view other than the one we already have.

Once bias sets in, research shows almost no amount of evidence to the contrary of what we believe will make us budge. It's a damn shame what delusion will do to you. If you are willing to look, you will find you are full-of-it, all day, every day.

PERCEPTION/WISDOM

All things in life, no matter how difficult or painful, provide something to gain. Your ability to take what happens and extract the benefit and beauty make all the difference.

When something happens that challenges your Resolve, ask yourself three questions:

- What have I been shown?
- How have I grown?
- How can I use this for the greater good, mine, and the world's?

OWNERSHIP/RESOLVE

We are here for three reasons and three reasons only.... to learn, to teach and to love. Everything that happens to you can be used to these ends if you will allow it.

Part of that process—the most important part— is to own yourself completely. You must own your power and your dysfunctions fully. This is your job alone, but it does help if you surround yourself with those who see your greatness, but love you for your less than desirable parts too.

One simple rule to remember is this: no one is going to accept you until you accept you.

This is why honesty, integrity, and authenticity are so important. They are not for the outside world. They are an internal declaration that you know, love, and accept yourself; that you are willing to let people see, and experience all of you, the same way you demand to see and experience all of them. It's not going to be easy, but no story worth creating ever was.

ENGAGEMENT/RESOLVE

"Do the things you hate. Make them hate you back," and "Turn your strength into a superpower and your weakness to a strength."

These are two mantras I often repeat in my head to remind myself of two things:

1. No one ever became less fearful by avoiding the things they fear, and
2. Consistent practice is the only thing that makes us better, both at the things we have no propensity toward, and the ones in which we are already proficient.

There is another aspect to this "exposure therapy." Putting yourself into a storm helps you figure out how to navigate that storm.

OWNERSHIP/WISDOM/SHARING

How do you handle feedback? If you are like most humans, you don't like it that much. Being the youngest of four, I received feedback all the time from my parents and my three siblings, who also thought they were my parents. And I HATED it!!

For much of my adult life feedback was a trigger, and took me right back to that little boy who was told by everyone what he could, can't, and should not be doing.

I started to realize something though. That trigger meant something. It was a smack in the face to pay attention, as emotions often are. I started trying to just use it to get better without judgment, which still isn't always the easiest thing.

Being an online influencer and running an online business is a funny thing. People don't have the same filters when they speak to you via email or in person.

I have been called a genius and a moron. I have been simultaneously thanked for all the free information and then told I am nothing but a crooked, used car salesman by two different people responding to the same email. I have been called humble and an egomaniac. I have had people ask me out while others called me bald and fat. And of course the science zealots, nutrition fanatics, and workout gurus have all responded to me in the kindest, most respectful way or called me a know-nothing ignoramus.

After all of this time, I just love the feedback, and I don't subscribe to the "it's about them, not you" mindset. It may be true that feedback often is more about the person giving it, but I try to make it about me. I don't take it personally, but I do make it personal.

I now see feedback as a gift, a learning opportunity. I don't take criticism or compliments very personally (I still like the compliments a little better of course); they just act as information sources. I just absorb the feedback and see if I can use it to my personal advantage.

Feedback is for you. There is a skill in seeking it, hearing it, not being emotionally reactive to it, and then using it if possible. Sometimes, the harsher the feedback, the better.

ENGAGEMENT/RESOLVE

Many people in the world of self-help and new age woo completely miss the direct access they have into the mind and emotions through physical training. Of course this is part of the appeal and goal of yoga, but it also works without the chanting and stretching.

Run 200m repeats or plow through 50 power cleans. It's the same thing. The connection between physical, mental, and emotional is a two way street.

July 14

PERCEPTION/OWNERSHIP/WISDOM/
ENGAGEMENT/SHARING

The three hardest things for a human to do:

1. Admit they are wrong.
2. Be charitable to the selfish.
3. Meet cruelty with compassion.

The reason these things are so difficult comes down to the stories we tell ourselves. In the first instance, we humans have a strong desire to win. Our Base Level selves make us feel like we are in competition with everyone else. We see other people as enemies rather than comrades. The story we tell is other people will hold it against us or get a big head. We therefore do everything to win including lying, deflecting, and changing the subject.

A better story to tell is the, "I am here to learn" story. It's ironic. We can't learn what we think we already know. In a strange way, know-it-alls actually end up knowing less and less over time, because they already think they know, so they stop learning about a subject. Admitting you're wrong is one of the most generous things you can do for yourself and others.

When people are selfish we want nothing more than to put them in their place. The story is the, "I'll show them" story. But the selfish are sometimes that way because no one was ever generous to them. By giving to the takers, we model a different way. Very few can do this, but the ones who do often make others less, not more, selfish.

When we are attacked, naturally we feel the need to fight back; often we should, to protect ourselves. But on occasion, we can realize that some people in pain want other people to suffer too. When we are able to recognize a person's cruelty as suffering, we can choose to meet it with compassion. This models a different way.

These are the three hardest things for a reason. Sometimes they expose us. I am certainly not advocating these actions 100% of the time. I am saying a Next Level Human does not just default to Base Level behavior. They recognize that sometimes it's appropriate and healing to use these strategies. They choose them, not for recognition or reciprocation, but simply to do their part to create a better world.

WISDOM/SHARING

---

learned from my mother and father that the only religion you need is kindness. It's both contagious and viral...nothing feeds the soul of the giver and the receiver more than kindness and generosity.

OWNERSHIP/SHARING

The way I see judgment is as the recognition of your own dysfunctions, past or present, in another.

Of course we humans love to judge and gossip. It feels good to be in this self-righteous mindset. "I can't believe they did that, how dumb." Or "I can't believe what an idiot they are." Or "They are so X, Y or Z." This type of behavior telegraphs our own insecurities and dysfunctions to the world. It says way more about us than the person we are judging.

I have done my fair share of this behavior over the years, but now I almost never do. I certainly rarely, if ever, utter this out loud and would never do this to someone I call a friend. Now when I catch myself judging in this way, I have two practices:

First I ask, "What is it in me that has this need to judge and feel better than?" When I look closely, I will almost always see the same patterns I have judged in my own present or past behaviors.

The second task is, simply acknowledge that we are all on our own path of learning, and it is not our place to police and judge people. My only job is to govern my own actions.

I have an honor code I strive to live up to - to be kind, generous, and honest especially when it is someone I call a friend. To communicate clearly and completely, so you never have to wonder how I feel about you. And to leave this world a better place when I am gone, either through my creations or my kindness. That is what it means to live truthfully and rightly.

I don't expect others to share my commitment, but I do expect to treat them with patience, respect, and without my biased arrogance judging their life choices.

PERCEPTION/WISDOM/SHARING

The most generous thing you can do for another is to hold an emotional space for them to express themselves, but few of us have this skill; this is expected since the natural default of the human brain is to judge, make assumptions, and take things personally.

Think about how selfish it is to make another person's feelings mean something about you? Of course we all do it, but if you care for a person you should instead hold a space for them to express themselves while trying to keep your own feelings out of it. I call this natural tendency to get caught up in someone else's emotions an "emotional trapdoor." As soon as we start making it about us, we become defensive, all the while leaving the person we care about with more emotional baggage then when they started. It's not helpful to them or us, yet it happens all the time. One way to fix this issue is to get out of the "right and wrong" mindset and instead, seek to understand.

Most people unconsciously want to be right and prove the other wrong. This is especially true if that person's hurt or anger seems to be about us (it rarely is; we are not in charge of how another perceives our actions - they are).

If we fall prey to the right and wrong mindset, we stop listening and start attacking or defending. Instead try seeking to understand. Realize it's ok, and even expected, that you will disagree with someone else's point, but if you really want to learn from them, you need to first express empathy for another. The best way to do that is to hear them out.

The great diffusion for emotions is to allow them to be expressed. Imagine you are a conduit to help the person shed their emotional baggage. Let the emotions pass through you without reacting. If you do this, you will almost always be amazed at how the emotional charge, which starts off being hard not to react to, quickly dissipates. At this point there is little that you need to say or do because you have already given your friend a gift most others are unable to manage. Once their emotional storm has subsided, there is now a unique opportunity for you to be heard.

SHARING

G enerosity, kindness, and honest, clear communication are some of the greatest pieces of spiritual wealth you can give.

A true friend gives freely without keeping score or "calling it in."

A true friend has empathy and compassion even when your actions hurt them.

A true friend is honest and clear in their communication.

PERCEPTION/WISDOM

Money-some say it is the root of all evil. I think it is the root of all possibility. As I have moved from a lower middle-class upbringing to someone who "has money," I can tell you some things I have noticed about those who do very well and those who don't.

Those with money are thinking about where they can spend it all the time, but they do it in a very different way than the middle-class or poor. They are not obsessed with saving and budgeting; they are thinking of investing in themselves or their business. They ask what can they do with their money to make it earn for them while they sleep? Money comes and they don't just spend it, they immediately take a sizable portion and put it back into their education or an investment that will earn later.

I see money as an entity different than most people. I don't see it as scarce or evil. I see it as an energetic statement regarding the value of my work and the success of my efforts at spreading my meaning. It's energetic feedback.

I can give you a few mindset shifts regarding business and money that were instrumental for breaking through the middle-class barrier.

- Money is not evil. Thinking this way makes you afraid of it and why would you attract something to you that you are afraid of?
- Money is a declaration of your worth and commitment to something. It is a way of amplifying the value you place on a thing and your corresponding commitment. The old saying "put your money where your mouth is" takes on new meaning in this way.
- Spending vs. investing. Both involve money leaving, but one brings money back.
- It is not revenue-expenses= profit. The better way to think of it is revenue-profit= expenses. Pull out the profit first and you immediately see if your business is viable or not.
- Those who don't understand business think there is money in ideas. Ideas are easy, but can you implement? -That is where the money is.
- A business is NOT about working for yourself; it's about creating something that works for you.
- Money isn't spiritual. What? Money has more spiritual power than most anything else on the planet. Realize this and earning, spending, and sharing takes on new meaning

OWNERSHIP/SHARING

G enerosity, kindness, excellent communication, honesty, integrity, humor, gratitude, empathy, optimism and the desire to create meaning in life...these are all my favorite traits in any human.

July 21

SHARING

I have these times when I will be participating in an activity. It could be after a workout, sitting in the house at the end of the day, while on a walk, or even when hanging out with my big, Italian-American family for one of our Friday night dinners. All of a sudden I will have this strange feeling of emptiness in my chest and a sense of disconnect. It can be triggered by an old song, or it can just pop up out of the blue.

It takes me aback at times and I have to check in with myself and ask what I am feeling. The feeling I am feeling? It's loneliness. This is peculiar because I have had many friends and family say things to me like, "I have met few people in my life who are loved like you are" or "I don't know anyone who knows you who has ever had anything negative to say about you" or "You have more friends than anyone else I know."

Despite all those comments, whether true or not, I have this feeling. Having worked in the health and coaching field for so long, I know this feeling is common. In fact, I know it to be nearly universal. To be human is to feel lonely and disconnected at times.

And then there are your friends - the people that when not physically near you have created an imprint of themselves in your psyche. They are a psychological buffer against loneliness. You know that if you needed them they would be there without question.

These relationships are built over years and forged through some pretty tough times. Doug and I attended high school and college together. We have fought each other, fought together, been a shoulder for each other, coached each other through breakups, been there financially, and we know all each other's best and worst parts. I know this dude would literally die for me and I would take a bullet for him without question. When hanging together I think, how can you ever truly be alone in this world when you have a connection like this one?

The thing about loneliness - it completely dissolves when we sacrifice for another. Only when we do for others can we recognize when someone else sacrifices for us. The antidote for your loneliness is being there for someone else.

SHARING

All your attention on the way you look...and the way others look. Are they pretty or not? Am I lean enough? Are they fat?

The funny thing about this is that there will ALWAYS be someone prettier or more handsome than you. And there will always be someone leaner, or more fit too. The older you get, the truer this becomes.

Is that really how you want to continue spending your time?

Do you really think years from now people are going to sit around saying that your good looks made such an incredible difference in their lives? Do you really think your attractiveness has anything at all to do with the quality of the person you are?

In the end, people will remember you for how you made them feel, how you inspired, what you taught, and how kind and generous you were.

OWNERSHIP/SHARING

People spend a lot of time adorning their bodies with piercings and tattoos, coloring their hair and working on their bodies. Yes, they are pretty or hot or sexy...for a time...and then it goes away.

Good looks are a lot like concession stand food. When you're hungry, it looks and tastes great, until a few bites in and you realize it all tastes the same and what you really want is some real food.

How about using that same idea, and beautify your internal world? Add some compassion, some listening, and some smiles. What you leave behind in your work, your words, your kindness, your integrity, and your legacy is what really touches people. More importantly, it is the only thing that will ever make you feel fulfilled.

How about focusing on being a better person? How about work on listening more and looking in the mirror less? How about giving more compliments than you seek? How about making people laugh or giving them a word of encouragement? There are a lot of physically beautiful people in the world, but there are far too few who see and bring beauty to the world.

Meaning is what we are searching for and it does not come from selfish pursuits or vanity concerns. It comes from making a difference in the lives of others.

You can do that whether you are fit or not. No one is going to remember you for your great body. They will remember the way you cared.

Our deepest meaning and source of connection can never be purely for self. Our legacy is about what we do for the world, not what it does for us.

OWNERSHIP/ENGAGEMENT/SHARING

E ach human has within them a deep knowledge that they are meant for greatness. Be the one who helps them realize theirs, and you will understand yours.

PERCEPTION/OWNERSHIP/WISDOM/SHARING

There is a secret about happiness that so many of us miss; I myself lost sight of this for a time.

It has to do with your intention. When you wake up in the morning, where are your thoughts about the world centered? Are they on that person who is not loving you the way you need? Are they on the people at your job who aren't respecting you the way they should? Is it a focus on those Internet people who are not liking or sharing your stuff? On the person who you feel you are more qualified than who is getting all the accolades?

Waking up in that state of focus makes the world seem like it's out to get you. What if instead of thinking about what others are not giving to you, you focus your attention on generating those things for them?

Look around at all the people who make you smile and you will almost always see they are focused on you and not themselves. As a result they are surrounded by positive energy, and people who want to be in their presence.

When your primary intention is to make a difference in the day of someone else, you are far more likely to receive what you are looking for.

I know a guy who stops and talks to all the homeless individuals he sees. He does not always give money, but rather just a kind, warm, and sincere hello from one human to another. I know a girl at a coffee shop who makes every customer feel seen and recognized. I know a person online who is more focused on giving likes, shares, and comments than getting them.

Here is the secret. Happiness is a boomerang. You put it out into the world with intent and it comes back to you in spades. Happiness and selfishness cannot coexist in my opinion. Besides, if you are not here to contribute to the happiness pool then what are you here for?

SHARING

To be allowed to help another is a gift.
Generosity is the act that gives equally to the giver as it does the receiver.

OWNERSHIP/WISDOM/SHARING

H as anyone told you how beautiful you are lately? I have this theory about compliments. Your ability to take one and to believe it is genuine is directly related to your love of self.

We have this very strange culture where critiques dominate compliments. Compliments are given too infrequently and when they are given, they are viewed with skepticism. I understand that actually. There are those who are people pleasers and offer compliments more for themselves than for others. I actually used to be one of those people and that type of compliment is more detrimental than beneficial.

I have noticed that now I give compliments more freely and genuinely than ever before. The compliments I offer are authentically the way I feel. They are not manufactured with hopes of you liking me. They are for you, not me. I have learned that offering a compliment that is not genuine is actually an insult and people can sense that.

Authentic compliments are like little packages of white magic. They are the simplest of ways to spread kindness. I believe kindness is sorely needed in the world and you and I have the power to promote and amplify it.

Then there are the ones we love, adore, or want to be close to. They, above all else, should get our honest feelings of adoration. Why do we not tell them? For me to say I love you or that you are so beautiful means something beyond a simple compliment, it is telling you that I choose to take a part of you and integrate it into me. It means I see something in you that makes the world expand for me.

The final lesson on compliments, love, and beauty; they are like energetic boomerangs. They only come back to those who initiate them.

OWNERSHIP/WISDOM/ENGAGEMENT/SHARING

G ive.
Give freely without expectation, need for reciprocation, or desire for thanks.

Realize that generosity is an energy currency that is meant to flow forward and away from you. You are the conduit. Let abundance flow through you and you will always attract it. It's like water; it follows the path of least resistance. Be the source of this currency.

Realize that most humans are programmed to take. Do your part to change this reality by giving so freely and in such large ways that others are at first shocked, but then inspired to do the same.

Be the gift; be the kindness; be the change.

OWNERSHIP/ENGAGEMENT/SHARING

Give to others what you seek yourself.

How do you feel when others act like they are better? It makes you feel small, doesn't it? Why would any part of you want to do this to someone else?

Smile a genuine smile at another human, your equal. Laugh, be kind, be generous, encourage someone's dream, be the person who is not less than or better than.

OWNERSHIP/WISDOM/SHARING

To me the desire for fame is a sickness and the belief that you are famous is repulsive.

You have power beyond your own recognition and here is the rub...to find it in yourself you must first find it in others.

So, in a very strange way, your need to be better than is the very thing keeping you from being more than you are.

OWNERSHIP/SHARING

Our deepest meaning and source of connection can never be purely for self. Our legacy is about what we do for the world, not what it does for us. A legacy you leave; not something you hoard for yourself.

PERCEPTION/OWNERSHIP/WISDOM/ ENGAGEMENT/SHARING

How hard is it to make eye contact with a person and smile? Isn't it as easy as frowning, or making no contact at all? Not only that, but when you smile, even if it is a forced smile, science says you will automatically feel happier too.

Think about how you feel when a stranger makes eye contact with you and gives you a genuine smile. It feels like a gift doesn't it? Almost like, "What did they do that for? Do I know them? Wow, that was nice!"

A simple act of warmth in this way is a two-for-one kind of deal. The person receiving the smile feels it, but so does the person giving it.

I have been experimenting with this action. When I am feeling a bit down, tired, or disconnected, I will go on a walk and wait to make eye contact with someone. I will then give them a warm smile. Sometimes they smile back and sometimes they don't, but either way I know they felt it. What's really amazing is how good it makes me feel.

Here is what I would ask you: kindness is one of the easiest and most impactful things you can extend in this world. It makes you feel good and others feel good. Why are you not doing it more? Why are you not being kind to yourself and others?

Your happiness is about the stories you tell yourself. Are you powerful or powerless? Are you kind and caring or cold and indifferent? Are you so much about your schedule, your importance, and your time that you can't acknowledge another human with warmth and kind regard? Is life really so bad? Is your phone so much more important than the human in front of you?

To me it's a simple choice; be a kind person. You win and they win.

PERCEPTION/OWNERSHIP/WISDOM/
ENGAGEMENT/SHARING

M any people are natural givers. They build their entire self-perception on the idea that good people give and are selfless.

It's a beautiful thought, but it comes with a potential downside. Not all people are selfless in their reciprocity style. When a selfless giver gets into a relationship with a selfish taker, the giver can be sucked dry.

When managing the emotional energetics of any relationship, we all need to realize that people fall into three basic categories: Givers, Takers, and Matchers. In psychology, we call these reciprocity styles. Social psychology research has shown that Givers fare the worst of any other social management style. They also fare the best. I know this sounds contradictory. I'll explain.

The difference between healthy Givers and unhealthy Givers is an awareness of social dynamics, and the ability to pivot to a different style of behavior when required. Healthy givers stay tuned into the social energy dynamics of their relationships. If the other person is overly needy, selfish and subtly taking advantage, a smart Giver will recognize it and adjust. Instead of remaining Givers, they will become Matchers.

A Giver who always gives will often attract Takers who always take. Think about it. Why would a Taker, who always gets what they want, ever have reason to change? They have their energy fed and will continue to enjoy that situation as long as the Giver allows it.

The taker will stay fat and happy while the giver starves.

There is only one way to deal with a Taker: become a Matcher. Once you become a Matcher, the Taker has no choice but to meet you halfway or starve themselves. This is what healthy, successful Givers do. They still give, but they are careful about how much and to whom.

The ability to switch reciprocity styles like this is essential. It is also another perfect vetting strategy in developing your Next Level Tribe.

PERCEPTION/OWNERSHIP/ENGAGEMENT/SHARING

Disconnecting is hard, but sometimes it must be done.

Self-awareness: When you have an issue with someone, look to yourself first. We often assume others are the problem, so wait for them to fix it. Resist this approach by practicing "extreme ownership." If you are involved, you are the one who must fix it.

The benefit of the doubt: If you stubbornly cling to the way you view a person, even if they change, you won't notice it. Try seeing their behavior from a different perspective.

When I was in college, my eyesight was failing and I waited to the last minute to get contacts. A friend thought I was a jerk because he waved to me and I ignored him. I couldn't see to know he was waving. Assumptions can get us in trouble.

New story: If you want people to change, give them a new way of seeing themselves. People often live into the way they are perceived by others. If you see them as lazy and they know it, they have all the incentive in the world to keep being that way. All humans know people's perceptions are hard to change, so they just throw up their hands and say "the hell with it." Treat them differently and they are more likely to start being different.

Vet them: after you change the way you see and treat them, see if they show up differently. Give them some time. If they show up like they always did, it is time to consider cutting them from your inner circle.

Be Next Level: A Next Level Human does not engage in Base Level avoidance and ghosting, nor do they do Culture Level gossip and bad-mouthing of others. To make it clear, simply tell the truth. Try this, "My emotional resources are drained so I am choosing to be less socially engaged in general and more involved with only my closest friends."

Boundaries: There are some individuals you can never cut out completely (family, in-laws, coworkers, etc.). Boundaries help. A Next Level Human is going to be respectful, but also make it clear what they will and won't tolerate.

OWNERSHIP

When you hear your friends complaining about their other friends who drain their energy, make them feel bad, depressed, or annoyed, and when they are done, you simply tell them, "But...YOU allowed them to treat you this way" ... then it gets very quiet.

OWNERSHIP/ENGAGEMENT

W hen you don't respect yourself you seek evidence of disrespect in others. When you don't trust yourself, you look for signs of dishonesty in others. When you don't take care of yourself, you point the finger at others.

And when you don't love yourself, it is difficult to feel any love from others even when it is clearly there.

When you see someone who lies, schemes, avoids, won't communicate, and has difficulty expressing compassion for those closest to them, the truth, more often than not, is that they don't know, like, or trust themselves very much.

These types are easy to spot. They have many superficial relationships and very few deep ones. They deflect with humor. They avoid difficult conversations. They ghost. They cut and run. They are fickle and full of it. I call these types Base Level and we all have it in us.

Self-development is the solution, although it's something Base Level humans usually don't do. Self-development is not new age, psychological woo, it is training for life and the only path to true self-responsibility. It is, very simply, the psychological equivalent of physical strength and conditioning with weights.

Avoiding your emotions, plowing through and rejecting those who can help is a choice to be a psychological couch potato. Instead of becoming fat and sick in the body, you get fat and sick in the mind.

WISDOM/RESOLVE

There are three philosophies that I have felt most drawn to over the last several years: Stoicism, Taoism and Adlerian. Each has one major tenet that instructs on how to achieve freedom. "Freedom," in philosophical terms, means personal, mental freedom. In other words, how do we each free ourselves from worry, fear, suffering, desire, and the rest?

Stoicism says, "If you want to be free, be ready for death." This is meant literally as well as figuratively. Yes, contemplate your physical death. Know it is coming at any moment. Use the knowledge to focus yourself on what is most important. Making friends with death gives you the focus to live for and the meaning for which to die.

It is also meant figuratively. All of life is on loan - money, material possessions, companionship, etc. Be prepared to live without what you currently have.

Taoism says to be free you must be like water. Water is adaptable and resilient. It can be yielding like liquid, boundary heavy like a solid and aloof like vapor. It can flow and crash and settle. In other words, life is nothing but change and water always goes with the flow or becomes what the environment demands of it.

Adlerian psychology says be ready to give up being liked. The need to fit in can become a psychological prison. To be free, we must each muster the courage to be disliked. Imagine if you cared little for what others thought, would you be living a different life? Would you have made other choices? What would you be working towards?

I love these three lessons and have taken to repeating them often in my head.

- Be ready to die.
- Be ready for change.
- Be ready to be disliked.

PERCEPTION/OWNERSHIP/WISDOM/ENGAGEMENT

Life happens to us, but we also happen to life. You would think this idea is self-evident but we humans have a natural tendency to miss this fact when things go awry. When we do, it is like voluntarily giving away our power.

Let me give you an example. Let's say you are in your car stopped at a red light. Out of nowhere another vehicle comes from behind and slams into you. The driver was not paying attention and you suffer the consequences with injuries, a long recovery process, financial considerations, and all the rest.

This did not "happen for a reason." It was random and pointless, like life often is. But who is responsible? The driver is obviously legally at fault, but it's unlikely they did this on purpose. They would probably be dealing with many of the same consequences you are.

Who is responsible? The only person who can be - you! Life happened and now you must happen back to life. This is a mindset of action a few people get, but most don't. The people who comprehend it understand that blaming, whining, and complaining do nothing but take their power away.

There are two different groups that emerge from events like this. One group is the VC or Victim Culture. The other is the GC or Growth Culture. The GC takes responsibility for all things in their awareness they wish to change. There is no blaming or complaining.

The VC constantly give away their power by blaming, complaining, and expecting someone else will do the job that can only be done by them. The VC wants to assign blame.

The GC finds the lessons, gets to work solving the issue, and decides for themselves what they will make it all mean. They take it on headfirst. In doing so, they are the ones who gather insight, resilience, wisdom and success. There is no room for blame in change.

PERCEPTION/OWNERSHIP/ENGAGEMENT/RESOLVE

W e are on the same team.

Do we see our fellow humans as comrades or competition? Do we seek the feeling of community or separation?

We should not establish vertical relationships where there is a division or hierarchy, but rather generate horizontal relationships where we understand people as different but equal. That's why I call it Next Level and not, higher-level.

We each have something to both teach and learn from others. You escape the feeling of competition by instead competing against your ideal self.

The strength to be rejected...

If we want to be free, we have to give up the need to be liked. This takes a huge amount of courage, but the degree to which we can tolerate being disliked is the degree to which we can realize our potential and chase our dreams.

Focus on purpose, not passions...

Passions come and go; purpose is the thread that runs through our lives and answers the question, "Why am I here?"

Be ready to die...

The consideration and contemplation of death focuses our attention. It solidifies the focus to live for and the meaning to die for.

WISDOM/RESOLVE

When I think about the idea of "easy," I think we get it all wrong. We search for easy as if it is something we find. When we see someone excel we think, "that is so easy for them," as if they just stumbled upon something that fit their talents perfectly. What we don't realize is easy is not something you find, easy is earned. The only way to advance to easy is to work your way there through blood, sweat, failure, tears, and fears.

I realize we would prefer to ignore this simple truth, but there is no getting around it. If you think you are going to find easy, you are sadly mistaken. The only real shortcut is knowing there are no shortcuts. If you're willing to create easy, to earn it; then you will be one of the few who may actually one day enjoy easy.

Stop searching for easy; easy is earned.

PERCEPTION/WISDOM

When one person says about another, "Now they are finally thinking for themselves," what they usually mean is; "Now they are thinking like me."

In truth, thinking for yourself without first considering others' opinions, is a sure way to become ignorant and entrenched in biased, dogmatic belief. That's because thinking is inherently social, and our ability to think well depends on other individuals.

Good thinking is like scaffolding. You learn a concept and add to it. One thought builds off of another. We formulate ideas by hearing other ideas and refining them based on our own knowledge and experience. Discussing and debating ideas is how we make progress as individuals and groups. The last thing you want to do is to be thinking in a bubble.

This is why becoming a Next Level Human requires that you associate with Next Level Humans. These types approach debate as an opportunity to enhance their knowledge base. Agreement or winning is not the goal, learning is. People have lost the art of civil debate because they enter into it with the wrong goal.

I realize debates can get emotional. The fact that you feel something about an issue is a good thing. Without that excitement you have no impetus to think about it. Feelings are a starting point to intelligent thinking, so long as the goal is to learn rather than win (Base Level) or fit in (Culture Level).

When I first started out in health and fitness, I would read a book or a study. It would then become my religion until I read the next book or study. That's not thinking. That's copying, memorizing, and regurgitating.

Thinking is one of the most difficult things for people to do because it means they must take their current beliefs and admit they may be wrong.

I try to remind myself of three things:

- Learning is the goal, not winning or appearing correct.
- Just because we agree does not make either of us right.
- Just because we disagree does not mean one of us is wrong.

PERCEPTION/ENGAGEMENT

Positive affirmation is an erroneous concept. It does not work as a standalone practice. Let me explain.

You can't say a thing and expect your brain to get it. It doesn't matter if you say it a thousand times over three years. The idea that you can wake up, say something positive to yourself and have that manifest in your life is delusional.

The brain responds more to your actions than your thoughts. This shouldn't surprise us. It is the very thing we do with others, why would it be different with ourselves? "Actions speak louder than words," remember?

Positive action NOT Positive affirmation is what works. Here is a tangible example. Over the last five years I have dabbled in Crossfit style workouts. When I first began, I could not do butterfly pull-ups, handstand push-ups, or snatches.

Let's do a little thought experiment. Which do you think would give me the most chance for success?

Experiment 1: For 30 days I do positive affirmations by waking up first thing in the morning and repeating to myself, "I am so good at handstand push-ups," or "I am mastering handstand push-ups every day." I also repeat this several times during my day or whenever I doubt my ability. This is all I do. Nothing else. No handstand push-ups are ever done at the gym.

Experiment 2: I wake up every morning look in the mirror and say, "I will never master handstand push-ups ever!" Or "I suck at handstand push-ups." But 3 times a week for a month I practice doing handstand push-ups in the gym.

Which experiment will improve my handstand pushups: Positive affirmation with negative action or positive action with negative affirmation? Even a child would bet all the money in their piggy bank on Experiment 2.

Even psychology research has proven actions change thoughts much faster than thoughts change action. Both can work of course, but one fails as a strategy most of the time and the other usually works.

Thinking about it may get you to try, but doing it is what matters.

OWNERSHIP

If you find yourself talking about other people's motivations, shortcomings and mistakes, you are not revealing anything about them; you are telegraphing your own filters, struggles, and biases.

It is an adolescent mindset. It's not inspiring. It's tired. There is little utility in it for anyone. If you want to elevate, and nothing says you have to, evaluate the human level in which you spend most of your time.

There are three types of people inside each of us:

Base Level. Motivated by fear. Me against the world mentality. This is your reactionary, lizard-brain self. It avoids, it lies, and it connives. It seeks control and stability. To your Base Level anything that is different is a threat. It's the one that goes off on social media rants and attacks the imaginary "they." It's scared and insecure.

Culture Level. Motivated by status. Look at me mentality. It's also tribe think. "Our way is better than your way." Or "wake up sheeple." Where Base Level seeks control, Culture Level seeks being right. Winning is more important than learning. This is the adolescent mentality. It can be summed up like this: "I am smart; you are dumb. I matter, you don't. My team has the answers, your team is clueless." It's the home of ignorance and arrogance.

Next Level. Motivated by growth. Operates by the 3 imperatives: to learn, to teach, to love (share). Where Base Level is self-serving and Culture Level is self-indulgent, Next Level is self-aware. It realizes you are no better than anyone else, but you are magically unique. You have signature strengths and the means to make the world a better place. Your Next Level self pushes you to create meaning and make a difference. Whether it's raising your kids, writing your books or loving the person right in front of you.

The next time you find yourself ranting, blaming, and complaining about "they," "these people," or "them," consider which level human you are being.

OWNERSHIP/WISDOM/ENGAGEMENT/SHARING

First off, life is not fair. It is at times cruel and destructive. You can't control it. You can't control other people. The idea that you can is an illusion.

Whenever I am in pain, feeling like life is not fair, and wishing for a different outcome, I do four things that set my mind straight.

- I just admit it. I submit to it. I will just say in my head exactly the insight I just shared. I will say, "Jade, you know this is how life goes. Part of life is suffering. Deal with it. It's part of being human."

- In the next breath, I provide myself a couple other reminders. I say, "Your suffering is not unique or special. A billion other people throughout history have felt and dealt with these very things." There is power in that for me. If they can do it, I can do it.

- This one is the hardest, but I look for the lessons. It used to be that I could only see the lessons with time and perspective. With practice, I can see some of them while I suffer. I have been able to do this because I gave up what I consider to be the utterly stupid mantra of "everything happens for a reason," and replaced it with, "Things happen and it's up to me to choose the reason." I decide how I will use my pain as a path toward growth. It could just as easily be used as a slide into reducing and shrinking myself. You don't find the meaning; you decide the meaning.

- Finally, in time, I live my way into even deeper lessons and insights. When I do, I find I am enhanced beyond what I could have imagined. It's like I was upgraded with a suit of armor and a dictionary download of new understanding. And the most important thing that brings it all full circle? I share what I have learned. I tell my story. I keep my eyes open for the individuals who are searching for me. They need my insight, and I am eager to give it. Then they can bring that to help someone else. Through the energetic ripple of giving, my pain has meaning.

SHARING

Some things we can share:
Our passion
Our energy
Our knowledge (teaching is sharing)
Our time
Our money
Our hands (helping hand)
Our words (communication)
Our truth (honesty)
Our kindness
Our superpower (that thing we are especially good at)
Our love
Our fears
Our courage
Our failures
Our triumphs

You may think we can also share negative emotions, like rudeness or anger. Maybe you can, but sharing to me means you take something from yourself and use it to enhance someone else, not degrade them. In this way anger expressed authentically could enhance a person by spurring them to take action. I feel that is a stretch, though. Sure it can work, but more times than not, negative emotions degrade.

I also think sharing is only sharing when it is done without any motivation for reciprocation or even a desire for acknowledgment. True sharing enhances both the giver and receiver without the need for any other exchange. Gratitude is not a requirement for generosity.

Generosity has become a sort of religion of mine. I love showing up in ways for individuals that they would never expect. Gifts are one thing. Money is great. But there is something simpler we all can do that costs nothing - just a smile.

Try this the next time you pass someone on the street or make eye contact in line. Smile at them as if they are a close friend you haven't seen in years. Smile at them like they are an adorable puppy. Do it with zero reservations or expectations. Watch how amazing you will feel. Be ready, people are often not prepared for this. Some may look away or look down. Do it anyway. Trust me, they still felt it.

There are few gestures that take energy, but give you back that energy ten fold. A warm, genuine smile is one of those things. If you really want to see it in action, look in the mirror. Smile at yourself as if you are your best friend. Sure it's a little weird, but it's a great way to practice.

OWNERSHIP/SHARING

A true friend = Kindness, vulnerability, communication, openness, integrity, authenticity, honesty, beauty inside and out.

PERCEPTION/ENGAGEMENT/RESOLVE

The major insight about life is that nothing is easy. Easy is earned. And weight lifting is the perfect metaphor for life. In fitness we have a principle called SAID (Specific Adaptation to Imposed Demand). In other words, your body adapts to the way you train it. Well, so does your psyche.

Just like with weight training, in life you must continually challenge yourself with progressing difficulty to improve and grow. Your muscles respond only to new challenge. The same is true with your mindset. With each new challenge, there's growth, and this incremental growth begins to snowball like compound interest.

Most people simply won't do it. They've never trained to have a resilient mindset. We are all inherently fearful, lazy, and ignorant. Some might see that as depressing. I find it inspiring. It's the secret to success.

All I have to do is be a little less lazy, a little less fearful, and a little more willing to question my assumptions and biases. Then I can achieve amazing things. And the weight room is my testing ground. A new PR (Personal Record) in the gym helps me prepare for new fear PRs in life.

Your brain is always watching you and judging the type of person you are. When it sees you attacking the gym consistently, day after day, month after month, it's more likely to believe and support you when you attack something new in life.

August 17

PERCEPTION/OWNERSHIP/ENGAGEMENT/RESOLVE

Do the thing you hate. Make it hate you back, and keep doing it until you redeem yourself.

The redemption story is the greatest of all human stories. Someone's fears or demons catch up with them. They can't avoid it because the world outs them in a very messy and public way. They lose friends, their reputation is destroyed, and respect is lost.

Everything does NOT happen for a reason. That is one of the silliest cultural mantras of our time. I think people say it because they get confused about the order of things. They forget that after falling down, they made the choice about what to make it mean.

Life happened and they happened back. Whether they were conscious of it or not, it was their power and the meaning they decided to give it that made the difference.

It is an important distinction, because the redemption story is not always realized. More often, these life events result in the destruction story. We all know people who are mere shells of their former selves after tragedy, loss, illness, or shame. - Perhaps because they are waiting for a reason instead of creating one?

This is why I say, "Do the thing you hate." Another way to say it is, "Confront the thing you fear" or "Own your dysfunction." In the gym, we purposely confront heavier weights, more challenging workouts, and more difficult levels of skill. We do that in hopes of growing, getting stronger, and mastering something new. That's why Semper Discendum is the only tattoo I have in plain sight. It is a reminder. It means, "always be learning."

What's true in the gym is true in life. We don't get to redeem ourselves by sitting on the sidelines ignoring our faults and avoiding our fears. We do it by learning from our mistakes, making amends (mostly with ourselves), and turning our pain into a path toward meaning for ourselves, and others.

When we achieve that we become more than we were before, except this time it's honest and real.

PERCEPTION/OWNERSHIP/WISDOM/
ENGAGEMENT/RESOLVE/SHARING

What is a Next Level Human?

- When you think, act, and behave as a virtuous person when no one is watching and with no need for recognition or reciprocation.
- When you judge yourself before judging others. When you see yourself as no better or worse than any other human. When you realize everyone has weaknesses that may be someone else's strengths and strengths that may be another's weakness.
- When life is not about winning or fitting in. When personal growth is measured above material gain.
- When you have the strength and conviction to stand up against injustice while keeping the moral high ground. When you don't deny sexism, racism, and bigotry, but call it out when and where you see it.
- When you can endure troubles and suffering and still be grateful for what you do have and for lessons you will learn. When your pain becomes your path. When suffering becomes a source of growth. When obstacles show you the way.
- When you are open to learn. When you don't let bias and dogma blind you from truth. When truth is more important than winning. When you can admit you were wrong and change your mind.
- When you are confident enough to know you are extraordinary, humble enough to know you are not THAT special, and aware enough to know your greatest contributions are things you do for others not yourself.
- When you realize blaming, complaining, and lying are forms of victimhood and poison to the soul. They represent your fear of taking responsibility and your desire to control the realities of others.
- When you are kind to other humans. When you smile at strangers. When you realize we are all in this together. When you can laugh and find joy in the small things.
- When you can shut up and listen. When people who are different than you are interesting, rather than threatening. When you expose yourself to change and challenge. When you don't deny facts and study both sides.
- When you realize being Next Level does not make you higher level. When you say what you mean, and do what you say.
- When you choose to create a legacy, not for yourself, but for others. If you are not here to help, why are you here?

OWNERSHIP/WISDOM

There are ways I assess and vet people. More importantly, there are ways to assess and vet myself. Self-awareness is THE skill that comes before all others. I can't be accurate in my assessment of others if I have not evaluated my own behavior as well.

If I see the same patterns repeating again and again, it is me. If this person is the only one I have difficulty with, it is more likely them.

If I am calling everyone a jerk, I am probably the jerk. If I am reluctant to call anyone a jerk ever, then I may be right in my assessment.

I judge myself first. After I have done that, I use a few filters to honestly evaluate others:

- History. If they have been lying, cheating, blowhards in the past, you may want to keep a closer eye on them. Sure, many people use personal failings to be better people (I would like to think I did), but history still matters.
- What others say. Do they sing their praises? Stay quiet? Advise caution?
- What they say. People who speak negatively of others not in the room are suspect from the start. Gossip is a character trait I avoid.
- Responsibility. There are two types of people in the world. The first type apologizes and displays awareness, consideration, humility, and generosity. The second person deflects, blames, and complains.
- Politics. I am looking for a person who does not align with a political team, and who has enough integrity to drop their allegiance when their person or team lies.
- Driving. This tells me about their tendency toward consideration, awareness, patience, and control.
- Service professionals. Do they display humanity or act superior? This reveals kindness, humility, generosity, and humanity.
- Arguments. Do you ever hear them say, "I am sorry, I was wrong and I understand your side?" This reveals respect and self-awareness.
- Honest Communication. Can they have the hard conversations and be honest about their intent?

PERCEPTION/OWNERSHIP/WISDOM/ ENGAGEMENT/SHARING

A s a human, you have a job to do. You have 4 jobs actually:

- To earn and manage money.
- To give and receive love.
- To gain and keep your physical health.
- To develop your spirit and mind.

All of these jobs are in service to the 3 imperatives: to learn, to teach and to love (i.e., share something freely that makes the world a better place.)

Base Level humans want to take. Whether wealthy, poor or in between, they feel they are in a battle against the world. They will work to rig the system in their favor. Some of this class of human make up the wealthy, greedy bankers AND those who exploit the system. Some become parents because they want someone who will love and support them. Others become parents to provide support and love. The former are the Base Level types.

Culture Level humans want your respect. They will do whatever they feel is necessary to elevate their status above others. If you show them respect, they may give it back, but they never give it first. The major reason for their actions is how they think others will view them. You can become a lawyer for your dad, the money, or the prestige OR you can become a lawyer because you are especially suited to serve justice. Those who do it for the respect, spotlight, or fortune are the Culture Level herd.

Next Level Humans want to grow themselves and the world. They are not interested in taking from others or being given something they did not earn. They want to do their jobs, not to become popular, but to become better and improve the world. They are the artists, creators, parents, lawyers and others who chose their professions because they feel called to them. They prioritize meaning over money and purpose over power.

If you find yourself confused about where you have been, where you are going, or what you want to do, then I suggest you take the Next Level path by asking, "What am I uniquely suited to do that will grow me and make the world better when I am gone?" The motivation to work your 4 jobs and achieve the 3 imperatives comes from this thinking.

PERCEPTION/OWNERSHIP/WISDOM/
ENGAGEMENT/SHARING

Have you ever been in a situation where you meet someone and they provide little acknowledgment at all?

How do you respond? You will probably feel an uncomfortable anxiety and a lack of connection to this person. This reaction will cause you to withhold and become unresponsive. This can even create a negative response that deteriorates the relationship before it can even get started.

This may be an appropriate reaction. Perhaps this person is indeed a cold, self-absorbed cretin. Maybe you should erect strong boundaries of social and emotional protection?

But what if they are under extreme stress at work? What if they are preoccupied thinking about a sick loved one? Maybe they have a social phobia, and exhibit these poor behaviors as a means to counter their fears?

My mother taught me this as a child. My grandfather on my Dad's side was a fairly conservative man. When I was young and tried to hug him he would shrink away and shake my hand instead. My mother would tell me, "Jade, don't let your grandfather do that. He needs your love the same way you need his. You hug him when you greet him."

I remember this being a slightly odd transition for my grandfather and me. But I recall years later when I was grown and in high school, he would look for a hug from me and often initiate it himself.

I have used that lesson for how to interact with people my entire life. As humans we make a lot of assumptions because we simply don't know. My mother taught me, if I am going to make an assumption about someone why not assume they are distracted, shy, or socially awkward instead of purposely being an ass?

Now I freely share myself with others first. When I see a human, I try to see them like a cute, but aloof, puppy who just needs to be pet or given a bone. Instead of waiting for them to acknowledge me, I recognize them. I give compliments, make jokes, laugh, and elevate my energy for the conversation.

It's a vetting system. It allows me to be real. My authentic self is warm, responsive, and interested in others. It also allows me to test them. Do they match my kindness or do they bite? I am a pretty introverted guy, but I believe this is my job as a human.

PERCEPTION/OWNERSHIP/WISDOM

This is all we have.

A friend of mine was struggling in his relationship. He was beside himself trying to understand how to live with his partner and their kids in the face of betrayal and a possible divorce.

I said, "Suppose you are going to die in a month. How would you treat them? How would you behave? How would you want to be remembered?"

My friend responded, "I would want them to know they were forgiven, that I loved them and that I support them. I would want them to see me as strong and supportive even in my wounded state."

"That is your answer of how to be."

PERCEPTION/OWNERSHIP/WISDOM/
RESOLVE/SHARING

All of life is on loan.

No other truth has helped me more than this recognition. If you want to be free, it starts with accepting two things: death and suffering.

I know this sounds morbid and perhaps scary. For me, it is no longer either. I am fully aware that I am going to die. It might be in a few minutes when I jump in my car. I know I will lose people I love. Perhaps they will die. Perhaps they will stop choosing to include me in their lives. Either way, I will lose them. It is inevitable.

My health is not fully in my control either. I try my best, but I can't predict what my genetics have in store for me. I will age and become unattractive. I may suffer a chronic illness. I could be paralyzed. I may lose my ability to remember and even reason. None of it is fully under my control.

My philosophy is to expect nothing and accept everything that is not fully under my control. The only thing I manage completely is the way I show up in the world. I will die and suffer, but I choose how I will be in those moments.

When I suffer, I choose to do so with dignity. That means I will accept the randomness and cruelty that may come my way. I will not blame, complain, or regret. I will use the storms in life to learn what I can and teach from it if possible. Regarding death, I will confront it like a warrior charging into battle, observing my honor code to the end.

Life happens but it better be ready for me to happen back. This is my choice and my power. It's yours too.

PERCEPTION/WISDOM

I just completed a handful of books on psychology and politics. Some insights emerged.

We have lost the skill of civil debate. We are paralyzed by team think. Our social media feeds and cable news (can we even call it that anymore?) keep us in an echo chamber bubble. Why?

First, we prefer certainty to learning. Having ideas challenged is not comfortable. It forces us to listen, consider, question, and research. Most people are happy not to do those practices. They prefer to be spoon-fed. Illusory superiority, the idea that we are better, smarter, and more virtuous compared to others, is always at play.

To remedy this:

1. Spend time trying to prove yourself wrong.
2. Argue the other side.
3. Use evidence-based, unbiased sources for your information.

Next, we think we are entitled to always feel comfortable. We can't grow without discomfort. We now live in a world where people point out micro-aggressions: "brief verbal, or behavioral indignities, intentional or unintentional, that communicate negative prejudicial slights." Unintentional? Aggression by definition is about intent. If I had no ill intent, I am not being aggressive. To assume ill intent where it may not exist is wrongheaded. Think about that for a second. Just because someone feels attacked does not mean they actually were. To assume aggression where none exists, then attack on that basis is the real aggression. Sometimes, people do intentionally attack. That is easily handled with strong conviction and stern boundaries. You are going to feel challenged at times. That's life.

"Choose not to be harmed - and you won't feel harmed. Don't feel harmed - and you haven't been." -Marcus Aurelius

Finally, the idea of good against bad - the danger of Tribal Think. Those on the other side are immoral, wrong, stupid, etc. You do realize they say the same about us, right? Seeing the world only in dichotomous, black and white terms blinds us. We alienate potential allies and amplify our enemies.

This does not mean we let injustices go. We cannot, should not, and will not. However, let's not be overly fragile, self-righteous victims either.

PERCEPTION/OWNERSHIP/WISDOM/
ENGAGEMENT/RESOLVE/SHARING

B e vulnerable. Practice gratitude. Be present. How many times have we heard these phrases?

It's good advice for sure, IF you are already feeling good. If your life is great, it is easy to feel great. It's also less risky and doable to be more open and available. But what if your life is falling apart and all you know seems to be crumbling down? When all you want to do is look at your social media feed and say, "Piss off you spoiled brats. That is easy for you to say. Try staying in your world of flowers and woo with this kind of debt, betrayal, loss, a dead-end job, terminal illness, etc."

There is a time and a place to pick dandelions, sip your kombucha and wax poetic about love and light. There is also a time to draw swords and charge into battle, a time to reflect, and a time to act. A time for woo and a time for woe, a time to be a philosopher, and time to be a warrior.

When the world is crumbling around you, the warrior mentality is what you need. I don't understand why this side of the equation is rarely discussed. It is a matter of using the right tool at the right time. Invoking gratitude and woo during the worst human struggles is like trying to use a paintbrush to remove a screw.

So what does a warrior do? First they are very clear on what they are fighting for. They have an honor code that acts as their anchor and lighthouse in the rough seas of life. It is a statement of what they stand for, fight for, bleed, scar, and even die for. It defines who they are and who they will become. This frames any struggle as a journey of growth and a fight to evolve. Do you have one?

Second, a warrior takes action. They rise to the occasion by doing the job they were put here to do. They take full responsibility for the battle. There is no wallowing, complaining, or blaming. They turn toward the storm and do what must be done.

Finally they understand that the past informs the present and the future directs it. The wounds they sustain are lessons and theirs alone to manage. They don't expect others to mend them. They eventually see those wounds as gifts of learning. Pain becomes a path to understanding and leads back to gratitude. And the cycle repeats.

PERCEPTION/OWNERSHIP/ENGAGEMENT/RESOLVE

S uffering is a normal consequence of being human.
Viktor Frankl talked about suffering as one of the three key sources of finding meaning in life. The two others being:

1. Our creative potential and expression.
2. Our experiences with people and places.

Suffering involves overcoming mental, emotional, or physical pain. To find meaning in suffering involves a choice. We realize that suffering happens to us. It's not something we control. But we CAN control our reactions to it. Do we crumble under its weight or do we beat it with dignity?

In warrior cultures this was often referred to as "dying a good death." They valued enduring physical pain and suffering; it served as training to overcome their fears and pains with dignity, but also fortified them mentally. As Frankl acknowledged in *Man's Search For Meaning*, "...those who master a hard lot in life with their heads held high are always the most respected."

Physical training is a proving ground to master this "transcendence of suffering." Physical exercise does not feel good to anyone. I don't think I have ever done a single workout I liked. What feels good is what comes after. The feeling of knowing you got through the pain, making it through a workout without giving in or quitting. When you do that your physical body becomes stronger, allowing you to push harder and further in future workouts. Soon you develop a mental state that matches the physical gains you have made. In time you realize that, when needed, this can even help you with emotional suffering. You keep your head up, you suffer through it, and you know your emotional muscles (resilience) are also being exercised and fortified.

PERCEPTION/OWNERSHIP/WISDOM

There are several different ways we can be better, Next Level Humans. One way is to interact without assuming ill intent. In philosophy this is called the principle of charity, where we assume the best intentions of a person rather than the worst.

Let's say you have family members who are always inquiring, opinionated, and giving advice. You could see this as controlling or you could view this as them caring and wanting to be supportive. You may not realize it, but how you perceive a thing can influence the behavior of that thing. People will often begin to behave in the exact ways you have decided they are, whether they started out that way or not. When you lose your charitable view of people, they often lose their positive opinion of you too.

We can also approach life with intellectual humility. Everyone is wrong at times. In fact the nature of life is that we are likely to be wrong more often than not. Do you always need to be the smartest person in the room? Do you question your own beliefs as vigorously as you question everyone else's?

To begin this process ask yourself, "Would I prefer to be right or do I want to learn and get better?" Also, keep in mind, just because we agree does not mean we are right. Just because we disagree does not mean one of us is wrong.

Finally, we can look at whether we see people as individuals or immediately assign them to groups. Do we divide people into us versus them, or do we take a common humanity approach? It is just as easy to find the commonalities in people, as it is to find the differences (I would argue it's easier).

You are Christian and I am atheist, but one religion we share is kindness. You are a Democrat, she is Republican and I despise both parties but what we share is a love for the ideals of this country. I am a white, straight male. You are a black, homosexual woman. As individuals we love books, sushi, and judge people based on their character above everything else.

There is an army of the self-righteous everywhere you look. History tells us these people always lose and always create devastation in their path. I want to be different. How about you?

ENGAGEMENT

Expect nothing; accept everything.

Make choices and take actions.

Forget your past. Wounds you pick at don't heal.

You get over your past by creating your future.

You are not special. Your pain has been felt millions of times by millions of humans.

You have a job to do. Answers emerge from doing.

OWNERSHIP/WISDOM

Have you ever heard of the law of attraction? You know, the idea that you sit down, take some deep breaths, say Ommmmm a few times and then wish upon a star— by envisioning what you want—and it eventually happens?

By this logic, if you want a fantastic, beautiful, romantic partner, you think about it a lot, and he or she will show up. Sounds like fairytale stuff, right? Well, it kind of is. The "law of attraction" has caused a lot of people to misunderstand how this actually works.

A more accurate term for the idea people are referring to when they invoke the law of attraction, is "the law of recognition."

Let's say you decide you are going to buy a Tesla. You had not thought about the Tesla before, but now you have researched it and are contemplating purchasing one. You think you may want one in red. Now you start noticing Teslas, don't you? As if by magic they are everywhere, and inexplicably, a high percentage of them are red.

This is not the law of attraction; it's the law of recognition. When you start thinking about and researching the Tesla, you are priming your brain to recognize them. Those Teslas— yes, even the red ones—were there the whole time. You did not call them into existence; you simply began to be aware of what was already around you.

This is how authenticity works too. Once you decide to own yourself completely, you immediately become visible to all the people who have been looking for that type of person. The way you carry yourself and the confidence you project will send a message to those around you.

You'll start recognizing the people you are looking for as well. This is the first stage of becoming a Next Level Human and building a Next Level tribe.

OWNERSHIP/RESOLVE

The key is to be insecure enough to know you must work, learn, and drive to get what you want, but, at the same time be arrogant enough to feel you can accomplish anything you want - confident humility.

August 31

PERCEPTION/OWNERSHIP/WISDOM

Information is simply noise without filters. Memory is one filter. Can we remember the salient points? Learning is another filter. Do we truly understand the information? Memorizing and learning are fairly easy. They take little work, and our brains are experts at these tasks.

Then information runs up against hard filters. These are the entrenched beliefs we have, most of which are unconscious. These hard filters include known psychological biases such as illusory superiority, rationalizing, halo effect, tribal think, and confirmation bias.

These hard filters keep us from deciphering the truth. For example, let's say we love our SUV. Our bias is strong toward that car (halo effect). We also think we are smarter and more moral than others (illusory superiority). Because we see ourselves as smart and good, we rationalize owning that SUV.

We might think, "Well I am contributing to US workers at GM and Ford." We may explain, "My kids are safer in this car." As this rationalizing continues, we will seek out in-group members who agree with us (tribal think). We will also seek out information that justifies our use of that car (confirmation bias).

The next thing you know, we are denying climate change is an issue and fighting against regulations mandating better gas mileage. We, having no expert knowledge in climate change, have found all the information we need to argue against 99% of scientists, who study the material for a living all because we love our SUV. And, so it goes with pretty much every political issue you can think of: guns, immigration, social programs, etc.

PERCEPTION/OWNERSHIP/WISDOM

People disagree because intuitions come first and reasoning comes second. Intuitions are snap judgments based on past experiences. For example, if when we were young, we hear our white mother react harshly to a black person while lumping all black people into her attack, we may see black people as less than, scary, or problematic without ever thinking about the logic behind it.

If we see our uncle objectifying women, our intuitions can cause snap judgments and behaviors toward women about which we are unaware.

It's a type of psychological blindness. We see our moms, our uncles, and ourselves as "good people" and become defensive at the idea that we may be racist or sexist. It takes an extraordinary human to say, "Wow, I see this cultural construct and I am impacted by it whether I realize it or not. I need to wake up."

Our morality can derive from experiences that we have never actually thoughtfully considered. Once we settle on a moral narrative, that story blinds and binds us.

It blinds us to alternative views that may be more true and moral. It binds us to tribes that hold similar views. In this way, extreme ideas create extreme bias, which creates extreme psychological entrenchment.

The only way out is to remove the blinders and become unbound to our current tribe. We force the blinders off by turning the tables back onto ourselves. We do this by examining all of our strongest beliefs- the ones that trigger our defenses the most- then we deliberately consider the other side and try to defend that viewpoint. Doing this almost always results in being less blinded and more open.

To disconnect yourself from extreme groups, stop looking for people who are like-minded. Look for people who are like-hearted instead.

I have friends vastly different from me in almost every conceivable way. The reason we connect is our hearts align on three fundamental ideals: the desire to learn and grow, a belief in kindness, and the willingness to admit when we are wrong.

A Next Level Human is one that insists on intellectual honesty and open mindedness. A Next Level person happily changes their position when warranted, and resists bias and team think.

ENGAGEMENT

C hange and Challenge - These are the things that make people feel alive and engaged. These are the elements that keep us growing and expanding. This is one of the reasons so many people look back at the time between the ages of 15 and 30 years old and think, "Those were the good ol' days"

For the vast majority of people, these are the years of new experiences: first loves, engagement in sport, lots of social involvement, first heartbreaks, college, marriage, kids, traveling, career, all kinds of things.

And then, for many, routine sets in. Life gets more familiar, maybe even monotonous. Your life is less interesting and the life of others becomes more interesting. You are more interested in eleven guys on a football team than your own growth. You are more into the Housewives and the Kardashians than you are your own life. You go from engagement in your younger years to escapism as you move into middle age.

But it does not need to be that way. Death can greet you at any moment. The ancient Greeks and Romans recited "Memento Mori," to remind them there is no time to waste; you may have zero time left.

Life is change and challenge. That is its very definition. We can't merely wait for the occasion. We should not think of rising to the occasion. We should be creating the occasion. Change and challenge are what expand your perspective, not comfort and stability.

If you are afraid, good! If you are unsure, good! If you are wondering and worrying, good! You are alive and well and that means you are still growing. If you are not, then all you need to do is begin now. Change something, anything, right now. Challenge yourself in any small way that makes sense starting now. This will begin the process.

PERCEPTION/OWNERSHIP/SHARING

When you find yourself in grief, loss, pain, and suffering all your intentions can easily be thrown out the window.

Have you ever had a situation with another where you wanted so badly to control the outcome that you ended up making it worse? Perhaps you even knew you were worsening the situation but you could not reign in the emotional conflict?

I like to think of emotional wounds like physical wounds. When you injure yourself physically, you will instinctually cover the area and apply pressure. You will then tentatively look at the cut to see how deep and extensive it is. Then you wash and tend to it. When it is bandaged or stitched up, you let it heal.

In this case, it serves no one to run around bleeding, expecting someone else to fix it. Even if it was someone else that cut you, you are the one who must tend to the incision. If you wait for them to help, you are going to bleed out. I realize it hurts doubly when people you trust cut you, but it is futile to expect them to heal your wounds. They can't, only you can.

With emotional wounds, it is more difficult to know how to cover the wound and apply pressure. This is analogous to removing yourself for a time to feel the emotions. Letting the emotions be felt is a lot like washing the wound. You can't cover a wound without washing. It may get infected. - Same with emotional wounds.

Some heartbreaks and betrayals can feel like having a limb torn off. We lose part of our identity when this happens. It is like learning to walk again, but these wounds can be a reminder.

If we are paying attention they call us back to creating our Next Level selves by integrating what happened into the greater meaning of life. How can you learn from this? What can you teach from it? Can you use it to make your part of the world better?

Relinquam amor. It means leave your love. It is the share principle. The greatest suffering can give rise to the largest transformations. Rather than fight the change this turmoil caused, turn into it. Use it to help others heal; this speeds your own healing.

September 4

PERCEPTION/OWNERSHIP

There are two states that can create change. I call them the "world of woo," and the "world of woe." One is rarely discussed, but it is more powerful.

You can find the inhabitants of Woo everywhere, especially on social media. They say: "own your life," or "live your purpose," or "radiate your bliss," or "think in abundance." I have made a lot of creative accomplishments by acting out these very same mantras. It can work.

But there's a problem. You are co-creator in your life. Life happens to you and you happen back. The reverse is also true, you take action and life has a reaction. If you have a good, successful life, it is incredibly naive to assume it will always be that way or to think that everyone has the same privileges. It's like the expression; "It's easy to be all good when everything is all good."

I bring this up for a reason. The spread of Woo is not a very helpful thing when life's random cruelty smacks you across the face. Sometimes you create your life. Sometimes life creates you. Sometimes you call forth, other times you are called upon.

Consider Viktor Frankl. He was getting his Ph.D. in psychology. He had a connected, loving family and every privilege. He was "creating his life" and "living his purpose." Then WWII and four concentrations camps landed on him. At that point, his life was being created for him. In times like these, all that positive Woo becomes useless.

In the world of Woo you are supposed to listen to your heart and follow your passion, but in this case his heart was the one asking him, "What do we do now?"

The world of Woe is also a magical place. It's painful, but it provides immense opportunity for growth. Hitting rock bottom is sometimes the only way to shed the old and create the new. To create out of pain and suffering is just as powerful, if not more so, than those shiny, new age mantras about bliss and gratitude.

Life can dole out some difficult and painful lessons. To not be a victim of your circumstances, no matter what they are; that is true magic and bliss. If we are going to create our lives, we must embrace and master both worlds; bliss and betrayal, pleasure and pain. Focus on one and the other may overtake you.

PERCEPTION/OWNERSHIP/WISDOM/ENGAGEMENT

Do you ever have that feeling of looking at a picture of yourself from the past and thinking, "Wow, I really look good there. Why did I think I was fat and disgusting at that time? I would love to look like that today!"

Maybe it's just me, or maybe you have to advance past the age of 35 before you experience that?

It's the same way with your mental state. When life is happening, we are changing and feeling challenged. We may not realize it at that moment, but later we may think, "Wow, those were the days!"

The thing we crave currently is not usually the thing we will celebrate tomorrow. In other words, we will choose comfort and stability over change and challenge every single chance we get. Yet, when we look back on those "comfortable and stable times," there is often little we can point to and say, "That enhanced and grew me." In fact, comfortable/stable times are more likely to be the times we regret.

Regret is one of the worst emotions a human can endure; yet comfort and stability are the primers of regret (more often than not). We regret what we did not do, or attempt, a million times more than what we tried and failed at. This is a truth few humans can deny; yet all of our thoughts, plans, and intentions revolve around procuring comfort and stability.

In my opinion, this line of thought is completely backward. Just because you are alive does not mean you are living. The very definition of life is change. In fact, life is nothing if not change, and it is our teacher. That challenge is our mentor. In nature, things either adapt to change and grow, or stay exactly the same and perish; such in life.

As people who want to grow (to learn, teach, and love)- to reach our Next Level- it's not enough to, rise to the occasion; we must create the occasion.

It's not, "leap and the net will appear," instead it is, "leap and weave the net as you fall."

If you are feeling stuck, lifeless, confused, overwhelmed, or lost, ...then realize the way out is not what is familiar and cushy; it is more likely to be what is different and difficult.

PERCEPTION/OWNERSHIP/WISDOM/SHARING

Consider this about pain. Pain is a call to confront something. It is a warning that something requires your attention. Pain often can show us the path. To ignore such a signal is to turn your back on growth and to reject truth.

Here is how it works: Intense hurt or loss strips us down to our bare nature. These emotions focus us in a way that makes us indifferent to what others think. That is a rare place for any human to occupy. Our inauthentic selves and psychological facades fall away in the midst of fear, hurt, or loss. Pain allows us to move past our superficial selves and closer to the fundamental truth of who we are.

It allows people to reach what psychologists call "depressive realism," which is the ability to see things exactly as they are. When something is painful enough, your psyche cannot hide from the pain and you are forced to confront it. More importantly, you are forced to confront yourself. You may not like what you see, but at least you are finally seeing it. When you arrive at this place, pain has done its job.

There are people we call wise, deep, or insightful. These are often the first people we seek out when we are dazed and wounded. Usually, they have almost invariably suffered through pain. They also know how to share the lessons of their hurt to speed the healing and learning process for you.

I believe this is a quintessential aspect of a Next Level Human, to get past our Base Level instincts of fight or flee, to transcend our Culture Level desires of maintaining the status quo, and instead, reach into our fear and imperfections and use our pain to teach and share with others.

The ability to do that is the essence of a strong and good human. - The type of human who uses their pain to illuminate a path for themselves and others. Ironically, that sharing is often the final stage of our own wounds healing too.

WISDOM/SHARING

The stoic philosophers discussed, "living according to your nature." To them, the one thing we humans have that sets us apart from all other creatures is superior reasoning. So, living according to our nature means putting reason above passions. Emotions and pursuits of passion are fickle and intoxicating; if we indulge in them too often, we can easily become lost in them.

The Taoist's talk about flow; they see our job as humans to live in balance. If you examine the yin and yang, most people will get lost in either the black or the white. The Taoists view the most important part of that image as the line that snakes between. In life, that is the path they say we should walk.

I love these two philosophies because they say nothing of God, rituals, or arbitrary rules. They simply give guidance on how to live without judgment, intolerance, or self-righteousness.

However, they do not fully examine our creative nature. We are not the only creators in the world. Look at a spider's web, a bird's nest, or dogs at play and you will see creativity. At the same time, we humans are immense creators. It simply flows out of every corner of our being. I believe the need to create is another quintessential element of being human.

Your work; what you build. The joyful humor you bring. The smile you offer up. The books you write. The podcasts you produce. The children you raise. The meals you cook. The language you speak. The love you make. The computer you program. The hair you cut. The car you fix. All of it is creative art.

In addition, art is meant to be shared. When you add your art to the creative pool of knowledge, we are all enhanced. That's why I love doing my work and love seeing yours too.

OWNERSHIP/WISDOM/ENGAGEMENT/
RESOLVE/SHARING

A job is thought of as a career, but it is best defined as the role one fills in society. There are 4 jobs every human must work regardless of career and whether they want to or not. These jobs are:

1. Manage finances.
2. Manage relationships.
3. Manage health and fitness.
4. Manage psychological and spiritual well-being.

It's like a three-legged stool with money, relationships, and health as the legs. Psychological self-development and life purpose are the floor and seat, providing the anchor and support for the three legs.

Without a meaningful why to live for, the other three jobs become pointless. Without self-development, it is difficult to integrate the other three at all. If you have ever sat on a stool that vacillates back and forth, only ever managing to keep two legs in contact with the ground, but never three, you have a sense of what a shaky spirit feels like when any of these jobs are ignored...

-The rich, "successful" businessperson, whose physical body is in shambles. -The beautiful model devoid of intelligence or kindness. -The religious devotee filled with self-righteous intolerance. -The witty friend, who uses humor to keep people at a distance, and distract themselves from their overwhelming sense of emptiness, and the social activists so blinded by anger they start to become the very thing they fight against. These are all examples of "stools" with broken seats, uneven legs, or on shaky ground.

It is not always easy to integrate our 4 jobs and begin living a Next Level life. When I think of this for myself, I simplify it into what I call the 3 imperatives: to learn, to teach and to love. Seeking to uphold these three imperatives inevitably stabilizes our stool.

Learning involves embracing change and challenge, and overcoming fear, laziness, and ignorance. Teaching involves patience, understanding, and compassion and disposing prejudice and bias. Sharing means giving your time, energy, or resources to help and bring joy to someone else. All acts that simultaneously develop self and bring meaning to life...the seat and floor; stabilizing the legs of our stool.

RESOLVE

Find your fears or they will find you.
Confront your demons or they will consume you.

Speak your truth or lose it.

Celebrate your failures knowing they can lead to future success.

Stop being afraid of what stands in your way because those things show you the way.

Do the hard thing now to earn easy later.

OWNERSHIP/WISDOM/SHARING

On sharing and receiving feedback:

The interesting thing about feedback is the more you are open to it, the more people will offer it. The better you are at receiving it, especially the portion that is rude or you disagree with; the more you realize it advances you.

Over time you begin to almost crave feedback, and you start to see it as something that can clarify what you know, and illuminate what you don't know. You learn to clearly discern when you are correct or when there is something you are missing.

Once you arrive at an appreciation for receiving feedback, you start to see the value in giving it more as well. If you perceive feedback as a gift others give you, you want to offer that gift in return. However, the way you disperse your input changes from an approach dominated by ego and self-righteousness, to an approach of reciprocity, teaching, and learning.

You discover that the way people receive your feedback is also very telling about them, and it illustrates core things about your own style of communication and level of understanding.

Slowly, over time you stop thinking of it as feedback at all. It simply becomes about learning, growth, honesty, and good communication. You no longer feel a need to give it, and you are no longer averse to receiving it. You are simply grateful for the way it enhances you in both dimensions.

WISDOM/RESOLVE

You know that feeling during a workout where you think "Why do I do this to myself?" Or after a workout when you find yourself on the floor squirming around to find any position that will take the pain and breathlessness away? These are the workouts that often make all the difference. -The ones most people simply won't do.

Not only these workouts, but also cold showers and ice baths. How about a weekend without food or grueling 200m repeats on a Sunday morning when everyone else is eating brunch?

You may not realize it, but manufacturing challenges like these in your life teach you to become more familiar with pain, change, and difficulty.

It is the principle of Resolve. You do it and you finish because you said you would and you know you must. You know if you do your brain works with you. It develops confidence in you and will work to support you. Give up, don't try, or give in, and your brain loses respect for you and will find ways to sabotage you next time.

In case you're wondering, this is essentially self-imposed, cognitive, behavioral therapy. If you are struggling with not being able to achieve something, ask yourself when was the last time you finished anything at all?

What we can endure physically is correlated with what we can handle emotionally. Physical perseverance translates into mental resilience.

I complete the insane workout because it helps me complete my book. I take cold showers because it signals I will do the things today that I don't want to do. I run those sprints and torture myself because I know at times life will require me to suffer, be strong, and finish anyway.

WISDOM/ENGAGEMENT/RESOLVE/SHARING

Be fearless, take action, learn the lessons, pay it inward, and then pay it forward.

PERCEPTION/OWNERSHIP/WISDOM

When I was back east visiting family, we spent a week together in the North Carolina Mountains. At one point I drove to get gas for the boat and Jet Ski we rented, but I realized the gas cans were leaking at the top.

I was going slow and driving carefully so as not spill the gasoline. The guy behind me was irate. I could see him in my rearview mirror. He was tailgating, driving a little erratic, and yelling. I did not get mad. I just thought, "He has no idea I have gasoline in here that is spilling. If he did, he would understand."

In college, a friend had just lost his brother. He was not being himself and was causing trouble at the bar where I worked. Another guy took issue with him and they got in a fight. I remember my friend getting knocked down. He just stayed down and cried. I looked at the dude he was fighting and said, "Man, he just lost his brother." I remember the look of anger vanishing and a look of sorrow replacing it. He suddenly understood.

My point is that we are all fighting our own battles. You have no idea what others are going through, how they are coping, or how they are contributing. It is easy to assume other people are dumber than you, have it easier than you, or are not as virtuous. Psychologists have a name for it, "illusory superiority." It is the natural human tendency to assume you know better and are better.

I don't know about you, but self-righteousness scares me. If I think I already know better than anyone else, I am unable to learn. This is why anything I believe strongly becomes a place of self-development for me. If I think I know, experience says I probably don't. I then ask more questions and read different viewpoints. That helps me understand more deeply.

Next-level human behavior does not assume the worst in people, but understands that people's beliefs, behaviors, and motivations are not always what they seem. I was not trying to annoy the driver behind me. My friend's behavior was unacceptable, but understandable when the truth was revealed. This is why I always try to point the finger at myself first. I feel it is a more useful operating system.

OWNERSHIP/WISDOM

D o you know the difference between a choice and a decision? A choice is "the act of selecting when faced with two or more options." A decision is "a conclusion or resolution reached after consideration."

Decisions contain considerations. Choices are just the act.

When I was in my twenties, I attended one, of what felt like a thousand, "self-help" seminars. I was called to the front of the room as the final activity in a grueling, four-day course. I was tired, annoyed, and did not feel I had gained much from the event.

Little did I know this final activity was a setup. On graduation night from this course, dozens of past participants join. What they knew, but myself and my fellow "classmates" did not know, was this exercise was supposed to test whether we "got it" or not. It was designed so that one person, in this case me, would be used to facilitate the discussion. Basically, this exercise was designed to make me fail so that everyone else could get it.

In front of hundreds of people the facilitator asked me if I knew the difference between a choice and a decision. He said, "Chocolate or vanilla? Make a choice!" I said, "Vanilla." He asked, "Why?"... "Because I have always liked vanilla," I said.... "WRONG!" He said. "That's a decision, make a choice. Chocolate or vanilla?"

I don't know what happened, but suddenly I understood. I said, "I choose vanilla because I choose vanilla." The room erupted in loud cheers of amazement. I found out later that it could take 10-20 minutes for that exercise. Usually the people in the audience get it before the one on stage being grilled.

That lesson about choices and decisions is important for health and fitness. If you desire success in this arena, you need to make choices, not decisions.

At a restaurant, most people will look at the menu, listen to the specials, or ask their friend about their selection. That's a decision, not a choice.

A choice means you know already. I choose chicken and vegetables. The menu guides me on the easiest way to do that. Will it be a chicken sandwich with extra vegetables and no bun, fajita with no rice/beans/tortilla, or a salad with chicken?

Decisions derail, choices prevail.

September 15

OWNERSHIP/SHARING

I believe we humans are here for three reasons: to learn, to teach and to love (share). I added share in parenthesis because I see it as synonymous with love, but without the romantic connotations. When I say we are here to love/share, what I mean is that I believe we have a duty to share our gifts and lift our fellow humans.

This concept of sharing encompasses generosity as well, but being generous raises many questions. Should we be charitable at our own expense? If we give with an expectation of recognition is that really giving? If we give to feel good about ourselves is that truly generous?

Several years ago when I was experiencing a tough, personal time, I had the idea to write myself an honor code. It was a way I would commit to living my life. One of the values I wanted to double down on was generosity. I wanted to "give so freely and in such big, unexpected ways that others would be shocked and inspired to do the same."

We each have within us a Next Level Human nature. When we operate from this place, we see other humans as benevolently connected to us. We feel "we are all in this together," and as a result we give freely, we battle against injustice, and we encourage all humans to flourish.

We also have Base Level and Culture Level tendencies that make us view the world as a place of "us against them." In this state we see other humans as taking from us or less than us. As a result, we work to undermine others consciously or unconsciously.

Generosity, especially when it is done without need for recognition or expectation, is a form of magic. It imparts to another human, "I see you, you matter, and you are worthy." Whether they can see that in themselves or not is unimportant. The fact that they feel love from someone else is all that matters.

I have this saying, "Be it until you see it." It has several meanings for me, but in this context it is like Gandhi's quote, "Be the change you want to see in the world."

Our physical bodies may be fed by food, but the kindness, sharing, and love of others feed our psychological and spiritual selves. That is what I want the world to stand for, so it starts with me, and you.

OWNERSHIP/WISDOM/SHARING

o you close the gap or open it? I talk a lot about the different levels of human we each have inside of us. If you want to know your dominant type, all you need to do is observe the way you are with other humans. Like Bruce Lee said, "To know yourself is to study yourself in action with others."

There are three very telling times to watch yourself and others: on your phone, while driving, and around service providers.

Base Level human behavior is motivated by safety and fear. Its motto is, "me against the world." Culture Level behavior is motivated by status and fitting in. Their motto is, "us against the world." Next Level Humans are motivated by learning and growth. Their motto is, "me bettering the world."

Base Level types are the ones on social media calling everyone dumb and going on rants.

Culture Level types stay out of social media discussions, but keep a strong air of private self-righteousness. Next Level types are reading the article and another article and another. They are too busy educating themselves to care about what is said in the comments.

Base Level types are rude to service professionals. Culture Level types are dismissive (unless someone is watching). Next Level types are kind, respectful and generous.

On the road, Base Level does not let others merge and closes the gap. Culture Level types just go with the flow. Next Level types let others merge, keep the gap open, and look out for their fellow driver.

Other Next Level behaviors? They leave their read receipts on for text messages. It's about transparency. They don't recline their seat on an airplane. It's about consideration. They tip big and give to the homeless. It's about kindness.

Your brain is always watching. Which type does it think you are?

PERCEPTION/OWNERSHIP/WISDOM

When people ask, "How are you?" What do you say? I used to reply in the standard, small talk way, responding, "I am good. How are you?" I would say this whether I was actually good or not of course, but isn't that what we all say?

Today the more likely thing to come out of my mouth, or thought in my head, would be, "I love my life. I couldn't be more happy." Sometimes I revert back to the standard answer, but it is hard for me not to notice this huge shift over the last six years.

The ironic thing is that I went through a divorce and heartbreak during this same time. I dealt with fatigue and weight gain. I experienced financial ups and downs. I had a lot of things to be unhappy about, or did I?

What I discovered during this process was that I was looking at happiness the wrong way. Happiness is not about what you have or can gain; it is about your ability to let things go. I have never dealt with depression or anxiety and I have had a pretty easy life. But I thought happiness came from having more things. A great relationship; Lots of money; Status and recognition in my field; Lots of friends; Family support; A great place to live, etc.

Some of those criteria make a difference I am sure, but what made the most difference was my ability to let things go; To stop holding on to old mistakes; To stop expecting someone else to tend to my wounds. I stopped looking for apologies and explanations from others. I decided regret was a choice and a waste. I started letting all the things I could not control go. That has made all the difference for me.

My two favorite philosophies instruct this principle in different ways.

Taoism teaches us to be like water, and flow. Be unattached. Take the shape that we can and change when needed. Crash, sit still, flow, or transcend, as life requires.

Stoicism teaches us to focus only on what we control and maintains that everything else is on loan.

OWNERSHIP

The chance you will die is 100% - there is no way to escape that fact.

Not only that, but the chances you will die with no one you know present are also higher than you would like to think about.

There is one person you can count on to be right there with you when you die -that individual is you. So you better make sure you create someone you will be proud to lie down next to when that time comes. They may be the only person you have. They are also the only person whose love and respect really matters.

SHARING

The answer to the question, "What am I looking for?" is the same for every human; to be loved, to be heard, to be seen, to be appreciated, to feel understood, and to be considered. It basically boils down to wanting a feeling of belonging, and having a supportive home with other humans.

Despite this universal desire, many humans fail to feel this way no matter how hard they try. In my experience, the answer to that question is also easy to understand - what many people fail to realize is that, the getting is in the giving.

How many times have you watched a conversation between people and thought to yourself, "Why do I feel so much tension in the air?" It's almost always because humans have a subconscious drive toward status. They want their status to be at, or preferably above, another person's, and they will use all manner of psychological jujitsu to achieve that. What they don't understand is their desire to connect with another human is undermined by their need to be right, smarter, more superior, or any other superlative.

There is only one thing required to connect and gather what you seek from another human; freely give them what you want instead. Let your ego's need to be seen and recognized go. Instead, give the other what you want them to disperse to you and give it freely.

Approaching things this way will almost always change your world. You will see two things happen very quickly. Either the other person will pounce and try to suck the kindness out of you, or they will soften and reciprocate the love back to you. It's almost always reciprocation, but when it's not, think of it as a perfect vetting opportunity. Who needs or wants that type of psychological vampire around them? This way you don't have to search for what you want, it's attracted to you while the other is repelled.

OWNERSHIP/WISDOM/ENGAGEMENT/RESOLVE

Things in life don't happen for a reason. Things happen and we must make a reason. That is the way I see it.

We can make a reason in many ways:

- We can decide to learn a lesson about what happened. For example, we pick up a knife and accidentally cut ourselves. We can then decide to be more careful around knives or learn how to use a knife more efficiently.
- We can take action based on what happened. Say you are walking down the street and someone tries to rob you. You can react by fighting back or letting your belongings go. You can then start a community watch club in response.
- You can make meaning out of what happens. Maybe you lost a loved one to a disease and you choose to start a nonprofit to help others with that disease?

In hindsight you link the two events in your mind, but often forget you made a choice. This is why you say, "Everything happens for a reason." You are drawing attention to the lesson, action, or meaning that came out of what happened. You are also forgetting it was you behind the choice and not some random, universal force.

In counseling and coaching I quickly realized how dysfunctional the saying, "everything happens for a reason" was. It is detrimental because it often leads to waiting, powerlessness, and needless, prolonged suffering.

If I am waiting for some magical, imaginary fairy to solve my problems, then I am literally giving away my power. I can't tell you how many times I have seen people wait for the lesson to materialize when all they needed to do was decide on the lesson, action, or meaning right there in the moment.

Nothing is easy. Easy is earned. You earn easy by realizing that you, and you alone, are the only person who can turn your suffering into something positive.

Your choices, your actions, and your ability to create a reason are how you grow and generate meaning for your life. It is the only way it has ever worked in my opinion. So it happened? Fine, you can't do anything about that.

Life is random and meaningless at times, but you get to exert your power and happen back by deciding what reason you will make of it.

PERCEPTION/OWNERSHIP/WISDOM/ ENGAGEMENT/RESOLVE

"If a man should conquer in battle a thousand, and a thousand more, and another man should conquer himself, his would be the greater victory." — The Dhammapada

Life is a battle. Not a battle against outside forces, but a battle against what comes from within. To become your Next Level self requires you fight this battle. In the fight you will find the wisdom you need. In fact, that's the only way to discover.

There are many definitions of wisdom. My definition? Wisdom is power and insight derived from suffering. Life is nothing but many different forms of suffering.

You can view the suffering as meaningless and cruel, or you can give it meaning by looking at it as training. When you train in the gym you understand that pain brings strength. You push yourself to grow yourself.

Growth in life is no different. It will test the fortitude of your mental resolve and ability to change and grow. It will challenge your honor code. As you suffer, you are meant to integrate the lessons and develop mastery over self.

You can't let passions distract you or arrogance and ignorance delude you. You must develop the ability to suffer and learn at the same time. That starts with knowing what you fight for. The values you hold, the legacy you want to leave, and the good you hope to create.

When you look back on your life you will be most proud of the suffering you endured with honor and the lessons that came from courage, not cowardice.

Make yesterday's hard today's easy. Do that by embracing the pain and learning from it.

ENGAGEMENT

H ere is a little background on making change. The first lesson is, you need to change as little as possible - one or a few things only.

The second lesson is the change has to be as easy or preferably easier than what it is replacing. Alternatively, it could be more enjoyable than what it is replacing. That would be even better. Both easier and more enjoyable would be best.

The final lesson is to make changes that have other beneficial change opportunities embedded within them.

For example, let's say I want to lose weight and become healthier. What are one or two changes I could make that are easy; easier and/or more enjoyable than what I am currently doing and have a trickle-down impact?

One change I could make is to eat two large salads every day. Just make that a rule. I could make this easy and enjoyable by finding a salad I like or buying pre-made, precut and/or pre-washed greens. This has the benefit of filling me up and displacing other foods. By making this one change I could potentially cut my daily calories by 25-50% without telling myself I can't eat certain foods.

I can choose walking. Maybe I listen to books while I walk so I am learning at the same time, or maybe I do my coaching calls while I walk (I do). Also, walking is incompatible with eating (for most) and lowers stress hormones. I can catch up with friends and family while I walk. Walking is also meditative when done slowly and in green settings like parks and forests.

Would this not have huge benefits in health? It could possibly have huge advantages in wealth and relationships too, if those books I am listening to focus on these areas.

The changes you make should provide a trickle-down effect, as opposed to what actions people often take. They declare, "I will stop eating all junk food" (not likely, it takes enjoyment out of your life and has no other benefit) or I will work out intensely six times per week (little enjoyment for most, inconvenient for most, costs money, etc.)

Think about things you can do, that are easy, fun, and multi-beneficial instead of things to *stop* doing.

PERCEPTION/OWNERSHIP/SHARING

We humans are "meaning making machines." We have a limited understanding of the world, and as such, we make up elaborate stories to explain what we don't know or understand. In hindsight, and with new understanding, these stories can seem naive and silly. We once explained thunder by assuming a giant god in the sky was swinging his hammer.

This is also where sayings like "God's plan," and "everything happens for a reason," and "the universe has your back," originate. We likely won't realize how silly these sayings are until much later. Of course some may never see them as what they actually are, made-up stories to make sense of a world that cannot be completely known.

It is unfortunate because the stories we tell determine the game of life we play. I see humans telling three different stories and playing three different games that result from these stories.

- Base Level: They tell the, "me against the world story." The games that derive from this story are the "lie, cheat and steal" game and the "profits over people" story. In other words, the Base Level type sees life as a zero sum game of survival. They are only concerned with self. Rich bankers who rig the system in their favor and poor criminals who take advantage of the system and the work of others fall into this category.
- Culture Level: They tell the, "me better than the world" story. The game they play is the "cars, money and mansions" game. They are status seekers and will choose team over integrity. Religion, politics, and team think behaviors are the hallmark of these types.
- Next Level: They tell the, "me bettering the world" story. The game they play is the "learn, teach and share (love)" game. They believe we are all in this together and life is about "meaning over money." They seek to be the best they can be to help make you and the world better.

Our lives are like energetic ripples. The stories we tell determine the games we play. Will the ripples of our lives crash into others, making their lives harder? Or will they lift others up and show them they matter and they have the power to bring unique beauty into the world?

ENGAGEMENT/RESOLVE

In strength and conditioning pursuits we have something we call a PR. PR stands for "personal record" and it is the way we measure progress in the gym. You can get a PR on a particular lift. For example, if I can squat 500Lbs, in order to progress I must attempt a new PR at 505.

Leading up to that attempt I am nervous. What if I miss the lift? Even if I get the lift, will I injure myself? This type of challenge is no small thing. Many people in the gym simply won't even attempt PRs due to these fears. This is especially true if you have ever injured yourself while lifting heavy weights.

Once in my early twenties while going for a PR on number of reps of 225 on bench press, I tweaked my shoulder and the weight fell toward my neck and chest. That type of harrowing experience sticks with you for a while. It took a long time to get back to where I was, but twenty years later I have beat my 225 bench reps PR at 24 reps.

Recently I spent time at a mountain lake with my family on vacation. We rented Jet Skis and a kayak. I was surprised to find I was slightly nervous climbing on the Jet Ski. I had only been on one once in my early twenties. It was a clear sign I have not been exposing myself to enough change and challenge.

I call this a fear PR. It is the idea that you don't rise to the occasion; you create the occasion. Just as our body needs to be exposed to new PRs, so does our brain. When I look around at my most successful, alive, productive times in life it was when I was in change or challenge.

So now I chase physical PRs in the gym and fear PRs in life, because my brain is watching and judging me all the time. If it sees me attacking life, it believes and supports me. If it sees me taking it easy, it doubts me and withholds confidence. I choose challenge.

September 25

OWNERSHIP/WISDOM/ENGAGEMENT

"If you let out what is inside of you, what you let out will save you. If you don't let out what is inside of you, what you don't let out will kill you."

This is a variation on an idea that shows up in many philosophies throughout the ages.

What it says is that to be happy, successful, and fulfilled you must be true to who you are.

This assumes you know two things.

1. Know yourself: knowing who you are requires a degree of self-awareness that is not taught and is often disturbing to examine. The best advice I have ever heard for "knowing yourself" comes from Bruce Lee, one of my favorite philosophers. He said "To know yourself is to study yourself in action with another." He was a philosopher and a martial artist. So you can see that he meant this both literally and figuratively. Your actions and reactions tell you more about who you are than anything else. You need to be honest about the good and the bad. I am a rule breaker, a contrarian, an out of the box thinker; I am intense, introverted and very unconventional. I don't give a shit about what most people think I can and can't do and I would choose freedom over stability or certainty any day. These traits have been both positives and negatives in my life. How about you?
2. Know your job: I have signature strengths and detrimental weaknesses. I have a knack for understanding and explaining complex ideas and topics. I also know a whole lot about a very narrow range of topics and not a whole lot else. I don't have much to talk about with people because I don't watch TV, I am not into movies or music, and I could care less about sports. My chosen job is a teacher - it suits my strengths and weaknesses. I read, I write, I learn, and I teach. I know my job. How about you?

I don't look to you or anyone else to tell me who I am. I know who I am and I own who I am. I do not choose what I do to impress you or make a bunch of money. I choose what I do because it is what I am good at and what I feel called to do. To let someone else define me or to work at something that does not speak to me is a death worse than physical death.

How about you?

OWNERSHIP/ENGAGEMENT/RESOLVE

Happiness is largely accommodated with two simple things:

1. Know what you want.
2. Be willing to risk it all to get it.

Both of these are difficult for many. When it comes to knowing what we want, we often defer to society's view as opposed to what we know we feel in our hearts. We think, "That job makes no money, we are too different to work romantically, or people will never accept me as an artist/banker/entrepreneur."

So rule number 1 is be in-tune enough with yourself to know what/who you want. The second part is the hardest. Be willing to risk it all and get pummeled in pursuit of your dream.

Sports are a great analogy. In life, like sport, you can practice your heart out and prepare better than anyone. You can then play the best game of your life, leaving it all out on the field, and still get beat and humiliated. That's life and that is what happens sometimes when you play all out. But that is the ironic thing research shows about happiness...the pursuit of happiness is an integral piece of happiness. Perhaps it's the most important part... It is what prepares you for recognizing happy, catching happy, and being happy.

It could be argued that just the risk and action, in and of itself, is the only thing required to generate happy. Like the famous poet Rumi said, "The lion is most beautiful when hunting for food."

Why not risk it and take a chance?

I'll take failure over regret. I'll take action over complacency. I'll choose to be brave and resolved in pursuit of my dream and the one I love. The question is, will you?

PERCEPTION/ENGAGEMENT

S tress is something we all hear a lot about; we are told to reduce it, to manage and avoid it. That is not bad advice, but it does show an incorrect perception about stress.

First off, stress is not always felt as an emotion. You can be happy and stressed. A great example is a new mother. She may be elated and yet under a huge amount of metabolic stress (nutrient depletion from supporting a baby for nine months and then breastfeeding, fatigue, and sleep deprivation from taking care of her new baby, uncertainty about a new life with a child, etc.). So, lesson 1 is stress may or may not be associated with a negative emotion.

Lesson 2 is the one that most people miss. To make yourself more stress resistant you don't want to avoid stress, you want to seek it out and learn to control it. Stress is a major primer of mental and metabolic resilience. Avoid stress completely and you can't adapt and get stronger.

Exercise, fasting, and cold water immersion are a few examples of controlled stress that can actually make you mentally stronger and more metabolically flexible as well. You want the challenge to be enough, but not too much.

Doing extreme diets for extended periods combined with harder, longer or more frequent exercise can easily overwhelm the body and tilt you towards stress overload and negative adaptation.

This is why pairing intense diet and exercise with relaxing, restorative, and regenerative practices are key. One of the best things in this regard is walking in the woods. The Japanese call this Shinrin-yoku or "forest bathing." Green lowers stress hormones. The clean air and rhythmic movement also aids the body (negative ions, increased oxygen intake, increased insulin sensitivity) and the brain (meditative, mental clarity)

Other restorative measures are massage, meditation, sex, laughter, creative pursuits (painting, writing, etc.), tai chi, naps, water therapy, pets.)

So challenge your body with exercise, just not too much. Challenge your brain with new, demanding, mildly fearful and nerve inducing subjects. Then quiet your mind and body as well.

OWNERSHIP/ENGAGEMENT

C hoice and action are often the only items required for peace of mind.
If you are wondering how you ended up where you are, it's choices and actions.

If you are confused about others, look no further than their choices and actions.

If you want to know how you get over, move on, achieve or overcome... choices and actions.

Anxiety, depression, frustration, dissatisfaction are almost always a result of being unable to make a choice, own a choice once it's made, or take definitive action.

WISDOM/SHARING

M ost people shy away from having conversations with people who have different beliefs, especially regarding politics or religion. It is simply too uncomfortable for them, so they choose to speak with like-minded people instead.

That idea scares me. By limiting discussions to only people who believe what you believe, you are basically saying, "I know everything I need to know. Anything you have to say is wrong." The fact that any rational human could believe they alone have all the correct information is terrifying to me.

I share my beliefs fully. I also seek and engage those who believe differently. I don't believe in God. I have a dislike for the Democratic Party. I have an even greater disgust for the Republican Party. I am probably best described as a Libertarian Paternalist. I believe in the individual's right above all else (so long as that right does not infringe on another's right). I also fully concede government must play a fatherly role in certain areas to keep individual rights protected.

I bring this up to point out that avoiding the viewpoints of others limits our own growth. Beliefs point to values and these values are what I seek to understand about others. Take climate change. Here is what a researcher says in regard to the debate: "People disagree not because they don't understand the science, but rather because their positions convey their values. Communal concerns vs individual concerns. Humility vs ingenuity. Harmony with nature vs. mastery over it."

When attempting to reach someone and understand them, focus on the underlying values behind their beliefs. There you will be more likely to find common ground, common growth, and common decency. There you are more likely to expand your pool of knowledge as opposed to what you are currently doing, voluntarily retracting it.

September 30

PERCEPTION/OWNERSHIP/WISDOM/ENGAGEMENT

Did you play sports in high school? Were you any good? I played football. I was good, but I was not great. I could have played for a small college, but I was not NFL material.

I missed 60+ days of school my junior year, but I came back for football practice. That's how much I loved football. However, I quit my senior year; I walked off the practice field two weeks before the 1st game and never returned. My coach angrily said I would regret that decision for the rest of my life. I didn't.

What I did was come to my senses. I woke up, and thought, "Football can't do a thing for you, Jade. Focus on school. Stop living the "dumb jock" story and prove to yourself you are smart." I started dressing differently, reading, and wearing fake glasses (my eyesight was fine).

I reinvented myself at 18. That skill of self-awareness and reinvention has become a superpower of mine since. Through heartbreaks, personal disappointments, business troubles, and the rest, I have used it to improve and grow stronger. We humans possess the power of reinvention.

The future we imagined can always be reimagined.

PERCEPTION/OWNERSHIP/WISDOM/RESOLVE

Have you ever felt rejected? A friend you trusted who you discovered was talking negatively behind your back? A lover you adored who chose someone else? A family member who is constantly unimpressed with you and your way of behaving?

You are human, so I know the answer is yes. Why are you still holding onto that? It's normal, of course; we have all had times where we are hurt so deeply it makes us feel completely lost and we don't know how to let it go.

The reason we feel that way is because we integrated these people into our story of self. They became a part of our identity. We feel like a part of ourselves has been torn away because in a very real sense, it was. This creates a crushing feeling that we have difficulty lifting our way out of.

Some people avoid the pain and stuff it away. Some people feel it and let it consume and own them. Others will become beaten-down, shadows of their former selves.

Then there are the ones who come back grateful, happy, and more alive than they ever were before. In the pain and confusion over what was lost, they remake themselves into something better, wiser, happier, and stronger.

These experiences force us to look at ourselves without the distraction of others. That loneliness may feel like an enemy, but it is actually a call to return to self.

It is questioning you. It is asking, "What will you do now? What can you become as a result of this? Who are you? What will you stand for? How do you use this to learn, to teach, and to love even more deeply than before, but without losing yourself?"

After a long, difficult breakup I remember when the honesty kicked in. I looked at the men she chose and thought to myself, "I would not want to be those type of dudes in a million years. That's not me and I love who I am." That simple realization woke me up.

I see rejection as one of the best tools that life has for smacking us in the face and saying, "Look in the mirror. Is this who you want to be? If so, own it. If not, change it. It's your weight to lift now. Show me your power."

PERCEPTION/OWNERSHIP/SHARING

S ome feel there is a war on masculinity. These people also make it clear they don't like it. Personally, I am glad. I think more people, especially men, need to join the fight.

Forget the weak masculinity of the past. We should fight the un-evolved who champion intolerance.

Should we defend the pompous, lying masculine of men like Donald Trump, or the manipulative, preying, Hollywood masculine of Harvey Weinstein? -The chest pounding, taunting masculine of some professional athletes?

These are the weakest forms of masculine, and the fact they exist at the level they do proves we are in a fight for the soul of man.

The alternative is no better. I don't care for the inauthenticity of the new age male either. Everyone gets a trophy just for participating? You should ALWAYS express your feelings and discuss your emotions? You should ALWAYS be tolerant, vulnerable, selfless, and kind? This thinking is also weak and naive. Real masculinity is far more intelligent and nuanced.

These ideas need to be buffered by focus, work, real achievement, emotional temperance and strong boundaries. A strong masculine identity incorporates the feminine, but isn't overpowered by it.

Think of a wolf pack. The dominant male is loving and protective. His power comes from integrating his strength with a mission larger than himself. If he is taking down prey, defending the pack, or focused on the hunt, he switches from loving to ferocious.

A leader knows their power is dependent on the support and love of their tribe. He is chosen, but also must prove his worth. He knows any two, united members could overpower him if he abuses his position. This is why only the balanced, strong, and compassionate wolf gets to lead. The violent tyrant is rejected. The self-absorbed softy is too.

Masculine is assertive as a default, but willing to relinquish its needs for the betterment of the tribe. Masculine does not fight for self; it fights fiercely for something it loves beyond self. Masculine is open and available to feel, but knows how to channel those emotions, not be hijacked by them.

PERCEPTION/OWNERSHIP/SHARING

Let me tell you about being vulnerable. There is a time and a place for it, and for a man, I would say those times are few and far between.

A few months ago I attended an event and I was the only man in a group of women. These were all Next Level women highly committed to learning and growth. They were discussing men, and their contention was that they would not want to date a man who did not cry. They asked me when was the last time I cried. I told them it had probably been years. I also confided that even then it was more of a choked-up, single tear.

I could tell they did not like this answer. One even said, "But I see you as such an evolved male." It was as if she was saying, "Maybe I should rethink the way I see you."

I was curious. I said, "Let me ask you. Would you rather"- I love "would you rather" questions- "have a man who cries once per month or a guy who rarely cries at all." Now they were mixed. They seemed confused and the answers were split.

This illustrates something I have noticed in the current "vulnerability culture." Women often say they want men who show up more like them (i.e., more vulnerable). But when their men show up that way, they tell me things like "He is soft," or "He is too needy."

My advice to you, men, is not to let women define what a man is. My advice to women is the male version of vulnerability shows up differently from a woman's. A man can feel sadness and cry or not. It's his availability to feel the emotion, rather than his reaction to it, that matters. One role men have burned into their DNA is the warrior mentality. In the heat of battle a warrior does not cry. He may feel sadness, fear, and uncertainty, but he knows crying will not help the fight and likely will result in sure defeat. So he transmutes those feelings to drive, motivation, and focus. He becomes an emotional alchemist.

When the smoke clears, or there is a lull in the battle, he may cry, or not. That is man. He should be loved, supported, and even celebrated for this. It is his power. It is the way he gets life done. To my fellow men, I would say be careful with vulnerability. I don't think that is the right word or approach for us. Be open, be available, be loving, and be authentic enough to cry, or not.

ENGAGEMENT/RESOLVE/SHARING

Answer this question for yourself. Life is about what? When you think about the purpose of life, what is it? Not your purpose; that is a slightly different question. What is life's purpose?

The way we each answer this question determines the way we experience life. Is life about winning? Is life about survival? Is life about love?

If you define life as about winning, what happens when you lose? What if you lose your job, your spouse, your lover, or your reputation? My bet is you feel lost. If you define life as winning and you are losing, then life can become pretty miserable. Perhaps you lose the desire to live as a result?

What if you define life as love? And what if you lose love or never receive love? Again you may feel lost, on uneven ground, and as if life is cruel and deems you unworthy.

There is a way to view life that avoids these traps and is far more accurate. The view that life is change. If life is change, then your job is to adapt. To adapt you must learn. That is a game everyone can play. That is a game everyone can win. You can learn. In fact, you are designed for it.

And out of that realization can spring your purpose for living. What have you learned that you can help others discover? Life's purpose may be to change, but your purpose can be to learn and teach.

Out of that desire to share your lessons and care for others springs love. In my view, sharing and caring above your own needs is the very definition of love, and defines why we are each here. I call them the three imperatives: To Learn, To Teach, To Love.

When I feel lost, fearful, scared, and like everything is changing, I say to myself, "Life loves change. If I am resisting change I am already dead. Let me embrace this, learn from this, teach from this, and love more as a result."

WISDOM/RESOLVE

A rule of life is that not all problems are solvable. This irks people because, as humans, we crave stability, certainty, and completeness. We want things wrapped up in a neat little bow.

But what we don't realize is that, in the unsolvable puzzles of life, there are discoveries that can't be experienced any other way.

I have had suffering, the same as you. I have watched people suffer too, through my profession as a healer, counselor, and coach. We all feel, but we all deal differently. Some run, some avoid, and some confront. I have made mistakes, hurt people I love, and been rejected by people I loved and trusted. I have watched people's lives altered by disease, betrayal, and death.

I wanted deeply to figure out the why behind my own suffering, both for myself, and to teach others.

In trying to answer this question, I found myself reading, studying, suffering, thinking, and experiencing through all sorts of new and uncomfortable directions.

The problem is, I never solved it. I still don't know the answer of why. I have watched other people get stuck in that why question too. But many, in their attempt to answer the question, become more as humans than they could have achieved otherwise. Maybe that is the entire point?

I may not have learned the exact why behind my pain, but I was taught something more valuable. If a problem in life can't be solved, all there is left to do is digress. That deviation is where we live our way into an answer that may be quite different from the one we were seeking in the first place. Perhaps what we find there is far more profitable.

Understanding why must be earned like everything else.

Meritum Securus (easy is earned).

October 6

OWNERSHIP/RESOLVE

Time is your creation. Whether you have it or not says more about your priorities than anything else.

"To say you don't have time is the same as saying you don't want to." --- Lao Tzu

OWNERSHIP/SHARING

You're having a conversation with a friend or colleague about another friend who is not present. I don't know about you, but these conversations always make me a little on edge. The reason? I believe gossip can poison you and your relationships.

Research suggests 80% of conversations are about other people who are not around. It is believed this evolved to keep our social groups cohesive and working together. It helped us identify people's strengths and weaknesses. It helped us sort the leaders from the freeloaders. It was integral for survival.

How do you tell good gossip from bad gossip? I think of three levels. There is chatting, dishing/venting, and shit talking.

Chatting is focused on you. You are expressing feelings about an experience with another person. The intent is to gain input from others to test your version of reality. An example might be, "They said X; I feel Y. How do you see it?"

Dishing is focused on the other person and goes on behind their back. It's sharing an opinion, story, or what you heard. It is the grey zone, sometimes harmless, sometimes not. When the intent is to hurt the reputation of another, and/or raise your own at their expense, you are on the dark side of gossip.

Shit talking has the unambiguous goal of tearing the other person down; there is malicious or destructive intent. It's meant to turn people against someone.

I am leery of gossip. I work diligently to stick only to chatting and more enlightened gossip, here's how:

- I ask a person's permission: "May I vent about something?"
- I state, "I could be wrong" or "If they were here they may see it differently."
- I don't say anything behind someone's back that I would not be able to say to their face.
- I don't allow shit talkers to berate others' characters verbally without telling them it's not ok with me.

The things people say about others who are not present says everything you need to know about their integrity, kindness, and self-awareness. I pay very close attention. If they are doing it to "them," they are doing it to me. Next Level Humans simply don't tolerate this behavior in themselves or others.

PERCEPTION/OWNERSHIP/WISDOM

"People cling to whatever opinion enhances the glory of their tribe and their status within it." This is a quote from *Enlightenment Now*, by Steven Pinker.

It speaks to our Base Level and Culture Level tendencies to ignore progress and abandon reason. We formulate an identity of self, and then we fight, lie, avoid, rationalize, and deny anything that challenges that identity. We do all of that while simultaneously complaining about our lives and our inability to change, never realizing it is impossible to create a new identity while defending our existing one.

Our Base Level selves choose the fight, flight, or freeze reactions. This results in ignoring opposing views, assuming other views come from ignorance, name calling, and of course, violence (real or threatened). Fear and bias are the quicksand of Base Level behavior.

Our Culture Level selves desire status and belonging above all else. This causes us to seek out only those who agree, to adjust our views to fit what's popular, and to choose appearing right over fact and truth. We vent, gossip, and disparage anyone who questions our identity or threatens our status.

If you want to see these two lesser selves in action simply put on Fox News or MSNBC. Watch as commentators on the left and right stick by the lies and rhetoric of their team's leaders. Or watch the social media discussion on a political post. All of this is an effort to defend their self-identity and team at all costs, and the costs are great. The sheep of Culture Level thinking are the champions of history's death toll.

There are those who have escaped Base Level bias and Culture Level dogma. These, Next Level Humans, seek change and progress over stability and status. They want their identity to evolve. They are happy to amend their viewpoints. They call out the behaviors of their Base and Culture Level selves. The truth is more important to them than being right. They identify lies when they see them regardless of which team is telling those falsehoods.

Becoming a Next Level Human requires constant questioning of your own beliefs more vigorously than any others.

PERCEPTION/OWNERSHIP

I don't understand. I am such a good friend to you and you could take or leave me. I am your friend, but I have no real evidence you are mine. The evidence I have suggests you willingly leave me in the dark and mislead me whenever possible despite the fact that you know I value honesty and direct communication above all else. I am your friend, but you are not mine. I don't want these types of friends, but I now realize that the kinds of friends you have in life are almost exactly the same kind of friend you have been to yourself.

Do you think about your needs or is your real "need" to be needed by others? Do you expect honesty from others...yet delude and mislead yourself? Do you allow yourself to take advantage of yourself by mismanaging your energetic resources, by pouring out for others but leaving nothing in emotional reserve for you? The bottom line is that until you start taking care of you and being your own best friend, your other friendships will continue to be a reflection of how you treat yourself.

We humans are not islands unto ourselves. We require connection, social interaction, and friendship. We all want the same things...

Most people learn how to be your friend through your example. If you are not happy with how people are showing up, consider that you need to show up for yourself first. No one is going to move that weight for you. It's 100% on you.

PERCEPTION/SHARING

D o you know why people love dogs so much? -They don't feel judged by dogs and they assume dogs are innocent. With this assumption comes the opposite insight that other humans are judging them and are not innocent.

This answer has always bothered me. I love dogs and when I see a person with a dog, I look at the dog and smile first before acknowledging the human. I don't like this about myself, but am grateful to the dog for being a conduit for human connection.

The truth is that dogs do judge and sometimes in a much harsher way. If dogs feel threatened they will yell and scream (i.e., bark) at you and likely bite you much faster than a human would punch you. If you were drowning in a lake, a dog would be much more likely to disregard your plight than a human would.

Then you might say, "Well, the aggressive behavior is learned. The dog is just scared or misguided." This answer has also baffled me; this infers that the smartest dog in the world is not even close to, or as mentally capable as a human, yet they learn this behavior and humans don't? Maybe you argue that humans know better and dogs don't? But dogs can be trained to know better through love and attention, can they not?

And that's my point. You can be compassionate, understanding, and loving toward a dog. You can say it was brought up in a poor environment. You will devote your time and energy to finding it a good home and providing it love, training, and free space to run. You call it merciful to put it down if it is suffering. You model love and it gives it back, most of the time. Of course some dogs can't be helped, just like some humans. That's rare in both cases.

Humans are exactly the same. Why are you suspicious, untrusting, rude, short, and judgmental to your fellow human? Is the answer because they are that way to you? Is that how you would treat a troubled, dirty, lost, and angry dog you ran into on the street?

If the answer is no, then consider you are nothing but a human in the clothing of a lost, mangy, miserable dog. You deserve love too or should you be put down, locked behind a fence, and denied access to what other dogs receive?

October 11

PERCEPTION/OWNERSHIP/SHARING

You are a liar. So am I. It's a default setting we forget is on.

I know all the arguments. I have made them too. "I don't want to hurt their feelings." Or "They would not understand." Or "Honesty is subjective anyway, how can we really know what's true?" Or "No harm, no foul." Or "It's just a little white lie."

I have been a liar, a cheater, an exaggerator, and an avoider. I still am in many ways. Nothing so engrained in our behavior as humans changes overnight. I am a work in progress. But I am fanatical about rooting out this behavior. I am grateful I woke up to the fact that, in no way, does dishonesty enhance my life or further my mission to help.

I believe lies, by omission or otherwise, are poison to the soul and relationships. Not the lies of others, these simply show you the relationship they have with themselves (although I personally no longer associate with liars of any sort). I am talking about your lies. Those are the ones that matter and keep you from truly knowing yourself.

Consider this; lies are you pretending to be someone else. This means the people you say you love, the ones you are lying to, can't possibly know you either. I don't know much, but I know every human wants to be loved and accepted. How can you achieve that when no one even knows who you really are, including you?

Lying is a barometer of self-love and acceptance. You show me a chronic liar and I will show you a person who doesn't like themselves very much.

I know…these words are triggering. Maybe you think there are perfectly acceptable reasons to lie? I won't even argue that point. Perhaps there are, and I certainly don't advocate spewing all your past transgressions everywhere. I will just ask you, is that really who you want to be moving forward?

Lying is the psychic equivalent of credit card debt. The more you use it as a way to mange your social interactions, the harder it is to escape your false self.

What's so hard about it? Simply stop deceiving yourself and others. It is a perfect vetting system. Tell the truth; if you are still loved, they pass the test. If not, at least you can own and love yourself.

PERCEPTION/OWNERSHIP/ENGAGEMENT/RESOLVE

If I gave you a choice...that the next five years would be the hardest of your life, with more suffering, loss, betrayal and heartache than you could fathom, but as a result you would be wiser, kinder, more honest, and contain super-human, mental strength and resilience, would you take it?

I suffered through some of the toughest personal challenges a person can go through and I would not change a single second of the battle. I came out of it better, stronger, braver, and with a greater lust for life. I did not realize the gifts at the time. This is why I am reminding you (and me) now. We have the ability to turn our pain into power.

People often ask me the how, why, and what of it all. I don't have an exact blueprint except to say...life happens to us all. It happens in very big, messy, cruel, and painful ways. But then we get to happen back in equally powerful ways.

Life will break you. It also can remake you.

The truth is, it feels a little disorienting at times. Even my family does not know me well any more because I have changed that much. I no longer believe in fairytales, yet I love more deeply than I ever have. I see gossip, lies, and manipulation and I no longer partake. I am both more open and more boundary heavy than ever. I am more confident and simultaneously more detached than ever. I know where I am going and who I want to be; yet I have few expectations on how to get there or who else may show up.

All I know is that I may die tomorrow. I realize this is morbid, but the thought focuses and energizes me. I have work to do. I am here for 3 reasons only: to learn, to teach, to love. My pain, suffering, and loss was the catalyst to my owning these jobs.

To know exactly why you are here- and to be doing exactly that- has a way of making death, not an enemy, but a friend who motivates and holds you accountable to your work.

I would take the suffering again if I could get a fraction of the life it gave me the first time, the meaning to die for, and the focus to live for. Often that is only found through what pains us. That's why I remember death and you should too.

October 13

PERCEPTION/WISDOM

When is the last time you examined yourself from a different perspective to see where you are wrongheaded and ego based? It is a very rare occurrence and it takes someone who seeks the truth rather than seeks being right. They have to also be honest and remove their ego from the equation.

Why would you want to do this anyway? As a human your brain is naturally prone to bias. We have a difficult time seeing past our delusional thinking. In fact, once we make up our mind, research shows very little can penetrate that bubble, even indisputable facts. It's the reason why supporters of a politician can watch them go on national TV, say all kinds of horrible things, and create a stronger sense of support.

Your brain does not want to see you as a complete bonehead, so it will find a rationale as to why the political nonsense makes sense to you.

This is what makes us so gullible and predictable. Very few of us can let our egos go and just simply say, "I was wrong and this is unacceptable. I will change course." Once a person has chosen a belief, for good reason in their eyes, they often spend the rest of their lives defending it, even if it is wrong or does not serve them.

How do we guard against this? By making it a part of our practice to seek out information that disagrees or challenges us. When I work as a coach, I call these perception PRs (Personal Records). Maybe I send you to an AA meeting even though you are not an alcoholic; maybe if you are an atheist, I make you go to church. Travel to other cultures, watch another news channel, go to a funeral, live a weekend as a homeless person, anything to force you out of your bubble.

You may think it's your circumstances that hold you back, but really it's your biased bubble that's holding you in.

ENGAGEMENT/SHARING

Oh, so you have an Instagram following? Congratulations, you are just like one of those popular kids I knew in high school. Still, what are you going to do with your life? How can you turn that into something that actually matters to someone other than yourself?

Oh, so you have a great body? Maybe it's your genes or maybe it's your hard work, either way no one is going to remember you for your banging body once you're gone. No one is going to say, "I really miss so and so, they had such amazing abs." Nah, my bet is they will think about how you made them feel and how you loved.

Oh wow, you have such a cute face! That's lucky for you, but beauty is an energetic thing and so is ugly.

It's great you're kind to the people who are close to you. It's great you take care of your children and put them first. What about everyone else? Do you let the driver merge? Give the barista a compliment? Pick up the trash on the sidewalk, say hi to the person asking for money, or tip the server out of kindness versus obligation?

There are Base Level people everywhere you look. They are like thick smog that saturates everyone in heavy, grimy dampness. One meaningful act can change all of that.

All you need to do to go "Next Level," is realize you are here for three reasons only, to learn, to teach, and to love (share). If you are not here to help, then why are you here? So we can all look at your adorable face, or your hot body?

Self-centered, mean, egotistical people are the psychological equivalent of bad breath; if you have it no amount of good looks can fix it.

OWNERSHIP/SHARING

On Next Level romance: authenticity is the most important thing. It is a word thrown around a lot and for good reason.

Authenticity means two things. First it means you know yourself and that takes a degree of self-awareness and questioning most people are unwilling or incapable of doing. Second, it requires the confidence to be exactly who you are (or change to be better if you choose); this is perhaps the rarest of human traits.

If you want a real, romantic connection, authentic is what you must become. True connection doesn't happen with disguises. Real love can't be generated out of false pretenses.

When most people fall in love, they don't fall in love with another person; they fall in love with the imagined better self they believe they will be. Or they fall in love with being what someone else needs.

In both scenarios their romantic partner never gets to know them at all. Their authentic self has been voluntarily pushed aside. Imagine waking up after years in a relationship and realizing who you present yourself to be is not the real you. Or thinking back to each failed relationship and realizing the real you never actually showed up?

This is why heartbreak can be so important. There has never been a better Cupid than romantic rejection. Only that kind of suffering can call you back to the questions required; "Who am I? Why am I here? What do I want?" True love can only be born out of knowing and loving yourself first. Suffering has a way of not just showing that truth, but teaching you how to live it.

Authenticity is the best synonym for self-love. It is aware and confident. It knows its strengths, is aware of its limitations and trusts its power. That is why it is so rare. It also happens to be the single most attractive quality in any potential partner. Authentic is honest, confident and a great communicator. It's basically romantic catnip for humans.

People will put all their effort into being or finding the perfect partner. But discovering the perfect partner is a direct result of knowing, creating, and being your Next Level self.

October 16

ENGAGEMENT/RESOLVE

A dversity, difficulty and suffering are required for stability, security, confidence and competence.

It's like Seneca said over 2000 years ago, "No man is more unhappy than he who never faces adversity, for he is not permitted to prove himself."

PERCEPTION/OWNERSHIP/RESOLVE/SHARING

How do you free yourself from past trauma? Getting rid of emotional trauma is not that different from healing physical trauma.

Let me provide an example. My hand has a huge scar on it along with a large knot of tissue. In my days as a bouncer I got in a bar fight. In a freak occurrence, I punched through a glass bottle and severed both tendons that extend the pointer finger in two separate places. I also severed the single tendon running to my middle finger.

That injury required extensive reconstructive surgery, rehabilitation that lasted more than half a year, and resulted in me graduating a semester late. I was told at the time that I might never have full use of that hand. Luckily the surgery, rehab, and my determination to get my hand strength back paid off. But I still have the scar and I suffer some pretty painful arthritis in that hand.

I don't deny the pain. I don't try to get rid of it either. It is there and I just make it a part of me. I integrate it into my story about myself and I use it as a reminder of who I want to be: a giver, a teacher, a motivator, and someone who inspires…not a fighter.

With psychological pain it is the same concept. I don't try to get rid of it; I use it the same way that my hand injury was a catalyst for positive change in my life. Who can I become as a result of the pain? How can this pain help me? How can I use it to help others? I may never get rid of it. It is with me. It happened. I happen back by choosing what it means. This way when it comes up- which it always does- I silently say, "Oh, there you are. Thanks for coming. And thanks for helping me learn, grow, teach, and love."

Your pain is a part of you. It's a mistake to deny it or expect it to one day be gone. It may never leave, so why not own it? Pain can be a powerful teacher, motivator, and catalyst for meaning. But you have to integrate it, not deny it. If someone has wronged you, the best revenge is not to be like them. Once you own it, it may still feel the same, but it's pain of a different kind; a healing pain, not a destructive one. You alone have the power to transform it.

PERCEPTION

What we humans sometimes fail to remember is this: the future you imagined can always be reimagined.

The ability to create your life means developing the skill of writing and rewriting your script as often as needed.

Stop letting society's beliefs about who, or what you should be determine your story. Stop letting past disappointments write your script.

Regret, remorse, grief, sadness, anxiety, or any other stuck emotion is a hint that you need to reevaluate the tales you are telling yourself and write some new ones.

OWNERSHIP/SHARING

I span two worlds. On the one hand, I come from a generation that urges us to shut up, do our job, know our place, don't get a big head, and be humble.

I also make a difference and a living by sharing my expertise. My life has centered on helping people make meaningful change through physical and mental growth. Social media has allowed me to amplify my reach beyond what my personal clinic, or even my books have been able to achieve.

Historically, I have had a love/hate relationship with the Internet sharing culture. But as I have interacted with so many Internet entrepreneurs and influencers, I thought I would share my perspective. These people who you become annoyed with due to their sharing- the ones you mentally berate for "seeking attention" or "who do they think they are" or "they are so self-absorbed and self-indulgent"- those people open themselves up to hate and criticism of a magnitude most people would crumble under.

You see them as self-absorbed or self-interested, but most I know are brave and purpose driven. Trust me, they are fully aware of what it all looks like to you. Most do it anyway, realizing there is someone out there for whom their story and lessons uniquely resonate. For all the hate they get, there are people they are helping and that matters more to them than looking good to you.

These are the ways we grow and share ourselves. You may not believe you are that special, but I think you are. You and I could say the same exact words and teach identical material, but you may be the only one some people will hear simply because you are you.

Which is more self-centered and self-indulgent, keeping your thoughts, wisdom, and gifts to your small inner circle? - Or sharing them with the world?

To me both are fine, but adding your touch to the larger pool of knowledge aids all of us. I am better for you sharing your gifts. We all are. You may be just the thing someone else needs.

OWNERSHIP/WISDOM/SHARING

So you are in pain? Someone was rude to you. A person disrespected you. A trusted friend betrayed you. You feel taken advantage of or were treated unfairly. Or the worst feeling of all, someone you love, respect and admire rejected you from their inner circle.

Most humans will go either Base Level or Culture Level in response. Base Level results in fight, flight, and freeze reactions. They will attack. Sadly these attacks can be against people who had nothing to do with it. Or they will run away. They may even run away from those who love them. Or they will avoid, ghost, or stonewall. Base Level tactics are like putting your hurt on a credit card; short-term you feel some relief, but in the long run you make it worse.

Culture Level will have you play the victim. You blame, complain, and run to your team members to get them on your side. You want them to reinforce the story of your wounds. It feels good to have others who will hate just because you say so, but this too backfires. How many people have repaired relationships with a person only to find their friends and family still hate them?

A Next Level approach has you look at the pain as a teacher. What can you learn from it? This is where you choose who you will be as a result. You are unique in the world and have gifts the world needs. Let your suffering be a reminder of what you have to share.

Your purpose is where your power lies. When you combine pain with purpose, you tap into an immense power to change yourself and others for the better. What if that was the whole purpose of the hurt to begin with?

RESOLVE

We are afraid and we treat fear as a bad thing. We are ignorant and we try to hide it. We are lazy and we beat ourselves up about it.

Here is how I look at this pattern: When I was a kid I played baseball; I was good from the beginning. It just came easy. I was so advanced in my first year that I played with the 12 year olds when I was only 8. I did not enjoy the game, and it seemed boring to me.

Football? I was good, but I wasn't great. I had to earn it. I remember my father sat me down before my first game. He laced a thin pencil over his middle finger, bracing it with his ring and index finger.

He explained, "See how my middle finger has to hold all the tension? If I slam my hand down on this table and I don't do it hard enough, I could break my finger." He then forcefully slammed his hand on the table and the pencil snapped. He said, "I didn't feel a thing, because I hit harder than it hit me. If you attack hard enough you don't break, they do. Jade, hit so hard you can't break."

He was being dramatic of course, but it made an impact. I was largely regarded as the hardest hitter on my football team, and that lesson has remained with me my entire life.

Now, when I am afraid, I remember to hit harder than it can hit me. I am tentative around spiders. The other day I picked one up by letting it crawl on me and took it outside. I didn't like to fly so I flew more. I was worried about money so I invested even more in me, and my business.

As a result, I discovered a way to make the money back. I still hate spiders, but not as much. I am no longer afraid of planes. Next Fear PR? - Oceans and sharks.

The way I interpret it is we feel fear to remind us about the virtue of courage. We are ignorant so that we remember to constantly seek the truth. We are lazy so we internalize that easy is earned.

The things we try to avoid are the very things trying to teach us. Now I commit to attack my fears so hard they become afraid of me.

PERCEPTION/OWNERSHIP/ENGAGEMENT

One of the most difficult things in the world is knowing who you really are. What's even harder is being it once you know.

PERCEPTION/WISDOM/ENGAGEMENT

We humans talk about happiness a lot. We ask those we care about "Are you happy?" We read books on how to become happy. We search for pursuits we think will make us happy (money, sex, pets, kids, travel, cars, houses, etc.).

Yet, happiness often still eludes us because we do not really understand what that emotion is. Happy is not a place you arrive. Happy is not something you find. Happy is not the same as pleasure.

Happy is something you generate. It's a lot like a hamster wheel. When you are on the wheel, engaged in pursuits meaningful to you, happiness occurs. If you stop, your engagement ends and happiness stops.

The degree of happiness comes from the difference between your objective reality (i.e., what is) and your subjective desires (what you want). To maximize happiness means to work to improve your circumstances while simultaneously removing your expectations.

The Stoic philosophers practiced negative visualization so that they contemplated and even expected the worst. This way if the worst happened, they were prepared. If the best occurred, they were surprised. This practice narrows the "happy gap."

To be happy is to be content with what you have, to be engaged fully in life, and to minimize expectations, wants, and desires.

OWNERSHIP/WISDOM

Why are you so triggered? Why so offended? And most importantly, why do you think you have a right not to be offended?

Think about that for a minute. Life is offensive by its very nature. Life is constantly going to reveal things you don't want to see. You will have to feel pains you would rather not feel. It is the height of ignorance and arrogance to demand not to be offended.

When I get triggered that's up to me to deal with it. I can't demand people don't do offensive things anymore than I can demand the weather not to rain on me.

Being offended is like stubbing your toe. It draws your attention. It alters your course. It makes you pay attention to things you were taking for granted. It is an amazing way to reality-check ourselves and decide what we stand for.

You don't have a right to be free of offenses. You don't get to not be triggered. Your angry, wound shopping is your dysfunction.

Anger is a useful emotion. Compared to sadness, it has more energy and therefore can be transferred into drive, motivation, and focus. It can also force you to examine your own unreasonable, self-righteous, spoiled nature.

However, being angry at everything is wasteful. It is like walking into a gym and yelling at the weights instead of lifting them. Feigning anger is even worse.

Your being offended by every little detail tells you something. Your wanting the world to take responsibility for not triggering you is self-centered and naive. Your having a real reaction to something you care about is why those emotions exist in the first place. They tell you something about yourself. They demand that you pay attention. Why would you not want that instruction?

I have learned to appreciate when I am offended or triggered and I give a silent nod of gratitude because it helps me clarify who I am, who I want to be, and what is, and is not, important.

Have you ever seen a spoiled, brat kid? Yep, bothered by everything, aren't they? Some adults never grow out of that mindset I suppose.

October 25

PERCEPTION/WISDOM/RESOLVE

Meritum Securus. It means, "Easy is earned." As humans we all have fears, failures, frustrations, pain, and suffering. In response to those things, what do we do? We often suffer in silence, grinning and bearing it. Or we try to avoid thinking about it altogether and just hope time heals.

There is a third path. The path of turning, looking into it and saying, "Ok, I see you. You have my attention. I am open to what you can teach me."

That path is rarely explored, but it holds the key to understanding your real power, who you are, and who you can choose to become.

Up until this point you may be operating as if life owns you, as if things happen for a reason. As if you are supposed to sit back and watch your life like a movie, being grateful for the good times and covering your eyes through the bad times.

But life does not own you. You own your life. Sure, part of it is out of your control. Life happens. But you get to happen back. All life events have something to teach. What if every person, place, thing, or event could be used to elevate yourself to levels you could not achieve otherwise?

My experience tells me this is exactly how it works. All the greatest stories of heroic humans were written partly with the pen of suffering.

The greatest power you can learn is how to write your own hero's journey. The first step is realizing you already have all the correct pieces in place.

OWNERSHIP/ENGAGEMENT/SHARING

What if you just simply told the truth? -About how you feel. -About your intentions.

-Even about your confusion, fears and failures?

The anxiety you feel when someone asks you a question disappears. The need to manage the emotions of others goes away. Most importantly, you are able to know yourself again. Your *real* self. And the people you call friends get to really know you as well.

In life we are simultaneously traveling alone while traveling together. This is an important element of learning and change. We honor our friends and ourselves when we choose to travel together in truth.

OWNERSHIP/SHARING

They are arrogant. He is so cocky. She is a know-it-all. Who does he think he is? You should know your place.

Imagine you acquire a brand new puppy. You want to teach him how to sit. Every time he sits, you give him a treat, tell him "good boy" and you give him some hugs and kisses.

This dog is super smart. Before you know it he is sitting without you even telling him. He becomes a master at sitting. This rubs you the wrong way. "Who does this dog think he is?" you say. He has gotten too egotistical. He thinks he is too good. Now every time he sits you judge him, withhold love, and ignore him.

Silly thought experiment I know, but this is exactly what we often do to others. We do it to ourselves too. You want to succeed, make moves, teach your expertise, and put your creations out into the world. At the same time you want to avoid being seen by others as conceited or arrogant, so you do nothing.

You want to share your work AND you don't want anyone to see you as arrogant or cocky? That's not going to happen. As soon as you start confidently lending your voice to the world, a sizable amount of people will see you as arrogant. Through the lens of insecurity, confidence and credibility appear as arrogance.

I have people unfollow me on social media because they see me as arrogant. They hear me talk and they think I am cocky. They see the way I stand or act and think I am conceited. I had a person, who does not know me at all, call me an "egomaniac."

Actually I am humble, grateful, and kind. I was raised to see all people as equals. I view myself as no better or worse than the next person. At the same time, I have special gifts and share those openly with the world.

I can't help that my confidence, loud voice, weird accent, baldhead and goatee make you see me as arrogant. I realize I have resting dick face, (male version of resting bitch face). I also refuse to soften my look, my passion, my purpose or my personality because others think it's about ego.

Confidence is inspiring to the secure and it is threatening to the insecure. Remember that the next time you are bravely adding your voice. We need you.

Most of us are inspired by you stepping up.

OWNERSHIP

Everything happens for a reason? I know people love that saying. I personally despise it.

Some people use different variations like: "Things work out for the best" or "There is no such thing as a coincidence."

It certainly is understandable. Who doesn't desire to believe in a benevolent world where someone (God) or something (the universe) has your back?

The problem? Any reasonable person who's lived just a little, and who contains even a shred of intellectual honesty knows it is not true. Life has zero interest in you. It couldn't care less about you and your beliefs.

Your sibling married a drunk, abusive alcoholic? Planes crashing into skyscrapers? Wars? Natural disasters? People shooting up schools? The Holocaust? Did these things happen because there is some divine, cosmic plan in which their unfolding makes sense? -I doubt it. Maybe, I am wrong? Maybe there is? All reasonable evidence says it's just us, scared humans, soothing ourselves.

If your child gets punched in the face for no reason, do you say, "It's ok honey, everything happens for a reason?" Of course not, that would be ridiculous. You would instruct them in some way. You would help them make meaning out of a senseless act. Maybe a lesson in turning the cruelty they suffered into kindness for others? -An insight in resilience? -A poignant example of how to defend oneself? Life happened, the lesson is how your child happens back. Why would we treat ourselves differently?

I don't believe things happen for a reason. I believe things happen and then we make a reason.

When the senseless, indifference of the world happens, we are left with our one true superpower...to create the reason. We decide what we will do with it. We choose what we will make it mean.

Some of the greatest achievements of humanity came from the worst tragedies. People did not simply say, "Everything happens for a reason." Instead they said, "We will not allow that to happen without having our say. Ok life. You happened. Now watch us happen back." That's what Viktor Frankl did. It's what we must do.

Don't wait for meaning to show up; create it. Make what happened matter.

PERCEPTION/OWNERSHIP/
ENGAGEMENT/RESOLVE/SHARING

What if every person who crossed your path provided an opportunity? What if every difficult situation, circumstance and relationship had, embedded within it, the exact components required for you to realize your Next Level self?

I don't mean this in some woo-woo, new age, "the universe has your back," kind of way. And I definitely don't mean it in a religious, "God's plan," way either. What I mean is, your ability to use what is available to you and create a reason out of thin air. Why did it happen? What can you make of it? You decide.

It's not, everything happens for a reason; it's, things happen and you make a reason. We have all heard stories of great tragedy turned to magic. A woman loses a child to a kidnapping. She then makes her life's purpose to include pictures of missing children on milk cartons across the country. She saves countless children as a result. If you were a child of the 80's, you will remember that campaign. It's one of my favorite examples of the "make a reason" principle.

Meaning in life is not found. It's chosen...It's created...It's generated...by you. It's choice and action. It's Engagement and Resolve.

Your suffering is not unique or special. People have experienced it since the beginning of time. What is unique is how the pain, fear, failure, grief, and heart-break will change you and how you will bring those new insights and lessons to positively impact those around you.

You have a unique set of gifts, experiences, and wisdom that only you can bring to the world. Those gifts are perfectly matched to a subset of people who need them. I could teach the same thing, only they would not hear me. Their ears are tuned to your unique voice.

This is how you choose to matter. This is how you bring meaning to your life. It's why your work and energy are so important. So, if you are a writer, write. If you are a teacher, teach. Show up for yourself and others. Make it mean something. We need your Next Level self. With it, the world is aided in ways it could not be otherwise.

PERCEPTION/OWNERSHIP/WISDOM

Humility is the precursor to wisdom; and to practice humility means seeing everything as your fault and your problem. Would you rather be right or free?

Let's examine two tough emotional conditions: resentment and regret.

Feel resentful? It's because either someone took advantage of you or allowed someone to take advantage. Or you are refusing to grow up by fixing the patterns you exhibit in relationships.

Resentment and regret are teachers. Regret is contrition for something you did. Resentment is anger over what you believe someone else did.

As Next Level Humans, it is essential that we learn the skills of emotional alchemy. Neither of these emotions will be useful over the long run. They can only, if you know how, be useful in the short run.

Emotions are like your spirit's GPS. Where are you positioned in the map of your life? How can these emotions turn you toward your Next Level self? How can they turn you away?

If you want to grow and get better you need to understand this. Regret is a choice. It belongs completely to you; you are in control of it. In that case it's a simple choice of whether to turn right or left. I don't choose regret. Simple as that; I feel it. It's instructive. But I will not let it scramble my internal compass. I let it teach me what neighborhoods to avoid, and then I let it go.

Resentment is trickier because it can involve others, so we believe they should have a hand in the fixing. But we can't control others. I make a right hand turn on Resentment rather than a left. This pushes me toward Anger and away from Depression. Anger can be used. Depression is a dead end. When I turn on Anger I see the traffic is too heavy and I may hurt others and myself. So I make a left onto Determination and then an immediate right turn onto Boundaries. Now, I am in the driver's seat again.

WISDOM/ENGAGEMENT/RESOLVE

"One way to guarantee freedom is to be ready to die." That is a quote from Epictetus who was born into slavery in the Roman Empire and became not only free, but also eternally famous. Over 2,000 years later we are still reading his work.

If you know anything about Stoic Philosophy you know Epictetus meant this very literally. The Stoics had a reverence for death. They did not fear it so much as revere it. Death gives the gift of focus and urgency. The only thing permanent in life is what you pass on to others. They live on; you don't. "What we do in life echoes into eternity."

Epictetus also meant it figuratively. Life is change. To resist that change is to go against nature. The Taoist philosophy talks about life as water. At times you will be a flowing river. Other times you will need to be calm and still. Sometimes you will need to crash and other times you will need to assume the shape of the circumstances you find yourself in. When you encounter an obstacle, water flows to the points of least resistance.

Water overcomes most everything, but only as a result of its ability to be at times transcendent (vapor), at times yielding and flowing (liquid), and at times solid as a rock (ice). To be ready to die means to be ready to change.

My two favorite philosophies are Taoism and Stoicism. Taoism describes the vision of the way. Be like water. Stoicism describes the practicalities of how to do that. Be prepared to die.

PERCEPTION/OWNERSHIP/WISDOM/SHARING

Maybe you can relate to the feeling that you are losing. Other people have passed you in success, smarts, good looks, etc. Like your life is not enough? I know you can, because you are human.

I have four major changes in Perception I use to deal with feelings of inadequacy, uncertainty, and insecurity.

1. Regret nothing ever. Regret is a choice. I simply will not choose it. No matter how I have disappointed myself, made an error, failed or anything else...I create a meaning for it and absorb the lesson. Regret is double pain and punishment and leaves nothing but misery. I won't do it; I own my faults, failures and misfortunes.

2. A lesson I adopted from Stoic Philosophy. -There is what I control completely, what I control partly, and what I don't control at all. I pour my heart into what I control completely. Everything else is on loan and does not belong to me. I enjoy it while I have it and am prepared to lose it at any time (health, wealth, relationships, and the rest). I control my thoughts, choices, and actions; that is all.

3. Change the way I frame a problem and the problem changes too. Life happens and I can't control that. But I get to happen back, and that I do control. I don't have to feel injured. I don't have to feel slighted. I don't have to feel cheated or betrayed. What if I choose to believe this is happening in the exact way necessary for me to grow? I will simply change my mind about what it means.

4. Focus on others. When all else fails, I focus on others. Nothing is new or different in this world. You suffer the same as me. My suffering is not special or unique. Neither is yours. Relinquam Amor means leave your love. When I give to, touch, inspire, and love another human, they are lifted and so am I. When all else fails to turn the pain around, I simply say quietly to myself, "Jade, why are you here?" Then I answer myself, "To help of course." Then I shut up, stop whining, and get to work.

This is how I journey from feeling like I am less alive and dreading life, to feeling alive and knowing I belong.

OWNERSHIP/WISDOM

It's funny how everyone you label as ignorant happens to have different beliefs than you. Do you find that peculiar? How is it that you have gathered all the right knowledge and experiences to give you alone the answers?

Is it feasible that there are some facts you don't know? Is it possible someone else has information more accurate than yours?

In my Facebook feed, I noticed a photographer post about how pictures make you happier. I read a gun rights advocate's post about how video games, not guns, kill people. I saw a person afraid of aging post how a new rainforest herb cures cancer. I posted about how donuts can save the planet from gamma radiation. See the trend?

As humans, we are naturally egotistical, self-righteous know-it-alls.

Exploring what you think you know is easy. It makes you feel smart, but in reality narrows your thought processes and keeps you confined to a box.

How do we reverse this trend? Socrates solved this for us more than 2,000 years ago. Ask questions that challenge the beliefs you hold. Explore information counter to the specific bubble in which you live. Perhaps I try a croissant and forego the donut. In doing so I discover croissants are delicious!

Or I can keep insisting everything I believe is the only way to think, like a teenager who insists that everything he learned in high school is THE truth. In fact, he makes it his business to prove that is all there is to know. Now you have to listen to him talk about beer pong, darts, condoms, and how good the North Forsyth High School Viking's football team is.

Maybe that's a silly example? But we see these behaviors in others all the time. Are we not falling in the same trap?

Once you switch from being a Culture Level human to a Next Level Human, the entire artifice falls away. Instead of being obsessed with defending your way so you can appear superior, you simply explore ideas for your own growth.

I know a few people who seek out things that challenge their beliefs, rather than reinforce them. They always have something to offer. I am tired of being an arrogant, narrow-minded schmuck.

OWNERSHIP/WISDOM/RESOLVE/SHARING

The Buddhists say, "Life is Dukkha." This word translates into suffering, pain, or dissatisfaction. The phrase is meant to help us understand that no matter what we choose, we must give up something else and suffer as a result.

If we are in a relationship we suffer from sharing space and losing some freedom. If we are single we suffer from not having companionship and a lack of deep emotional connection.

If we are poor we may suffer from lack of material things and experiences. If we are rich we may suffer from overabundance and false friendships. The point is, no matter your choices in life, there are ways you will suffer.

Why do we try to avoid this when it is unavoidable? It is impossible to remove some forms of suffering. We must work. We must suffer loss. We must study and strive if we want change. We must disappoint and be disappointed. We must die.

The trick is to be conscious in our choices, solid in our values and clear in our intentions. If we are going to suffer regardless, at least we can choose what we will suffer for.

Vivere Est Militare is tattooed down my side. It means life is a battle. It's a reminder we must choose what we are here for. What do we stand for? What's worth putting it all on the line for? What is our code of honor? What is the battle we choose to fight?

My fight is for kindness, generosity, honesty and compassion. -For equality, knowledge, experience, and wisdom. -For teaching. -For those I love. -For my writing, my books, and other creations. What's yours? What are you here to suffer and fight for?

Knowing what you will fight for can change your entire life experience. It can change others too.

OWNERSHIP/ENGAGEMENT/SHARING

Remember to step into your work with confidence and conviction. Stand up straight. You know why you are here.

A true creator creates not to be seen, or accepted, or celebrated. They create because they must.

Keep in mind it is the same for critics when they show up. They are critics because they are not true creators. They critique because they don't have the fortitude to create. A critic and a true creator cannot exist at the same time. You are either one or the other.

To be the creator you have to understand that you have made a conscious choice to not be a spectator. You have also chosen not to be a critic.

You have chosen to create for you and you alone, but in that process you provide the space for spectators and critics to show up. Without you, they would have no job. Your work keeps the spectators entertained and the critics distracted.

When the critics appear, and they will, listen to them if you wish. Use any of their input if you can. Then wave goodbye to them from your place on the playing field to their place in the stands.

November 5

PERCEPTION/OWNERSHIP

What a person thinks of me is none of my business, unless I choose to make it my concern. First I must ask myself, "Who is this person to me?

Do they impact my life? Do they impact the lives of others I care about?" If it is neither, then I smile and let them pass. Their opinion is of little use or consequence.

If I choose to care, I do so with an eye toward myself, or another I care for. I inquire, "Does their opinion matter to me? Can an opinion harm me or another I love?" I also ask, "Does their opinion have use for me? Can their opinion show a truth from which I could learn?"

These questions are challenging because a negative opinion can cause an emotional sting. These questions are not designed to remove that pain. That pain is best left alone; it needs to be felt. Pain is instructive. It helps me ascertain if it matters and if I care.

It's like the pain that occurs after I twist my ankle. That pain stops me and draws my attention to this body part. I must ascertain whether or not the ankle needs mending. I test it out by slowing down, bending over to touch the ankle, looking at it and cautiously moving it. If I determine everything is fine, I move on and continue the game. If I find it is indeed injured, I remove myself from the game; attend to the injury and weakness. If I am smart, I will rehab and strengthen the ankle to ensure its former strength or better.

This is how I like to view emotional hurt. Pain points me inward to examine my thoughts, assumptions, and stories. Do I care? Why do I care? Should I care? What must I do to be less triggered? Do I need better boundaries to protect myself?

People are practice. The pain is the path. What a person thinks of you matters only if you choose. What is it about them that makes you think so highly of them? What about you makes you think so lowly of yourself?

I want people to like me too. I want them to see me as smart and to fall in love with my gorgeous, bald head and sparkling eyes. It's human. But more importantly, I want to like them. If I am too busy asking the question, "Do they like me?" I forget to ask the more important question, "Do I like them?"

WISDOM/ENGAGEMENT/RESOLVE

In the gym we don't avoid the tough stuff; we chase the tough stuff. We do this by periodically exposing ourselves to lifts we have never achieved before. This is scary and exhilarating at the same time. We are always pushing the boundaries to improve. We pay particular attention to our weak areas.

Why not treat your emotional weaknesses the same? I had a friend who took flying lessons as a way to conquer a fear of flying. I call that a fear PR. You can conquer those same fears you have regarding rejection, loneliness, and boundaries.

Afraid to be alone; start learning to be alone. Start with movies, then dinners; try a weekend at a hotel alone, then perhaps a trip to a completely foreign country where you do not speak the language...alone.

When you feel completely taken over by the need for acceptance by others, it is because you are not choosing, challenging, celebrating and changing yourself. You are waiting for someone else to do that for you. It's not their job. It is 100% yours.

Consider that they may be your best life teacher if the emotions they cause in you allow you to understand where you must venture.

People are people, yes. People are also practice. Relationships, especially the romantic type, are some of our best teachers because no other relationship is laced with so many expectations, assumptions, and inaccurate stories. One simple example is the "you complete me" story.

Sorry, but the idea that someone can complete you is asinine. We must complete ourselves and we do that through change and challenge, the same way we accomplish it in the gym.

Relationships can aid you with that job, but they can't do it for you. You can't complete me, but you can help grow me.

OWNERSHIP/WISDOM/ENGAGEMENT

You know how a sports team practices to get better? -The same way you hit the gym and eat well to improve your health and fitness. But how do we get better socially? How do we practice?

Most individuals approach this by saying you should get out more. Socialize. Engage. Get along. Seek common ground and be pleasant.

I don't believe this is bad advice, but that approach is only one step, and I think there are additional, better ways. One of those is counterintuitive. It involves NOT going out. Instead, it is about staying in and keeping yourself company, try reading, thinking, journaling, and exploring your own thoughts, motivations, and insights. I know people who need constant social stimulation and interestingly, I have noticed they often have more social difficulties. I think you must know and like yourself before anyone else can.

What is it you really believe? What is it that matters most to you? What are YOUR values? Not the co-opted values of your family, political team, church, or culture?

The final step is learning how NOT to get along - how to disagree, how to speak your truth respectfully (or disrespectfully when required), and be open to an alternate truth. One of my favorite ways to get my practice in this realm is by bringing up politics and religion. Given I am anti-Democrat and even more anti-Republican, as well as a rational agnostic, who is largely anti-religion, this gives me ample opportunities.

Feedback is a final method I use. When most people ask for feedback, they are really asking you to tell them how good they are. When I ask, I get the most out of the "negative feedback." This tells me as much about the other person as it does myself. My reality is one version among many, and it moves closer to the truth when that reality is scrutinized and battle tested by bumping into other people's reality. How do you get better socially?

OWNERSHIP/ENGAGEMENT/RESOLVE/SHARING

My Next Level Human Coaching Curriculum has 6 powers I take people through. They go by the acronym POWERS:

P= Perception
O= Ownership
W= Wisdom
E= Engagement
R= Resolve
S= Sharing

In this coaching model, we don't simply sit around discussing things. Instead we use the As If Principle. People refer to the "Law of Attraction," which is misunderstood and incorrect in my opinion.

The idea that you are going to sit on the ground, visualize something, think of it all day and then have it magically show up in your life is just dumb to me.

If I want a donut - which I do right now- no amount of wishing and thinking is going to make a donut delivery guy show up at my doorstep. I want it? -Then I need to get out of bed (I am still laying here), put on my shoes, and prove to the world I want it with real effort and real skin in the game (i.e. money).

I know many people who call themselves writers and authors who technically write circles around me, but if I take action and finish the book, then my brain, and the world goes, "Damn, Jade really **IS** a writer!" If I don't finish, then I am a pretender no matter what I say or think.

These are the Powers of Engagement and Resolve. You choose. You act. You finish. When you publish, that is the Share Power.

It is not the Law of Attraction; it is the Law of Action (by the body) and recognition (by the brain). Do that enough times and you are the thing whether you are thinking about it or not.

PERCEPTION

This is what I wrote down in 2004 as I drove cross-country after finishing medical school:

1. Create a workout that reaches people all over the world.
2. Build a lifestyle company that teaches people how to eat, exercise, and live and think for optimal health and happiness.
3. Create a silent, six-figure business that requires only a few people to run and runs on its own.
4. Stay real, stay true to yourself, love/learn/teach, and give back as soon as you can.

I am writing this from memory as I have since lost that notebook, but this is the basic idea. At the time I did not know how I would do this, and I did not realize the Internet would become my tool. As I look at this list, it is sort of magical and incredible to think I actually accomplished all of these goals.

But here is the trick as I look back now. -My ability to do this hinged on one superpower I have always had; I call that superpower, Perception.

I have the ability to see things others do not and to believe I can do things others cannot, and most importantly, the ability to rewrite my story again and again to accommodate for change.

When the boot camp I started was not growing fast enough, I rewrote the script to include workouts in gyms. When that did not seem to generate revenue, I rewrote the script to release a book and incorporated the workouts online. In other words, my ability to rewrite the stories of my business and my life has served me well.

The only thing certain in life is uncertainty. The future you imagined can always be reimagined. I truly believe this and I embrace this belief in every endeavor.

We need to write our own story, but more importantly we must be able to rewrite it again and again. The person you love rejects you; rewrite your story. Your business fails, rewrite the script. Discover you are a selfish person; rewrite the story. You and the people around you don't believe you can do it, rewrite your story. Rewrite the story you are telling about whatever haunts you.

Like Marcus Aurelius says, "You have control over your mind not outside events. Realize this and you will find strength."

OWNERSHIP/RESOLVE

I think about death every morning, not because I am sick, and not out of fear. Not for attention. Not because anyone I know recently died. Not out of a morbid curiosity. I think about death because death is my counselor, coach, and mentor. It provides me with the focus to live for and the meaning to die for.

There is a quote by a famous Polish freedom fighter, Witold Pilecki, which I love. Before he was put to death, and after breaking into, and then escaping from, Auschwitz (to gather intelligence during World War II), he said, "I lived my life so that at this moment, I would meet death with joy, rather than shrink back in fear and regret."

The stoic philosopher, Seneca had similar thoughts. He was ordered by the Roman emperor to take his own life. His followers were devastated. He said, "Men do not care how nobly they live, but only how long, although it is within the reach of every man to live nobly, but within no man's power to live long."

Contemplating death is one of the most powerful tools we have to cut through the superficial and meaningless to clarify what really matters. Where is it that we can apply our signature strengths in a way to make a difference?

What we really want as humans is to matter. This is why we fret so much about others and how they view us. This is why we feel jealousy. This is why we feel pangs in our chest if we think someone does not like us.

We have it all wrong. The question to ask is, "Do we like ourselves?" The pursuit of the adoration of others distracts us from looking at ourselves. The refusal to contemplate death keeps us from asking ourselves what really matters. And it keeps us from realizing our time is already running out. What are you waiting for? How could you begin living life right now that would cause you to greet death with a smile?

I doubt money and good looks will satisfy you. I bet learning, teaching, and loving (sharing) will.

PERCEPTION/OWNERSHIP

What is romance really about? Why is it so wonderful? How can it be so incredibly painful when it is lost?

Romance taps into the place inside us that needs to belong. We are social creatures before anything else and there is no stronger drive than to feel we matter.

Romance also taps into two of the most important needs of our human brain: certainty and relatedness. Having someone, anyone, is better than having no one as far as many people are concerned.

Romance also provides us with the three P's, what Viktor Frankl called the three wills: The will to power, the will to pleasure, and the will to purpose.

Romantic relationships not only provide us with stability and connection, but also make us feel more powerful than some of us feel alone; two seem better than one. And, of course, what on earth is better than an orgasm?

I love romance. I believe in love, but romance is a slippery slope. When we are in romantic relationships, we necessarily give up a part of ourselves. This is where both the wonder and the pain of romance originate.

If you subscribe to the belief that part of your purpose here is to choose your meaning and how you will matter to the world, then you can immediately see how romance could aid or hurt that sacred contract with yourself.

PERCEPTION/OWNERSHIP/ENGAGEMENT

M any people subscribe to the "you complete me" model of romance. This is where the danger lies. If you complete me, you also control and own a part of me. Perhaps the very part of me that my contract demands I must complete myself.

These are the relationships that keep you from yourself. The pain of them ending is a wake-up call back to yourself and a return to the contract only you can complete.

The romance that aids that journey is the one that says, "You grow me," not, "You complete me." It is a romance that walks along with you, but does not become you.

Only you can become you. Your romantic partner can help point you in the direction, but the journey is yours alone.

PERCEPTION/ENGAGEMENT/WISDOM

One of the greatest obstacles to wisdom is, not what we don't know, but what we think we already know. We humans have a glitch in our brain. You can think of it like a computer virus.

This "virus" causes our brain's "software" to run in ways that don't serve us. When we have an opinion about something, this brain glitch makes us easily see things that agree with the opinion, but miss things that don't.

This explains why people's opinions, whether right or wrong, are often self-perpetuating. In other words, they become strengthened and repeated over time, rather than questioned. That is a huge problem if you want to develop true knowledge and Wisdom.

If you are trying to absorb new information, gain wisdom and grow to new heights of success and meaning in your life, having an open mind is crucial. The fact that your brain is naturally close-minded is a HUGE impediment to personal growth.

This is so pervasive that psychology researchers have given it a name, "selective attachment theory." The more, well-known name for it is, "confirmation bias."

I love the definition given for "confirmation bias" at Wikipedia. They define it as, "The tendency to search for, interpret, favor, and recall information in a way that confirms one's beliefs or hypotheses, while giving disproportionately less consideration to alternative possibilities."

In other words, you unconsciously perpetuate what you currently believe even if those beliefs are completely false. If you are someone wanting to change, what I just said should scare you. It certainly does me.

There is a way to combat confirmation bias. I call it *contradiction* bias and it has become my diligent practice. This practice involves questioning all information you read, hear, or are exposed to in any way; most importantly and critically the things you are already convinced are true.

OWNERSHIP/ENGAGEMENT/SHARING

Life, death, and time; these are the only three things of certainty in your existence. You know you are alive. You know you must die. What you do with the time in between is all that matters.

I like to think of it like a pebble dropping into a pond. Once that small stone sinks, life is finished. It only has one chance to make an impact. So do you.

Will the ripples you create even last? Will they be a destructive force that makes it harder for others? Will they be a powerful source of inspiration that lifts others and helps them to shore?

What you do with your time is all you have between life and death; then it is done.

Are you more concerned with a bank account filled with cash or a large bank of generosity for others? Are you more concerned with being right, being seen, and being safe or do you seek the truth, acknowledge others, and inspire through courageous action?

What we do with our time is up to each of us. I have worked in the healing profession long enough to know that we want our lives to have meaning and matter above all else. We want our time to make a difference.

The only way to accomplish this task is to move past Base Level fear and Culture Level status to Next Level sharing.

Legacy is not about ego, or cars, money, wrinkle-free faces, or the impossible quest for perfect health. Legacy is about what you do with your time that others benefit from long after you're gone.

Next Level Humans use their time for three things only...to learn, to teach, to love (share).

Working toward our Next Level inspires us to make meaning, not just money.

OWNERSHIP/WISDOM/ENGAGEMENT

Have you ever read Rilke's, "Letters To A Young Poet?" It is a very short read. For those into self-development, it is incredibly rich with lessons in self-awareness, humility, ego, focus, delusion, and more.

> "If your everyday life seems poor don't blame it, blame yourself. Admit to yourself that you are not enough of a poet to bring forth its riches."
> ~Rainer Maria Rilke

This quote is one of my favorites. The implications are profound.

OWNERSHIP/WISDOM

One of my struggles over the last five years has been listening. I find myself quick to interject when others are talking. They will be speaking and that sparks a thought in my head. I want to share and then I often interrupt. I am no longer listening to them because I am too busy listening to my own thought. Maybe you have experienced this too?

I have a tattoo on my left shin that echoes this sentiment. Semper Discendum means, always be learning. To learn means you must listen first. You cannot speak and listen at the same time. If you can't listen, so many lessons and insights will escape your comprehension.

I think the refusal to listen comes from the need to be right and the fear of being wrong. But the sting of being wrong also holds the motivation to learn what's right.

I am not sure why we humans are so averse to admitting we were wrong; there are few human attributes I respect more. Admitting we were wrong, or are not good enough, is NOT giving up. In fact, it is the first step to improvement.

The inability to admit our faults or ignorance is the same thing that chokes our personal growth.

WISDOM/ENGAGEMENT/RESOLVE

M y friend, Bruno, and I were talking about the practice of intentional manifestation, the idea that we can consciously bring into existence that which we think about, focus on, and most importantly, act upon.

Bruno brought up an important point. We don't really seem to celebrate our successes. In fact, it is almost looked-down-upon to get charged up when we achieve something we set an intention to create. No one wants to appear to be boasting or bragging, therefore, often our successes fly under the radar.

By "under the radar," I am not speaking about attention from others; I mean recognition by our own brains. The brain is watching, and judging us, all of the time. It judges our own personal behaviors in the same way it watches and judges others. What it sees us doing, and what it feels us experiencing, is important feedback that determines its future belief in us.

Success is, to some degree, a habit. By celebrating our successes, we are potentially programming the brain for future success. It's similar with failures. By replaying and then debriefing the brain on the lessons learned, we program failures as lessons, not disasters. In this way we are coaching ourselves to achieve.

So take big risks and attack what you want. When you win, throw your arms in the air and scream "YES!" Go out with friends for a celebratory dinner. Buy yourself a remembrance of the accomplishment. Do NOT let the moment pass without acknowledgment.

When you lose, the same applies. Do not let failures pass by without scrutinizing and studying them for the lessons.

PERCEPTION/OWNERSHIP/WISDOM/ENGAGEMENT

What did you learn?
What meaning can you make out of it?

What will you create in your life as a result?

I spent some time in Cabo, Mexico at my Next Level Man Event and these are the big questions we covered.

A Next Level Human is a person who understands that life, by its very definition, is growth. They know that the natural default will be to resist change. As a result, they seek out growth, not just rising to the occasion, but also creating it. The mindset is that our job as humans is not to stay the same, but to change. The lessons of that change can then be harnessed to grow, to teach, and to love (share).

It's not easy because humans are story-making machines. We may not be completely aware, but we walk around with stories about the world that impact everything we do, defining much of what we can and cannot achieve.

These "stories" are often completely unconscious and borrowed from our family and culture. If we are to achieve our next, best level, we must become aware of the narratives we are telling and consciously write new ones capable of producing the meaning we seek.

However, thinking is not enough. Without action, the "Law of Attraction" becomes the law of retraction.

Sitting around in lotus pose planning and thinking positive thoughts can never deliver what real-world immersion can. Only action can be reality-tested by life. Only real wins and true failures produce the Wisdom required for Next Level growth.

The narratives you tell yourself are often the only stories you will hear life reading back to you. To experience a new, richer story means giving up the familiar and acting as if you are that new story, starting now.

OWNERSHIP/SHARING

I believe that in our culture we often celebrate all the wrong things and give attention to all the wrong people. Why do we celebrate megastars who make a living pretending to be heroes, when we have examples of real-life heroes everywhere?

My mother is my hero. She did not have it easy. While I will not get into details, let's just say she was not a favorite in her family. Some people get special treatment and some people get especially abusive treatment. My mother fell into the latter category.

There are several ways people respond to that type of upbringing. They can become the thing that abused them, they can give up and become a victim, or they can grow into something immensely beautiful. My mother is an emotional alchemist for herself and others. She took the hurt, jealousy, pain, maliciousness, and lies and turned them into kindness, love, compassion, and caring. Anyone who has ever crossed her path, has been touched by someone rare, unique, and gifted.

I love you so much mom. Thank you for being my greatest example of how to turn pain into magic for the world.

PERCEPTION/ENGAGEMENT/RESOLVE

Life occurs; that is what it is designed to do. We are at once both fragile and solid like rock. We are simultaneously weak and strong beyond our imagination. Humans realize their power only when we are blasted by the storms of life.

In response to what happens to us, we respond differently.

The weight room is my favorite example. -Imagine you go into a tough workout. Not once during the entire thirty minutes do you feel in control. You bloody your chin, you tear your hands and you throw up in your mouth a little at the end. It leaves you on the ground frantically searching for a position to ease the breathlessness and pain.

It is miserable- for a time- and then it's not again. You made it through and you feel as if you have reached a place inside that is a new powerful point, a new personal record of physical endurance. You will definitely try this workout again. Not right away of course, but eventually, sooner rather than later.

But what if, instead, you decided that was too hard? You are not going to ever do that workout again. Furthermore you are not going to do those exercises either. In fact you are going to give up weight training and take up knitting instead. Sounds silly, right? Except that is exactly the way many of us respond to psychological pain.

Life is suffering. That's what it is by design. I expect it to be and I would not want it any different. My strength comes from my suffering. My pain illuminates my path. My misery produces my meaning. I am better, kinder, stronger, smarter, and happier as a result.

PERCEPTION/OWNERSHIP

I remember playing football in high school I was a junior on a very talented team that could not seem to win a game. I remember the feeling distinctly. We would do well the first couple downs and usually score first. Then as soon as a play went wrong, we just fell apart and never recovered. After about the fourth game, we just expected a loss.

Interestingly, something strange started happening to me. Without the expectation of a win and with everyone else seemingly giving up, I decided to just focus on me. I started to play the game from a different perspective. My play started to improve, and I took it upon myself to simply play my position the best I could.

I would prepare all week. Study the game plan. Stay conditioned. And play with all the intelligence and physical effort I could muster. Guess what happened? Nothing! We still got beaten almost every game. I played the best football of my life and no one even noticed.

I don't pay attention to the game anymore. Stressing out about 11 dudes I don't know, will never meet, and have nothing to do with seems nonsensical. But the game did teach me a lot.

I think it is something all sports teach. It's a universal lesson. You can do your best, plan your best, practice your best, play your best and still get utterly beaten. That's life; it does not give a damn.

When times are hard and things go wrong, it's easy to become disillusioned. Yet, I can't help but notice that the challenges we face often seem perfectly matched to our growth needs. The way your spouse shows up turns out to be the thing you have struggled with for years. The devastating heartbreak is the experience that could, if conquered, grant the true independence and confidence you always wished for. The financial difficulty you feared helps you finally learn to earn, manage, and save money.

Is it that life or God seems to give us exactly what we need? Or is it that we humans have this superpower to attract the lessons we need to grow naturally? I think it's the latter.

I believe in the power of you and me to make meaning out of misery.

OWNERSHIP

When it comes to interpersonal relationships Base Level humans want to control. Culture Level humans seek to conform. Next Level Humans look to connect.

People have all three types within them. In fact, we typically grow through these phases as we mature. Children are a bit more Base Level. This is a natural place to be in an uncertain world. Only through loving parents, consistent care taking, and freedom of exploration do kids begin to transition out of this.

Teenagers are mostly Culture Level. They want to fit in and take two main strategies to do so. They either fit into an existing group or they create their own group. They have recognized their sense of self is partly contingent on other people, but they concede too much. They spend more time subconsciously adjusting to their peers and too little time attending to the exploration of self. Sadly most adults are still stuck in adolescence.

Next Level types have realized that control is an illusion and developed the courage to be disliked. People are seen as rich sources of potential growth and learning. People who are different are seen as interesting rather than threatening. Life is no longer a competition or popularity contest, but a compassionate and creative endeavor. The Next Level Human still has Base Level Or Culture Level tendencies, but is continually growing into a majority Next Level state.

Age has little to do with it, since age does not necessarily mean emotional maturity. And because we humans often wear masks, it can be difficult to discern. This is why the best places to catch a person's true behavior is when they are under stress or anonymous on the Internet. Watch people driving in traffic. Do they tailgate, close the gap, or get angry? How do they behave behind a computer? Are they a troll? Is everyone stupid but them? Is it always, "Look at me?" Or are they trying to connect and add value? What about behaviors in long lines, crowded airports or when they're hungry?

Stress feels threatening and can auto-trigger Base Level behavior in the less mindful. This is why stress is a great way to discern the degree of Base Level someone still has.

PERCEPTION

H ave you ever heard someone say, "I can't believe they think that way! They are so ignorant!"

Ignorance is likely not the correct explanation. Let's use political examples, global warming, conspiracy theory, vaccines, and terrorism. You might think lack of education (i.e., ignorance) is the reason?

But terrorists are NOT poor, uneducated people; they are often middle class and even affluent (especially the leaders). Climate deniers can have above average science backgrounds. Vaccine crusaders may have strong medicine knowledge.

But if not ignorance, then what?

Bias and Dogma:

Bias is an unreasoned judgment about something. Dogma is what people believe is true. A biased/dogmatic person favors certain ideas over others without proper evaluation (bias) and is convinced they alone are correct (dogma). Bias leads to ignorance since information is rarely scrutinized. Dogma creates arrogance because, in the eyes of the person, there can be no other explanation. This is why I say bias and dogma are the parents of ignorance and arrogance.

Want to avoid bias and dogma? Be aware of these 4 brain tendencies towards delusion:

1. Anchoring bias- the 1st thing you learn about a topic often becomes your belief, even if wrong (i.e., your parents believe your brother was harmed by vaccines, you then maintain the belief even after becoming a scientist and seeing the actual evidence to the contrary).
2. Bandwagon effect- the more others repeat it, the greater chance you believe it, even if it's untrue. This is most true if they are "team members" (i.e., why more climate deniers are Republican).
3. Confirmation bias- you seek and believe ideas that confirm your stance while avoiding and disbelieving information that challenges it, despite the facts.
4. Backfire effect- if someone provides solid evidence against your belief; you will believe your stance more strongly than before, even if it is wrong.

The first step to guard against these brain biases is to be aware of them. This is why science is important. Unlike opinion, which is self-perpetuating, science is self-correcting. It helps us by providing a system that checks against bias and dogma.

OWNERSHIP/WISDOM/ENGAGEMENT/RESOLVE

When I hear the doubters and realists say, "It can't be done," I know what they really mean. What they are really saying is, it won't work for them. They telegraph their fears and limiting beliefs.

Here is one concept I figured out early in life. We humans are inherently lazy, ignorant, and fearful. You might think that depressed me. On the contrary, I realized I just found the secret to success.

I gleaned all that was required was to be a little less fearful, a little more willing to grind, and a little more eager to learn. The courage to take risks, the work ethic to muster what needs to be done, and the open-mindedness and curiosity to learn what you don't know.

OWNERSHIP

I am incredibly fortunate to have cultivated a tribe of family and friends who are on another level. We have taken to using the term "Next Level Human," to make a distinction between our Base Level tendencies.

We don't gossip, at least not in the way others do. We simply don't tolerate it from each other. We don't hate or troll on people. We see that as the ultimate sign of a weak and insecure person. We don't ghost, placate, bullshit or lie. We communicate, even the tough stuff, most importantly the tough stuff.

Our thoughts about your beliefs are the same as my thoughts about diet and exercise:

You should believe exactly what it is that works for you. The thing that brings you peace, stability, happiness, and meaning... so long as your belief does not infringe on anyone else's ability to also freely choose how they live and what they think and believe. If that is the spirit of things, then we are fully supportive of your politics, your religion, your opinion, and your actions.

SHARING

Life is a shared experience. You are not an island unto yourself. Your fellow human is an extension of you. Their base self is a reflection of your base self. Their higher potential is a reflection of your Next Level self.

It is your duty as a warrior to protect your tribe, to see it to its highest evolution. You must leave the world better than you found it.

Your legacy is your creations. Your creations embody your love. Your love is what you must leave.

PERCEPTION/OWNERSHIP/SHARING

B asing your self-esteem on your looks is like basing your career off of what you knew in high school.

Good looks are of little credit to the person. Their parents gave them a nice face? That was lucky for them. Nature will take it away.

Sure, they can inject it, stretch and lift it, but in the end it will just be a puckered-up, stretched, old face. I get it, I had a hair transplant because I like a bit of a shadow on my bald dome. It makes me look better to myself. But it makes me think that what's really unattractive, is the incessant need to be physically attractive.

We all are turned off by neediness, and yet our neediness is telegraphed to the world when we base everything off of our physical appearance. It's like a beautiful, sports car with no engine, useless except to view.

If I were to tell you to follow my diet advice, and I kept posting pictures of myself 100 pounds overweight, eating a pound of fried chicken every night, I would have zero credibility to you. Likewise, if I post pictures of my ripped abs, collagen lips, and hair transplant and then say, "Accept who you are, love yourself," you would probably see the incongruence in that as well. Real body acceptance is showing up as you are.

We have to be careful here though. What's wrong with wanting to improve your physical appearance? Nothing, a little vanity is required even for good health. But taken too far, vanity just makes you a superficial, shallow, but amazing looking human.

Besides, beauty is an energetic thing and so is ugly. Our physical looks are of little credit to us, but our character and kindness is something we control and can be enhanced as we age.

I see pretty faces everywhere. Mine is not one of them. I am a sucker for cute as well, just like you are. But what takes my breath away, what I want to get close to and what I personally find irresistible is real body acceptance, authentic kindness, confident intelligence, and compassion for all people, no matter how they look.

OWNERSHIP

Honesty= lack of deceit or untruthfulness.
Loyalty= giving firm or constant support to someone.

They are not exactly the same thing. Although I think we would all agree they are related. Which is more important to you, honesty or loyalty?

Because it can be challenging to separate the two, here is an example: You have a business idea or invention and it is your purpose to see this thing through. Out of excitement, you openly share the idea with many friends. It's a fast and effective moneymaker that you and your friends could quickly execute.

These friends, including your best friend, are out together and your idea comes up in conversation. That impromptu meeting turns into a conversation of how they can adapt the invention for themselves and cut you out.

What would you prefer...

1. Honest, but not loyal: Your best friend tells you the entire story and everything that was discussed. She also admits she was engaged in planning how they could use the idea for themselves and did not stick up for you or point out to anyone the invention was yours.
2. Loyal, but not honest: Your best friend does not tell you about the meeting and denies it to your face when you tell her you heard about it and you know she was present. However, during the meeting your friend was an adamant supporter of you, insistent that the idea was yours, and she would have no part in it. In fact, she told the group if they executed the idea, she would no longer be their friend.

Now, I realize this is a hypothetical and a tough choice, but if you had to choose, what would you want... loyalty or honesty? And let's assume this friend is always this way. She lies to you frequently, but is always loyal. Or, she always is honest, but frequently disloyal.

For me, it's loyalty over honesty any day. And yes, normally they would go together, but I am asking for you to consider them separately.

Who makes up your inner circle?

OWNERSHIP/SHARING

I was third in line at Whole Foods. An older, frail woman in her 80's was at the checkout counter.

As the cashier, a young guy in his 20's, swiped her items, she kept getting confused and telling him she did not select the item he was scanning. She questioned the prices. Then she asked for items she did not place in her cart. Then she could not figure out the new checkout terminal.

I am not joking; this ordeal probably took around 5-10 minutes. It was an agonizing process for all to watch. It was also one of those busy times where the place is packed and there were not enough lines or staff to take care of everyone. Basically, the other five people in line and I had to accommodate and deal with this frustrating situation.

I watched as the people in line switched from annoyance to agitation to anger. And then something really interesting happened. The guy behind the woman and in front of me turned to me and said, "Can you believe this shit!" I said, "No, I am in awe of this cashier."

By this time I was simply observing the cashier. He was so kind and patient. He even started asking the woman before every item he scanned, "This looks good. Would you like this?" And he waited patiently while she confirmed or rejected items she already put in her bag. He was pleasant, considerate, and funny. All of a sudden, everyone in the line was laughing and smiling. Anger turned into understanding and compassion.

When I finally checked out, the cashier said, "So sorry for the wait." I just looked at him and said, "Are you kidding me? Thank you for that. You are so inspiring. You made my day. I want to be just like you." He was confused, but I meant it.

Behavior is not always our own. Actions can affect more than ourselves. Showing up in this way leaves a mark on others, so does behaving in the reverse. Actions are like energetic waves that can lift, teach, and inspire or push down, crush, and defeat. Frequently, those waves reflect back on you.

If your life is not embodying what you want and people are not treating you how you wish, ask yourself how you can treat the world differently first.

PERCEPTION/OWNERSHIP/WISDOM/ ENGAGEMENT/RESOLVE/SHARING

To me, easy is something you earn. To me, pain is the path.

Think about your hurt as similar to your hunger. Hunger is what drives you. Hunger is what creates urgency to seek food. Hunger makes food, which would be otherwise ordinary, delicious and extraordinary.

Without hunger you would feel no urge to feed yourself and you would waste away.

I don't have a complete answer to how people can thrive in life, but I do think part of it is to recognize that... hurt, pain, struggle, suffering, wounds, and all the rest are an essential part of life.

These challenges push us to grow, take responsibility, and care for ourselves. They are also the parts of life that allow us to feel the pain of others, and to be compassionate.

Those who face pain and suffering and respond by growing stronger become our heroes.

Maybe thriving means embracing, rather than avoiding, the struggle? Maybe it's not just about rising to the occasion, but creating the occasion. Maybe it's not just about accepting what you are going through, but loving the process.

What if you could treat your pain like an old friend who tells you what you need to improve rather than what keeps you comfortable and safe? Anyone would be lucky to have a friend with these qualities.

OWNERSHIP/WISDOM

S top looking to be recognized by others. You must constantly move forward when no one else believes but you.

Once you decide to own yourself completely, you immediately become visible to all the people who have been looking for that type of person. The way you carry yourself and the confidence you project will send a message to those around you. You'll start recognizing the people you are looking for as well.

When you are fully occupying your authentic self, others recognize you, and you recognize them. But this process takes time. Being real takes guts and requires you to weather the storms of doubt that will come your way. People you have never met may immediately get it, but your current tribe members may have some initial doubt. Can you blame them?

Let's say you decide you are going to become the next great American cupcake maker. This is who you really are, what you really love, and what you are genuinely committed to. But you can't expect that people will immediately start treating you that way.

It just doesn't work like that. Authenticity needs to be proven, first to yourself and then, to others. The initial skepticism we may encounter is part of the process. It is as if life is saying, "It is easy to be real to yourself. It is easy to be motivated when no one is watching. It is easy to be all-good when everything is all-good. Before others recognize, you need to prove it; this means confidently moving forward when no one else believes but you." Then slowly everyone else starts to see you that way too.

Before anyone else realizes the amazing pastry chef you know you are, you have to start showing up every day with flour on your apron. You need to see yourself churning out delicious icings. Even then, you will encounter mostly haters.

But, the more you show up as you, the more you will become visible to those around you, and the more they will be recognizable to you. The more they see you, the more they get you. More importantly, the more you will start to see yourself the way you want to be seen."

SHARING

One of the things I want to work on is acknowledgment.

Acknowledgment is something we all appreciate, right? When someone really sees us and then can tell us, it's one of the best gifts in the world. Especially when it is authentic and unexpected.

My friend, Ronnie, has been a third older brother to me. I have known him since the age of 12, and we have been training partners for over 20 years. Do you ever play that game where you choose the 3 people you would want with you if you had to go to war? The people you know would not hesitate, ensuring you would never have to look over your shoulder, because you know they would be there? I have been lucky in my life to have more than a few... Ronnie is one. I love him; appreciate his honesty, humor, and admire his work ethic.

And Amanda, she has become one of my closest friends over the last two years. She is beautiful, loyal, and selfless. Imagine waking up day after day, early as hell to run a gym and train with little to no pay... simply because you love it and you know others love it too. What you do and who you are is so special. I adore you.

Are there people in your life that deserve your acknowledgment?

Relinquam Amor = Leave love

RESOLVE

B eing afraid of death is the same as being afraid of living. I am not writing that to sound clever or wise, I feel I have witnessed it.

Once I was in Santiago, Spain when an elderly man in his late 70's, recognized me as a fellow American. He was on a bike, had on a backpack and informed me he was biking across Europe.

On that same trip I met a women in her 80's walking the famous Camino De Santiago. She too was alone, but vibrant and alive. I asked her if I could take a picture with her, and I asked her secret. She told me something along the lines of this, "I became more fearful of not living than dying, and then I realized they were the same."

Contrast those two with the average people their age, stuck in their homes glued to shows about other people's lives. I would argue that young people are equally susceptible to this trap.

I know it sounds backward, but fearing death makes you not live. You don't fly because of plane crashes. You don't drive because of car crashes. You don't hike because of bear attacks. You don't swim because of sharks.

Sometimes I wish I were afraid of choking so I would stop eating so much. I joke of course, but you know what I mean? The fear of death is worse than death because it keeps you from living. Embracing death means embracing life.

I love the idea of death. I imagine a hooded figure playfully trying to catch me while I duck and dodge, laughing and learning the whole time. When he does catch up, I want us both to collapse on the ground in exhausted laughter saying, "Damn that was fun!"

Death gives us the focus to live for and the meaning to die for.

OWNERSHIP/ENGAGEMENT/RESOLVE/SHARING

As humans we can count on few things in life, but there are two things we can be sure of; we will suffer and we will die.

My close circle-of-friends and I often talk about this openly. We discuss the painful things we have and have not yet encountered in life. We also discuss our deaths and how we would like to perish. It does not seem odd until a newcomer enters the conversation. You can see the emotional squeamishness others have with these ideas.

I was talking to my nephews about death and how I overcame my fear of flying, which I now see as silly. The first thing I realized was that fear was stopping me from exploring the world. I started to fly more, not less. The next thing I did is a little stranger; I chose the exact way I would go out. Let me explain.

Several years ago I came up with an honor code and a code of conduct. It contained declarations of honesty, courage, kindness, and generosity. It was born out of my personal suffering, and was my way of making meaning out of misery.

The code also defined for me my behavior in the toughest times. If I am going down in a plane crash, dying in a car wreck, or fading away in a hospital bed, I will turn my attention to what my life has been about; teaching, inspiring, and supporting other people.

On the plane I will turn to the person next to me, take their hand and say, "It's going to be fine. You can do this. I got you, we will do it together." In the hospital I will make sure the staff knows their work is important and needed. If there is an act of violence I want to run in to help, not flee. I will work to comfort and care for others even as they care for me.

I may not have a choice in what ultimately happens to me, but I have a choice in how I will behave as it happens. Many people are afraid because of the uncertainty. Not me, I know exactly who I will be.

Just before I learned to drive my father said, "Look at all the people driving; if they can do it, you can do it." That's how I feel about suffering and death. Simply by being human, I have the capacity to enter both realms with courage and Resolve.

OWNERSHIP/WISDOM

People say you should not discuss politics. They say these conversations are never fruitful and almost always end up in arguments. I disagree completely.

Politics is one of my go-to conversation topics when I am learning about a person. It is the perfect vetting system and one of the best barometers of the quality of a human. If I want to pursue a business relationship with you, become friends with you, or date you, the way you speak politics tells me all I need to know.

I value intelligence in a person. I value honesty. I value kindness and good communication too. Perhaps more than anything else I value open-mindedness, independent thinking, and a strong, identifiable honor code. A discussion of politics makes these qualities, or lack of them, immediately apparent.

You might think I am looking for someone who aligns with my political team. Instead, I am looking for a person who does not align with a political team at all. If they jump on a political bandwagon, it tells me something. If they focus on a single issue, it tells me something. If they say nothing to "get along," it says something. If they watch only Fox or MSNBC and use team-talk terms like "fake news," "liberal media" or "all conservatives are dumb," it tells me they are ignorant; or at least not smart enough to think for themselves.

If they vote for someone who ends up being a complete jackass, do they admit it and withdraw their support or double down? Do they believe in conspiracy theories? Do they even understand the issue they oppose or support? Do their values hold up when their "team" talks-the-talk but does not walk-the-walk?

People always ask me how to find other people who are Next Level Humans rather than Base Level; to me, political conversations sort it out better than any other topic of discussion.

December 6

OWNERSHIP/ENGAGEMENT

It can be a struggle moving away from those who either don't value you as a person or who don't share your core values. By struggle, I mean it can be painful to be rejected by another or have to reject another. Often that is exactly what is required to grow.

Here is the process I have followed:

- Define your meaning. Many people treat purpose as if it is something you find. To me, it is something you decide. Choose your meaning. Mine is to be a teacher who inspires and moves people to change. Once I own this I have also created a blueprint for what type of people I will have in my life. -Those who are life-long learners. Those who can teach me and expand my perspective.

- Define your code. How will you conduct your life? How will you show up? What will you fight for, suffer for, bleed and scar for? I choose the religion of kindness. I choose generosity. Honesty and good communication are also how I will show up. Once I put this code into action, it acts as both an attractant and a repellent. When I own my self fully, others see me clearly and I also see them. I then work to recruit my social tribe as if I were a scout trying to build a championship team. What superstars do I already have? Who do I need? How am I contributing fully to my social circle?

- Define your boundaries. This one is the hardest because it involves firm lines in the sand. Admittedly this has been my weak point in the past. Now I am solid. I will give you a few chances and I am always open to an apology and explanation, but once you cross the line, it is difficult for me to ever revisit you. I will not tolerate liars or avoiders. -Those who can't communicate and are unwilling to learn. Bigots and racists, mean, rude, and selfish people.

Sometimes individuals remain in our circles because they are family, or family of friends, or friends of family. It's not that I don't engage, but I limit my interactions to the superficial, and retain only a small opening for anything more.

PERCEPTION/OWNERSHIP

R egret is a choice. I simply do not do regret - period.
Regret is for the second guessers. It is living in the past. It is choosing to stay stuck.

No thanks.

OWNERSHIP

Pleasure, Power, and Purpose. Viktor Frankl called these the "3 wills." These are the concepts we humans chase, whether consciously or unconsciously.

- Pleasure is about feeling good. Getting a naked back rub by your beautiful lover on top of a stack of gold bullion while being spoon fed tiramisu? -Yeah, that would be great, but does it mean anything to you or others? What are you going to do with those feelings other than seek them again?
- Power is about feeling in control. We want to be better, smarter, stronger, and prettier. Signing your *NY Times* bestselling book, while instructing people what to do during a CNN interview about how great you are? -But, what are you going to do with that? Did it feed your ego rather than feed someone else's soul?
- Purpose involves feeling like your life matters. The will to meaning is the highest calling of a human. What would you be willing to fight, bleed, scar and die for? What will the world look like after you are gone? Will you have made a difference? Will you be proud of the way you showed up? Are others better off for you having lived?

There is nothing wrong with chasing pleasure and power at times. The issue is that without purpose it is easy to get lost in a hedonistic, egotistical, and singular focus on pleasure or power. We all know people like this. Time and time again we see people's lives ruined by the dysfunctional attachment to drugs, sex, alcohol, food, money, power, and corruption. This is almost always a result of abandoning purpose in favor of the easier, and more fleeting pleasure and power.

Meaning over money. It's a mantra I use to remind myself what matters. Do I care how many social media followers I have or do I care how many I've helped? Do I care about proving I am a nutritional expert, or do I care about helping people become healthier?

Meaning is something you choose. You just decide. I want to teach and inspire people to achieve the change they dream of. Yes, I want to make money while I do it too. But even if I didn't make a dime I would do it anyway, because meaning matters more than money...to me.

OWNERSHIP/WISDOM/ENGAGEMENT

Humans are, at their core, social beings. We require social interaction and connection with other humans. At the same time we know our social circles can impact us dramatically, negatively and positively.

As I have been sharing more about my Next Level Human Project, I am repeatedly being asked, "But Jade, what about other people? How do you manage them while working on yourself?"

There is nothing you can really say to change another human. Instead you do 3 things, primarily:

1. Be the person you want to be fully. The behaviors of Next Level Humans are honesty, integrity, communication, kindness, transparency, and consideration among other things.
2. Know what is about you and what is about them. This is easy to do. If they are the only person in your life where you encounter drama and difficulty, it may be them. If it is a pattern you continue to see with multiple people, it is more likely you. Either way, it's your responsibility to change, not theirs.
3. Enforce strong, defined boundaries. Next Level individuals know what they will, and will not, tolerate. They won't ghost or avoid (the behaviors of those with the psychological maturity of a preteen). Instead they simply let people know clearly what is okay and what is not. This is the final vetting process for who remains in your circles and who doesn't.

Here are some of the behaviors of my Next Level friends:

They are themselves.

They respectfully speak their truth.

They are open to your truth. They listen to understand.

They communicate fully to be understood.

They turn read receipts to "on" in their mobile devices. This, like everything they do, is a commitment to honesty and transparency. They do not engage in gossip, and will defend their friends even if those friends are not present.

They treat others with kindness as a default, but will not hesitate to call out bigots or racists. They realize that by being Next Level and having firm boundaries, the right people are automatically attracted into their circles, while the wrong types are repelled.

OWNERSHIP/WISDOM/ENGAGEMENT

I often talk about the 3 levels of humans. It's my way of understanding, and helping the people I work with, identify some of their natural human tendencies. -Base Level, Culture Level and Next Level.

It is also not a judgment or a "better than" thing. Most of us are doing the best we can. It's not easy being human, and we each have our own lessons, to teach and to learn, that begin with self-awareness.

Base Level and Culture Level are often stuck in an adolescent mindset. There are 3 hallmarks to adolescence:

1. The tendency to see the world only through your eyes and only according to your needs. Adolescents perceive themselves as the center of the universe
2. The tendency to need approval from others and to adjust behaviors in ways to fit in or control the way others see us. Adolescents can get so lost in this that they have no idea who they even are.
3. The tendency toward extrospection versus introspection. To an adolescent, everyone else is clueless and dumb. They are experts at picking apart other people's dysfunctions, yet completely blind to their own.

I think much of our adult human struggle is about overcoming adolescence. Periods like a "midlife crisis," can be interpreted, like philosopher Alain De Botton says, as the "final attempt to escape adolescence." Of course we all know far too many people who never move beyond this state of being. I would argue that most humans don't.

This is where self-development comes in. The pursuit of self-development is itself a barometer of the adolescent state of mind. Those who need it most believe they don't need it at all and have a negative reaction to the very idea of self-study and growth.

A Next Level Human, on the contrary, has the mottos of "always be learning," and "always be growing." They are seeking to be more open, more aware, and more intentional.

Self-awareness and self-growth are the psychological equivalents of physical exercise to improve health and fitness. They require the same discipline and consistency. They both require pushing the body, physiologically and psychologically, out of its comfort zone.

OWNERSHIP/ENGAGEMENT/SHARING

I t's not what you have done that has the most power, but rather what you are left to do.

I call this the "Nobel Effect" after the scientist who invented TNT, Dr. Nobel. This explosive device is arguably responsible for more violent, human death than any other invention. Yet, the man who invented it, in his last statement of legacy at his death, left his vast monetary resources to sponsor a yearly accolade, the Nobel Prize, to be awarded to those scientists making the greatest discoveries and contributions toward the promotion of peace.

Here is a man who saw his contributions and sought to right the balance. We can judge for ourselves if, in the end, his accomplishments were for the greater good, but I celebrate the intention he brought to the legacy he wanted to leave. I find it fitting that Dr. Alfred Nobel's last name is so similar to the word noble, which is synonymous with honorable, good, charitable, moral, and ethical.

When I look at my past and see my mistakes, failures, and missteps; I often think of Nobel's story and resign to make the rest of my time matter more by sharing more, communicating more, learning more, teaching more, loving more, giving more, and being more.

Don't let your past define you, let it inform you on how to be better next time…more noble.

PERCEPTION/OWNERSHIP/ENGAGEMENT

I adore the work of Brené Brown and have devoured all of her books. I just don't think the term, vulnerable, serves men well for several reasons.

1. From a purely semantic point of view, most men view vulnerability as a weakness. While Brené Brown and others have done an excellent job explaining why it is not a weakness, most men won't get it. It's limiting to keep using a term that already has an entrenched meaning for men. Just change the term...I like emotionally open, mature, or available.

2. Men feel more in their power when they are taking action - telling them to be more vulnerable is tough for them. They interpret it as you telling them you want them to be your girlfriend versus your man. I hear the same from women. If their man is too talkative and too emotional, they ultimately see him as weaker.

3. Last, and this is just being petty, idea hijacking can get you in trouble. You read a book, think it's great, and start preaching its ideas like it's the Bible. The next thing you know, the term vulnerability is being thrown around like popcorn at a movie theater. This has two effects: 1) The idea stops being questioned and improved upon. 2) The idea loses some of its power and purpose.

For men there is a time to be vulnerable, soft, and thoughtful and there is a time to be a warrior, take action, and put emotions on the back burner.

PERCEPTION/OWNERSHIP/ENGAGEMENT

I f the two of us were to become friends, I would have to know you to trust you, and I would need to trust you to like you.

That's how it goes for me now: know—> trust —> like.

I suppose sometimes the "liking" and "trust" are hard to tease out; which one comes first is not always clear.

When you ponder this, there is another level: our relationship with self. Before I can know, trust, and like you; I must know, trust, and like myself.

Our brains are watching us all the time. We judge ourselves the same way we judge others, only more harshly. If we tell ourselves we will do something and then don't, our brains say, "Yeah, you are lying. I don't trust you." It's the same when we exaggerate, tell white lies, and pretend to be someone we are not.

Have you ever caught yourself telling someone something about yourself, and then walk away from the conversation saying, "I just completely made that scenario up?" It's okay if you have; you're human. We humans do that kind of thing more than we would ever want to admit. The problem is, it is not benign. I have stopped doing this. I am relentlessly rooting out this behavior in myself.

I am committed to being 100% who I am and sharing that with the world. I realized that is the only way to know, trust, and like myself and in turn have people really know me, rather than the person I am trying to project.

As humans we want to be loved, appreciated, considered, and connected. We want to matter. However, how can someone love the real us if we don't know who that is or never let them see it? Therein lies the problem.

It is essential to comprehend that we can easily become what we pretend to be. If we are a liar, an avoider, and a cheater, this is what we will feel like on the inside. As tough as it is to admit, this is who we are, until we decide not to be. Believe it or not, people eventually see who we really are anyway. If we delude ourselves, other people will eventually come to see us as exactly that.

December 14

PERCEPTION/OWNERSHIP/WISDOM/ENGAGEMENT

You have to know yourself to be honest with yourself and you must be honest with yourself to learn the lessons in life, improve, and grow.

How many people say, "I am such a jerk. I really need to work on that? How many people assert, "My fault. I messed up. I apologize and I am going to work on that?"

Base Level humans always assume they are the smartest people in the room; they blame every one and everything else. The idea they could be the one who is wrong is near insanity to them. They are the most biased and most dogmatic.

Culture Level people rarely admit their mistakes and believe in "toxic people." These toxic types are the problem, make them behave a certain way, and as long as they avoid toxic people, they assume they are fine. When they do discover they are the problem, it comes only after repeated patterns. After seeing things repeated again and again in their lives, they MAY finally get the point and start closely examining themselves.

Next Level Humans assume they are the problem from the start. They take the opposite stand and ask, "How did I contribute to or cause this? How can I fix this? How can I learn from this?" They don't believe in "toxic people." They only believe in toxic attitudes and realize theirs is the only one under their control.

Next Level Humans set firm boundaries on what they will tolerate in themselves and others. They do this by constructing a strong honor code and personal code of conduct. This helps them decipher when they are falling short or when others are encroaching.

Next Level types know when to care, when it's on them (it usually is), when to give the benefit of the doubt, and when to tell someone to get lost. To them, people are practice.

When their boundaries are crossed, there is little chance of going back. But no matter what happens to a Next Level Human, their motto is "Semper Discendum" (always be learning). The lesson is always there, and they know they are ultimately the cause, and the solution.

PERCEPTION/OWNERSHIP/WISDOM/ENGAGEMENT

What do you do when you feel disrespected, discarded, taken advantage of or done wrong? What's interesting is that these feelings almost always come from being more invested in a person than they are in you. As humans, this is one of the worst feelings.

There are two ways to handle this predicament. One way is to hold on to the hurt and carry it with you into your future relationships and interactions. Using this approach, the next person you meet in a similar relationship becomes a mannequin for you to dress in the clothing of your last hurt. If you have ever had someone treat you a way you are not, consider they may be dressing you with their old histories of hurt.

This is what I call the VC or victim culture. These types are quick to paint the world with broad strokes of their pain. They will project onto you behaviors that actually belong to someone else. You ask a genuine question of concern and they think you are prying, questioning, and distrustful; which is a sign they have old baggage. It's not healthy for you, them, or the new relationship.

The other approach is to not carry baggage, but instead set firm boundaries. Using this approach, the pain is not carried beyond the original insult or person.

This is what I call the GC or growth culture. Instead of assuming all people are the same, these individuals create clear markers so they recognize if, and when, someone is crossing them. They use the last insult as a growth marker. They place it in the ground of their psyche and watch to see if others encroach.

Boundaries are a hugely important tool of an individual's honor code. I can put up with a lot of things and consider myself a patient, kind, and understanding person. At the same time I will not tolerate rude, dismissive, selfish, or victim-type people in my circle. Once those boundaries are crossed a few times, I shed that person, and their baggage, from my life.

I set boundaries; I don't carry baggage. Which approach do you use?

ENGAGEMENT/RESOLVE

L ife is just like the gym.

Sometimes I don't lift with any intensity for longs periods – I just don't feel like it. I can average no more than two training sessions a week over that time. These details reflect some of the things that go on in my business and personal life.

Sometimes you just settle in, do what you need to do and don't obsess or worry about it. Then you get a good workout in and it helps you take action and get unstuck in life.

Or it happens in reverse. Like when I make a difficult choice or take definitive action in life; it manifests as motivation and movement in the gym.

OWNERSHIP/WISDOM/ENGAGEMENT

Did you ever notice how there are certain people who evoke reactions that others don't? I am not talking about being attracted to one person over another, or how we just connect more with one friend over another. -Those are examples, but I am talking about the dark side of that coin.

Have you ever cared about, respected, and admired a person who did not reciprocate? As a result you felt less than, needy, ineffective, and insecure. Sure you have, you are human. I have too.

Most who know me know one of my superpowers is that I couldn't care less what the vast majority of people think of me. "Oh you like me? Great." "Oh, you don't like me? Great." I guess that's one reason I do well in this career field. I am very clear that you, being triggered by me, positive or negative, is about you.

But then there are the select few people who, for reasons not always comprehendible, I care deeply about their opinions. These are people I consider, think about, and adore; who are not concerned about me in the slightest. These types are my kryptonite and end up draining my emotional resources.

They appear far less nowadays, but I notice the opportunity for growth when they do. This is because they highlight the truth for me. As humans we are social creatures and we must walk a line between looking at ourselves in relation to self and others.

When we attach with another, romantically or not, we are often attaching to a story about a more perfect **us** they help us envision. A lesson they can teach. A trait they exhibit that we want. A way they once made us feel.

These people are our greatest teachers. They illuminate the ways we try to outsource love of self. When these types show up, I am now grateful because I can work on the areas of doubt, unworthiness, and fear they helped illuminate. Other people can't be your torch, but they can be your matches.

To love you is their choice, but ultimately it's your job.

OWNERSHIP/SHARING

I have been in the healing profession for a long time, in many different roles: as trainer, as doctor, as counselor, as coach. I can tell you that growing from pain is not the norm. Many people succumb to it and end up shells of their former selves. Others remake themselves and thrive.

They end up becoming something so much better than what they were, and something they never could have reached without the pain.

But how do we do that? I believe the first step is Ownership. Own what happened. Accept it. Then decide where you will carry it and what can you make out if it.

One of the reasons people get this wrong is their mental framework. Some are able to own it while others struggle and can only view it as outside of their control. The saying, "everything happens for a reason" it is a poor invocation when dealing with the rough stuff. It is perhaps one of my least favorite mantras because it takes you completely out of the equation and makes you a victim of circumstance.

The way I think the quote should be phrased is: "Everything happens, you create the reason." To me that is far more accurate and places the responsibility in the only place it belongs: with you.

I believe this is the highest form of spiritual alchemy. Take the pain, hurt, frustration, sadness, anger, and make magic out of it. What's the lesson you can learn and then teach from it?

Turn the pain into a light so bright it illuminates the path for others.

OWNERSHIP/ENGAGEMENT/SHARING

Your inner dialogue tells me how you see yourself. The subjects of your conversations telegraph where you're probably headed. Your consistent actions portray who you really are or who you are bound to become.

Your inner speech can reveal which level of human you closely are mirroring: Base Level, Culture Level or Next Level.

Base Level types are con artists, liars and avoiders. Their inner chatter sounds a lot like "Who does that person think they are?" They hate on others because they hate on self. These are the types you see on social media calling names, getting triggered, and not realizing they are the things they hate. Their actions -There is a reason they are critics and not creators: They say a lot and do nothing.

Culture Level types have an inner dialogue of prom, marriage and kids. They play high school sports. They go to college. They get the degree, the job, and the family. They fall in line. They say, think, and feel what the culture says, thinks, and feels. Their outer conversation can best be described as beers and ballgames. Their actions are restricted by what they think others will say or feel about what they do.

Next Level types possess the same human tendencies of fear and dysfunction. The main difference is that they do something about it. Their inner dialogue is one of possibility. They feed that voice and story. Outer conversation is around positivity, creation, support, and a sense they can spin magic. They are too busy chasing a better self and world to be wrapped up in the lives of others. Their actions are found in learning, teaching and loving.

You show me what you say to self, what you say about others and what you do with your time and I will show you your level of life. Of course, we all dive Base Level on occasion, but where does your level typically reside? The good news is Next Level is a practice, something I strive for and still often fall short.

To get there: Stop hating. Stop talking smack. Stop copying and start creating. Do it for you, your children, your family, your friends, and the rest of us.

We are watching and learning from you. We need you the same way you need us.

December 20

SHARING

D on't let fear, considerations, ego, or circumstance keep you from loving who you love. Is it really "love" if there is a requirement for reciprocation? My love for you does not require your involvement; that's what makes it real.

But love manifests in many different forms, and while the sentiment above pertains to romantic or family love, that is not really what I ultimately mean.

I think the greatest expression of love is synonymous with legacy. Imagine your spirit crashing into life and leaving fields of energy long after you have come and gone. Will those fields be insecure, arrogant, or angry wastelands that drain those in its path, or will they be compassionate, inspiring gardens that cultivate, enrich, and inspire others to their next, best level?

Legacy is about leaving the world a better place when you go. Are you intentional about what you are doing here?

Leave your creations, your teachings and your love behind for others. What we leave is not for us to see. I love that thought, and it is my intention to make it worth something, not for me, but for them.

PERCEPTION/WISDOM/ENGAGEMENT/
RESOLVE/SHARING

The truest test of life is, whether or not you can learn from your experiences and find the benefit in your mistakes and misfortunes.

Success psychology confirms this theory. The number one determinant of success is not IQ, social savvy, or emotional intelligence; it's the ability to leverage stress and hardship as the catalyst to grow.

This has been true for me. There is nothing I am more grateful for than my mistakes, struggles, and misfortunes. A marriage, a divorce, love, betrayal, heartbreak, loneliness, and confusion- these have led to greater kindness, better communication, more warmth, enhanced understanding, new insights, deeper compassion, more capacity to love, and a commitment to honesty. As well as a new direction and defined meaning, by helping others who are struggling understand that pain is the path.

You may not see it now, but the suffering you are trying to overcome, is the catalyst required to help you level up as a human.

You are dying right now, death comes for us all, but what does that matter if you are already dead on the inside? Death too is something to celebrate. It's a reminder. It is what gives us focus, urgency and purpose. How? Realize, it's not rise to the occasion; it's create the occasion.

Memento Mori.

OWNERSHIP/SHARING

About ten years ago my now ex-wife, but still best friend, Jill and I, were driving back from a fitness show in the middle of the night. We gave three young female competitors a ride. Since I was driving and trying to keep myself awake, and I am known equally for serious conversation and nonsensical shenanigans, I asked a ton of random questions that alternated between the bizarre, hilarious, and serious.

The answer to one of those questions has remained with me since. I inquired, "If you could be anything in the world, what would you be?" I fully expected answers like, "Be the person to cure cancer," or "Be the inventor of clean, renewable energy" or perhaps just, "Be an amazing, loving mother." What I received were three answers exactly the same, just varying in context. One said, "A hot, famous model." Another said, "A hot, famous actress." The final one said, "A hot, famous, fitness competitor."

I still think about this, and it bothers me. Not one wanted to do anything of meaning or substance. If those girls are like many people today, they probably have a huge social media following and have achieved their dreams. They have become "famous," in a way, at least in their own minds.

Except being someone who has an Internet following does not make you famous. At best, it makes you one of the popular kids in an oversized high school. And the problem is the same, what are you doing? What's your purpose? And honestly, who gives a shit?

I am not famous, I don't think I am famous, and frankly I don't want to be famous. What I want is to make a difference using my signature strengths in only the way I can. I want to contribute to the world beyond myself.

When I am gone, I want my energetic signature to have touched others and to have helped in some small way. I want to be remembered as kind, generous, and an individual who taught someone else something that made their life better. I would rather genuinely do that for a few people and never be noticed by anyone else than the reverse. I believe this is what we are here for, to learn, to teach and to love. Big social media following or not, I think this is where you find fulfillment.

December 23

PERCEPTION/OWNERSHIP/SHARING

Some people don't care if you care. In fact, I have learned some people even seem offended if you care. "What business is it of yours?" they think.

Some people will judge you for caring. Some people will hate you for caring. For some people, your caring means something is wrong with them. Some people don't want you in their lives. Your caring is neither welcome nor wanted.

So what are you supposed to do? -Care anyway.

It's what you feel isn't it? Just learn to do so without their involvement.

Isn't it ironic how we can say we love a person, and yet as soon as they stop being the way we need them to be, our love stops? Is that really love or caring?

Love is not about what that person is doing or can do for you. If your "caring" is hiding behind your needs, that's not really caring at all.

So care, just realize that sometimes your caring means you won't be included. And realize too that this kind of caring is never sustainable unless you care for yourself first.

PERCEPTION/OWNERSHIP/WISDOM/SHARING

When people are wounded, they usually take one of two paths:

1. They block it out, go about their business and don't speak of it again. Of course this often takes the life out of them in the process.
2. Others become bitter, angry victims, whose entire identity becomes what happened. These types suck the life out of everyone else.

And then there are the types who see the pain as the path. They use it to learn, teach and love. They go Next Level and are able to enhance others, despite pain no human should have to endure.

Walk the Next Level path. The world needs you.

PERCEPTION/OWNERSHIP/ENGAGEMENT/RESOLVE

If you think back on your life, you will find that the most distressful times often come from some type of loss of identity.

As humans we have key needs for status and certainty. Our sense of identity incorporates these two imperatives of the human psyche. When we lose a thing we have attached to strongly, it is incredibly painful and life-altering; so much in fact, many never recover, becoming psychological shadows of their former selves.

However, with every great loss arises the opportunity for enormous gain. It simply takes realizing the truth; life is, by its very nature, change. In other words, your identity is meant to transform. There is no way of escaping.

So the trick is to realize that life happens and you get to happen back. You can create a new identity. The life you imagined can always be reimagined.

It helps when you have things in your life that provide a thread of identity, a lifeline you can hold on to throughout. It's doubly helpful if that thing helps build emotional resilience and mental fortitude. This should be something that is yours and not attached to another person, place, or thing.

Fitness has always been that passion for me. It's who I am. It's part of me. I lean on it heavily during times of change. It has acted as a catalyst for me each time I confronted loss of identity and it will continue to be. What is your lifeline?

OWNERSHIP/ENGAGEMENT

What you think about me is often, but not always, a reflection of what you think about yourself. You have probably heard this concept in the world of new age psychology.

The idea is that we project onto others our feelings, behaviors, and beliefs about the world. For example, if I am dishonest and selfish and believe the world is not safe, then I will often default to perceiving others exactly that same way.

Psychology research does hint some of this is accurate. For example, those who frequently tell lies are much less trusting of other people. Liars assume we are all liars.

But there is a problem with this idea of, "It's always about you." Sometimes it's not. Sometimes the other person is the issue. We know this intuitively, which is why we are a little uncomfortable with fully owning the idea of, "How you see me is how you are." That is not always true.

This is where self-awareness and self-responsibility are called upon. Those who practice self-awareness are more adept at understanding where the problem resides. They also realize, no matter where the problem lies, it is still 100% their responsibility to fix it. Simply because we are the only person who can guarantee ourselves it will be solved. Good luck waiting for someone else to do it instead.

So, how do we determine if it's them or us? My default is to assume it's me first and take responsibility. But at the same time, I reality check the situation. -I ask, "Do I do this with others? I ask, "Does this person exhibit this same issue elsewhere? If I am honest, the answer is often very clear.

Finally, regardless of what I discover, I either work to alter my behavior or labor to remove my interactions with that person. Either way, it's on me to change or protect me. I can't change someone else, that's impossible and a waste of my time.

PERCEPTION

R esearch shows there are three specific elements that determine an individual's success.
They are:

1. What your social circle believes of your abilities.
2. What you believe about your abilities.
3. Your ability to see stress, pain, failures, and fears as growth enhancing.

All of these things fall into the rubric of Perception, your way of seeing the world:

1. It is all about the stories you tell yourself, about yourself. -Are you too arrogant to know your limitations? -Are you too insecure to know you are capable of accomplishing what you want?
2. Do you let other people's stories about you stop you? Do you adjust your social circle so you are surrounded by believers, not haters, those who inspire you, support you, challenge you, and are cheerleaders for you?
3. Can you reframe the most painful experiences in your life, so the lessons are apparent, and then use the lessons to level up and grow to your Next Level? -If you can do all of those things, you have mastered the super-power of Perception, the first and most important step in self-actualization.

We humans are telling ourselves stories about others, the world, and ourselves every single day. The stories you believe will determine the quality of life you live. Everybody has the capacity to dream and believe anything they want. The life you imagined can be reimagined.

If you feel stuck in life, the solution is simple: flip the script and reinvent yourself.

OWNERSHIP

If you want to know someone's true character it is pretty easy to assess. Simply examine their behavior when they are stressed and when they interact with strangers while in a "protective bubble." -For example driving a car, interacting online or with a service professional. In these three cases the person is able to "hide behind," the doors of their car, the computer screen, and money respectively. The degree to which they are hidden from others often determines the degree to which their dysfunctional personality will be displayed.

For example, in this case you would expect to see the person be the most rude to least rude in this order: internet > car > service professional. This is based on the degree of anonymity.

To really know a person, observe how they behave when they are stressed or in a hurry. Or when they are in a protective bubble. Or when they are in a high status position. Do they all of a sudden act like nothing else matters, but their needs? Do they become rude, short, selfish, or demanding? I bet you know a ton of people like this?

Some qualities of a Next Level Human:

- They treat service professionals with respect and often tip well, a sign of kindness and generosity.
- If they are asked for money on the street, they will make eye contact and be polite whether they are in a charitable mood or not, a sign of humility and humanity.
- They let people merge into traffic, a sign of generosity and consideration.
- They treat humans as kind as they treat animals, a sign of sanity and sociability.
- They don't recline their seat on an airplane, a sign of consideration and awareness.
- They leave their read receipts on, a sign of honesty.
- They don't ghost people, a sign of maturity, confidence, and good communication
- They don't talk behind people's backs, a sign of not being a jerk who will do the same thing to you.

WISDOM/OWNERSHIP/ENGAGEMENT/RESOLVE

Why are you afraid of being attacked? Our greatest lessons come from being challenged.

It is natural as humans to want to be liked. In fact, I would say it is one of our most central imperatives. We require that. It makes us feel like we have a comfortable place of belonging. And, at the same time, we all know the dangers of taking that need too far.

Imagine you are a professional fighter and you want to be the best. Now imagine you avoid any actual contact with other fighters. You never allow yourself to be attacked. This assures you remain small. You will be in the dark about your actual abilities. You will have no accurate measure of your resilience and resolve.

I would go further and say your ability to overcome a massive kick to the head will be low or nonexistence. Resilience and resolve are skills you build from real-world feedback that can only come from fighting an actual opponent. If you're really serious about being great, you will crave the opportunity to be challenged by the best.

Mentally and emotionally, it is the same. If you feel brittle in these areas it is almost certainly as a result of you avoiding any conflict. You are scared because you don't know the reality of what it feels like.

Fear is funny that way. The only way you see its true face is by looking into its eyes and saying, "Yeah, I see you. Let's see what you're really made of." You confront the thing and it immediately becomes something different, usually less scary.

So the next time you are attacked, take a second to consider that you are refining your Next Level skills of patience, discipline, willpower, listening, emotional control, and rational thought. Here is one way to do this:

The next time you are challenged, don't take the Base Level approach of trying to win, avoid the Culture Level approach of looking for support, and instead, go Next Level by seeking to grow. You can do this very easily by asking questions. Calmly ask your attacker why they feel that way? Keep asking questions. Make them look their own emotions and arguments in the eyes. They will almost certainly seem smaller and less threatening. More importantly, you will learn something you can use. That's what you are here for anyway, and conflicts are great teachers.

PERCEPTION/ENGAGEMENT/RESOLVE

I had a long conversation with my colleague for his podcast, and I turned on my recording device to capture some of the convo. I am glad I did because it quickly dovetailed into psychology - my favorite subject.

Below is the answer to his question..."Jade, what do you do when things get overwhelming? How have you used strength and conditioning?"

My contention is we suffer most when our stories, which are tied to our identities, are disrupted. Our lives are nothing if not one, big, long story we tell ourselves about who we are, why we are here and what our job is.

The problem is we think, in spite of all evidence to the contrary, that things will remain the same. We don't like thinking outside of our stories, because that's uncomfortable. We hate acting out of our comfort zones even more.

But life is nothing if not change. You will get punched in the gut, smacked across the face, and kicked in the balls. You better be ready for it. That's life. Your only choice is whether it will grow you or shrink you.

Strength and conditioning has always been the constant thread and anchor in my life. It's the thing that I lean on, and it's the thing that teaches me. It is the perfect metaphor for life. To get strong, to prevail, you must embrace challenges and reach new PRs (personal records). In life we must do the same. Fear PRs, perception PRs, Wisdom PRs, pain PRs and the rest.

Strength and conditioning is the training ground and life is the proving ground.

PERCEPTION/RESOLVE

The journey is a solitary one; in the end it comes down to you. Given we humans crave certainty so much, it's normal for this realization to result in a fear response. We start thinking, "What if I am alone?" Or "What happens if they leave me?" Or "How will I manage if I lose my support system?"

Our brains are always playing these fear scenarios in our heads. They prevent us from taking risks, making moves, and growing forward.

In psychology research there is a phenomena called post-traumatic growth. It is perhaps THE most powerful force for change that exists...And yet it occurs out of traumatic experiences.

Only a certain type of person makes it through these types of experiences in a way that enhances them. As a result, they end up trusting themselves more, needing others less, and developing the superpower of Perception, the ability to see stress and change as growth enhancing.

Wounds are viewed as something to avoid, but I have come to see them as something to embrace. Have you ever torn your hands during a workout, only to watch a protective callous form over the next several days? That callous does not make you more timid and scared, but it actually allows you to go harder next time. It's like your own self-constructed battle armor.

I approach psychological wounds the same way. They don't cause me to run away from love due to fear of hurt or rejection, rather they allow me to feel more and go deeper with an acute knowledge that I can handle what comes next.

Made in the USA
Middletown, DE
23 February 2022